Japanese L

Also available from Continuum:

Japanese Language in Use: An Introduction
Toshiko Yamaguchi

Japanese Linguistics

An Introduction

Toshiko Yamaguchi

continuum
LONDON • NEW YORK

Continuum

The Tower Building   80 Maiden Lane
11 York Road   Suite 704, New York
London SE1 7NX   NY 10038

First published 2007

British Library Cataloguing-in-Publication Data
A catalogue record for this book is available from the British Library.

ISBN: 978–0–8264–8789–6 (hardback)
      978–0–8264–8790–2 (paperback)

Typset by RefineCatch Limited, Bungay, Suffolk

Contents

Preface

Japanese Linguistics: An Introduction grew out of my experience of teaching Japanese language and linguistics over the past five years in Singapore and Malaysia. The writing of this book began with a collection of materials for an introductory linguistics course in 2003 at the National University of Singapore. This book is written as a course text designed for undergraduate students who have completed basic Japanese grammar and want to acquire more advanced and systematic knowledge of the Japanese language. No previous linguistic knowledge or training in linguistics is assumed, but what is assumed is an enthusiasm for learning the language in an authentic context and a desire to learn how to explain the language using linguistic concepts. As such, key concepts are given in boldface to draw the reader's attention.

Since this is an introductory textbook for students of Japanese, it does not contain technical terms from linguistics theories. Instead, it compiles notions that help learners to understand authentic texts. 'Authentic texts' here means texts that are composed naturally. That is to say, unlike those in most textbooks on Japanese language and linguistics, they are not created for pedagogical purposes. All the authentic texts used in this book are written discourse extracted from various sources (e.g., newspapers, short stories, children's books, dramas or comics). In Chapter 7 (Text 7.4), I have used an excerpt from a drama that consists of conversations, but this will not fall under spoken discourse (despite its oral style), as the conversations displayed there are created through written language.

This book has a forthcoming companion volume entitled *Japanese Language in Use: An Introduction* (abbreviated as JLU in the main text of this book). The present volume focuses on the structure of Japanese language comprising topics concerning sounds (phonetics and phonology), words (morphology and lexical semantics) and sentences (syntax), including chapters on vocabulary and writing systems – areas especially important to Japanese language. The forthcoming volume deals with pragmatics, discourse, culture and conversation – areas of linguistics concerning how the language is used. The combination of both volumes is considered to be a hands-on introduction to Japanese linguistics. If the reader intends to study the language methodically, I would strongly recommend beginning with the first book and moving on to the second. The second book may be read independently by anyone who is already familiar with, or well-versed in, the notions and distinctions explained in the first book. The point is that each book is organized in such a way that it can be read independently and that the two books can also be paired perfectly to achieve desirable learning outcomes.

This book promotes the active commitment of students to language learning – students do not read passively but instead perform as active participants tackling the tasks in the activities of each chapter. The role of the activities is not to ask students questions and expect 'one right answer', but to give them an opportunity to traverse the subjects in linguistics. The purpose of the activities is to get students to recognize forms and their functions in the language in authentic texts and to practise explaining the usages of the language. Most activities are followed by commentaries that discuss the main subject matters of an activity. Some activities have no commentary or provide only suggested answers. Commentaries are, by their nature, my own projections or opinions – they are not model answers or definitive accounts. When readers come up with alternative proposals, commentaries become the place where the two standpoints can be compared. Through the combination of explanation, activity and commentary, I hope that students develop their own strategies to work effectively on the authentic texts – that is, the way the language is actually used – based on their newly acquired knowledge of linguistic concepts.

The texts used are treated differently according to their level of difficulty and their significance to the task in each activity. For some texts, a full English translation is given, accompanied by a Japanese transliteration. For others, one or the other is given, while for still others, neither a translation nor a transliteration is provided.

I owe a great debt to many people for the warm encouragement they have provided during the writing of this book and their interest in it. I wish to especially thank the following friends and colleagues who read parts of the book at different stages of its composition and commented on it: (in alphabetical order) Andrej Bekeš, Ad Foolen, Sing Hon Ngiam, Yoko Otsuka, Magnús Pétursson and Jean Sévery. Comments by two anonymous reviewers were invaluable for the refinement of the book. All the errors and omissions that remain are, of course, my own responsibility. Lastly, the book could not have been completed without the permission of the publishers and copyright holders to reproduce a range of copyrighted materials for the text. I express my utmost gratitude for their kind understanding.

TY
March 2006

Acknowledgements

The author and the publisher would like to thank the following copyright holders for permission to reprint their material:

Kuma no Ko Ūfu, first published in Japan by Popular Ltd, 1977. Copyright © Kanzawa, Toshiko and Inoue, Yosuke. With kind permission of Popular Ltd.

Kuruma no Iro wa Sora no Iro, first published in Japan by Popular Ltd, 1977. Copyright © Aman, Kimiko. With kind permission of Popular Ltd.

'*Calling You*', from *Ushinawareta Monogatari*, first published in Japan by Kadokawa Shoten Ltd, 2003, pp. 5–47. Copyright © Otu, Ichi. With kind permission of Kadokawa Shoten Ltd.

Hagoromo, first published in Japan by Shinchosha Ltd, 2003. Copyright © Yoshimoto, Banana.

Hiatari Ryōkō, first published in Japan by Shogakukan Ltd, 1996. Copyright © Adachi, Mitsuru. With kind permission of Shogakukan Ltd.

Itsumo Misora, first published in Japan by Shogakukan Ltd, 2001. Copyright © Adachi, Mitsuru. With kind permission of Shogakukan Ltd.

Doraemon: Kandō-hen, first published in Japan by Shogakukan Ltd, 1995. Copyright © Fujiko Production.

Doraemon: Nobita Grafity, first published in Japan by Shogakukan Ltd, 2002. Copyright © Fujiko Production.

Ī Hito, first published in Japan by Shogakukan Ltd, 2004. Copyright © Takahashi, Shin. With kind permission of Shogakukan Ltd.

Fuzoroi no Ringo-tachi III, first published in Japan by Magazine House Ltd, 1991. Copyright © Yamada, Taichi.

'Traveling the world by car', first published in Japan by *Newsweek Japan*, 2002, pp. 64–93. Copyright © *Newsweek Japan*. With kind permission of Hankyu Communications.

Kanji in Context, first published in Japan by *The Japan Times* Ltd, 1994. Copyright © Inter-University Center for Japanese Language Studies. With kind permission of The Japan Times Ltd.

The extracts from *Asahi Newspaper*, first published in Japan by Asahi Newspaper Ltd, 1940, 1985, 2002–2005. Copyright © Asahi Newspaper Ltd.

The extracts from *Yomiuri Newspaper*, first published in Japan by Yomiuri Newspaper Ltd, 2004. Copyright © Yomiuri Newspaper Ltd.

The extracts from Asahi.com, first appeared in Japan by Asahi Newspaper Ltd, 2003–2005. Copyright © Asahi Newspaper Ltd.

How to use this book

Presentation of Japanese words, sentences and authentic texts

1. Japanese words in the main text are romanized in italic and given an English translation. English translation is not always given, particularly when the word is merely functional (see んだ in Entry 2 below).

    > Portuguese words such as *carta, tabaco, pão de Castella* and *tutanaga* were adopted as かるた *karuta* 'Japanese-style playing card', たばこ *tabako* 'tobacco', かすてら *kasutera* 'sponge cake' and トタン *totan* 'corrugated iron'. (Chapter 3)

2. When the same Japanese word is used for a second time in the same paragraph, it appears without romanization and English translation. In the text below, ドラえもん and のび太 (in lines 3 and 4, respectively) appear alone because they are mentioned for the second time.

    > Try to explain what information のび太 *Nobita* and ドラえもん *Doraemon* share in this drawing and why they use んだ *nda* here. ドラえもん possesses a magic mirror with which のび太 can see more than what is visible to the naked eye. (JLU: Chapter 1, Activity 2)

3. Example sentences are presented with their romanization in the second line and their English translation in the third line.

    > あの子 はだれですか。 (Chapter 5, example (11))
    > *Ano ko wa dare desu ka.*
    > Who is that child?

4. When a word or a phrase is emphasized in an example, it is presented **in boldface** in the Japanese example and its English translation.

    > 私の**親**は田舎で農業 をしている。 (Chapter 5, example (9))
    > *Watashi no oya wa inaka de nōgyō o shite iru*
    > My **parents** live by farming in my home town.

5. × means that the example is unacceptable.

> × 佐藤さんが私から本をもらった。(Chapter 7, example (36))

6. △ means that although the example is not completely unacceptable, an alternative given in the text is more appropriate.

> △ ぼくははな夫をころされた。(Chapter 7, example (22))

7. Authentic texts are presented in a box, the majority of which are transliterated in *hiragana*. Some texts are translated into English. Authentic texts are accompanied by their source (e.g., © year copyright holder/title (page), name of the publisher).

> 原田さんとも時々、話をした。彼女は大人で、どんなこ
>
> とでも相談に乗ってくれた。大学での生活や、一人暮ら
>
> しをする上で経験した悲喜こもごもを話してくれた。

(Chapter 7, Text 10)

Methods of romanization

8. The Hepburn system has been adopted. This system was devised by James Curtis Hepburn (1815–1911), an American missionary who arrived in Japan in 1859, and it is nowadays the most widely used method to transcribe Japanese into the Roman alphabet. The table below compiles basic and palatalized sounds. It reads in horizontal rows from left to right. One row consists of one, two, three or five sounds. Each sound is presented in the Roman alphabet (the first column) and *hiragana* (the second column). These two presentations are separated by a dotted line. Shaded rows indicate voiced sounds as opposed to their voiceless alternatives.

Basic sounds										Palatalized sounds					
a	あ	i	い	u	う	e	え	o	お						
ka	か	ki	き	ku	く	ke	け	ko	こ	kya	きゃ	kyu	きゅ	kyo	きょ
ga	が	gi	ぎ	gu	ぐ	ge	げ	go	ご	gya	ぎゃ	gyu	ぎゅ	gyo	ぎょ
sa	さ	shi	し	su	す	se	せ	so	そ	sha	しゃ	shu	しゅ	sho	しょ
za	ざ	ji	じ	zu	ず	ze	ぜ	zo	ぞ	ja	じゃ	ju	じゅ	jo	じょ
ta	た	chi	ち	tsu	つ	te	て	to	と	cha	ちゃ	chu	ちゅ	cho	ちょ
da	だ	ji	ぢ	zu	づ	de	で	do	ど						
na	な	ni	に	nu	ぬ	ne	ね	no	の	nya	にゃ	nyu	にゅ	nyo	にょ
ha	は	hi	ひ	fu	ふ	he	へ	ho	ほ	hya	ひゃ	hyu	ひゅ	hyo	ひょ
pa	ぱ	pi	ぴ	pu	ぷ	pe	ぺ	po	ぽ	pya	ぴゃ	pyu	ぴゅ	pyo	ぴょ
ba	ば	bi	び	bu	ぶ	be	べ	bo	ぼ	bya	びゃ	byu	びゅ	byo	びょ
ma	ま	mi	み	mu	む	me	め	mo	も	mya	みゃ	myu	みゅ	myo	みょ
ya	や			yu	ゆ			yo	よ						
ra	ら	ri	り	ru	る	re	れ	ro	ろ	rya	りゃ	ryu	りゅ	ryo	りょ
wa	わ							o	を						
n	ん														

9. Special attention should be paid to the following sounds: し, じ, ち, つ, しゃ, しゅ, しょ, じゃ, じゅ, じょ, ちゃ, ちゅ, ちょ, are presented as 'shi', 'ji', 'chi', 'tsu', 'sha', 'shu', 'sho', 'ja', 'ju', 'jo', 'cha', 'chu', 'cho', respectively.

10. When a small つ is romanized, the consonant following it is doubled, for example, 真っ赤 as 'makka' and ちょっと as 'chotto'. When the doubled consonant contains 'shi', 'chi', 'shu' or 'sho', the doubling is presented as 'sshi', 'tchi' 'sshu' or 'ssho'. For example, キッチン is given as 'kitchin' and キャッシュ as 'kyasshu'.

11. Long vowels are presented by a macron placed immediately above the prolonged vowel. For example, 重要 is given as 'jūyō' and シーズン as 'sīzun'.

12. Long vowels are not indicated with macrons in English text. For example, くまの子 ウーフ is presented as 'Kuma no Ko Ūfu' in Japanese text, but is given as 'A Bear Cub Uf' when it appears in English text (see Chapter 3, section 3.7).

13. When a special consonant ん is followed by a vowel or a consonant /n/, it is separated from the vowel/consonant by a hyphen to

avoid a mispronunciation of the two independent sounds. For example, 音韻論 is given as 'on-inron' (see Chapter 2) or 女 as 'on-na' (see JLU: Chapter 3, section 3.5.7).

Presentation of complex expressions

14. When compound words are a composite of two or more smaller compound words, they are separated by a hyphen. For example, 親子電話 is given as 'oyako-denwa'.
15. When compound words are a composite of a compound word and a single word, they are separated by a hyphen. For example, 腕時計 is given as 'ude-dokei'.
16. When compound words are a composite of a compound word and a character, they are separated by a hyphen according to the meaningful units they consist of. For example, 日記帳 is given as 'nikki-chō' and 決勝戦 as 'kesshō-sen'. When the compound word has an idiosyncratic meaning as a whole, it is not separated by a hyphen. For example, 春一番 'the first storm in the spring' is given as 'haruichiban'.
17. When compound words consist of two characters, they are not separated by a hyphen. For example, 水泳 is given as 'suiei' and 花畑 as 'hanabatake'.
18. When grammatical markers are attached to a word, they are represented as part of the word. For example, while 書いた (containing the past tense marker 'ta') is presented as 'kaita', 殺された (containing the passive marker 'are' and the past tense marker 'ta') is presented as 'korosareta'.
19. When complex predicates (containing a connective て) are romanized, they are presented as being attached to the verb but separated from what follows it.

> 犬 が死んでいます。 (Chapter 7, example (51))
> *Inu ga shinde imasu*

> このレッスンの単語を復習しておいてください。
> *Kono ressun no tango o fukushū shite oite kudasai*
> (Chapter 7, example (62))

When complex predicates do not appear as parts of an independent example but are referred to in the main text, they may be presented as a single unit.

> いってしまいました *itteshimaimashita* (JLU: Chapter 4, Activity 1)

20. Particles are presented as separate units. The first example below

contains から, は and ぜ. Copulas are treated in the same way. The second example below contains a copula だ.

> 明日 から、酒 はやめるぜ。
> (JLU: Chapter 4, example (39))
> *Ashita kara, sake wa yameru ze*
> I will stop sake beginning tomorrow.

> シンガポールはマーライオンが観光名所だ。
> (Chapter 7, example (4))
> *Singapōru wa māraion ga kankō-meisho da*
> Speaking of Singapore, the Merlion is a tourist attraction.

21. When a grammatical marker (e.g., copula だ) appears in a meaningful unit, it is represented as part of the previous element.

> それで今日 はあくびばかりしてるわけだね。
> (JLU: Chapter 1, example (4))
> *Sorede kyō wa akubi bakari shiteru wakeda ne*
> That's the reason why you are yawning all the time today.

Notes on romanization and phonetic and phonological transcription

22. Romanization is not identical to phonological or phonetic transcription (see Chapter 1, Table 1.1), although they resemble each other occasionally. The former provides the hands-on pronunciation of words based on English phonography, while the latter adopts IPA (the International Phonetic Alphabet) and is used to describe the sounds. Specifically in Chapters 1 and 2, the reader should pay attention to the differences between these presentations. Examples below are presented in the following order: (i) romanization, (ii) phonological transcription, and (iii) phonetic transcription:

> 布団 'Japanese-style bed quilt'
> (i) *futon*   (ii) /huton/   (iii) [ɸɯ̥toɴ]

> 月 'moon'
> (i) *tsuki*   (ii) /tuki/   (iii) [tsɯ̥kj̊]

Abbreviations

23. The following abbreviations are employed in the book:

JLU	*Japanese Language in Use* (Yamaguchi 2007)	In all the chapters
SV	Sequential voicing	Chapter 2, section 2.2.4
V	Vowel	Chapter 2, section 2.4, Activities 5 and 6
C	Consonant	Chapter 2, section 2.4, Activity 5
Cy	Palatalized consonants	Chapter 2, section 2.4
N	Special consonant	Chapter 2, section 2.4
Q	Geminated consonants	Chapter 2, section 2.4
R	Prolonged vowels	Chapter 2, section 2.4
NJ	Native-Japanese words	Chapter 3, sections 3.1, 3.4 and 3.6
SJ	Sino-Japanese words	Chapter 3, sections 3.2, 3.4 and 3.6
FL	Foreign loanwords	Chapter 3, sections 3.3 and 3.4
E	Element	Chapter 2, section 2.3.2 Chapter 5, section 5.5
C	Classification	Chapter 5, Activity 2 (Table 5.3)
R	Reference point	Chapter 5, Activity 2
Com	Compound	Chapter 5, Activity 3 (Table 5.4)
A	Affix	Chapter 5, Activity 3 (Table 5.4)
P	Prefix	Chapter 5, Activity 3 (Table 5.4)
S	Suffix	Chapter 5, Activity 3 (Table 5.4)
V1	First verb in the compound	Chapter 5, section 5.7
V2	Second verb in the compound	Chapter 5, section 5.7
SP	Subject–Predicate Structure	Chapter 7, section 7.2
TC	Topic–Comment Structure	Chapter 7, section 7.2
G	Grammatical noun modification	Chapter 7, Activity 5
A	Appositive noun modification	Chapter 7, Activity 5

Index

24. An index is provided at the end of the book. Key concepts are **in boldface** in both the main text and the index to draw the reader's special attention.

1 Speech sounds

This chapter will give you a brief overview of **phonetics**, or 音声学 *onsēgaku*. Phonetics deals with three aspects of speech sounds: nature, production and perception (see Matthews 1997: 277). This chapter focuses on the rudiments of production, that is, how and where speech sounds are produced. You will learn the basic names of speech organs in the vocal tract and their functions, as well as different classifications of speech sounds (e.g., voiced versus voiceless; consonants versus vowels; place and manner of articulation). A sound knowledge of the production of speech sounds is a prerequisite for the understanding of sound structure in Chapter 2. The main purpose of this chapter is for students to categorize and identify the speech sounds.

1.1 What are speech sounds?

Sounds are anything we can hear in our everyday life (e.g., 'noise' on the street, 'snoring' by my room-mate, or a fellow student 'grinding' his teeth in class). Our concern is with **speech sounds** that occur when we speak by means of language. Speech sounds are produced when air is pushed out of the lungs and passes through the vocal cords and vocal tract. When the airstream exits the vocal tract, we perceive the sounds of speech. Speech sounds differ from sounds resulting from, say, coughing or crying in at least two ways. First, they serve the purpose of verbal communication: by articulating speech sounds, a speaker conveys information to the hearer. Second, the articulation of speech sounds follows well-defined patterns within the system of a given language (see Chapter 2). Each language has an independent inventory of speech sounds; the inventory of Japanese speech sounds is not the same as that of English, Chinese or Malay. What most languages share, however, is the property that speech sounds are, under normal circumstances, produced while we breathe out but not while we breathe in. As Table 1.1 shows, we identify 23 speech sounds in Japanese. Place of articulation (section 1.3.3) indicates the places where the sounds are articulated, while manner of articulation (section 1.3.4) indicates the manner in which the sounds are articulated. Voiceless sounds are in the upper part and voiced sounds are in the lower part (section 1.3.1). Nasals, liquids and glides are all voiced sounds.

Table 1.1   *Inventory of speech sounds in Japanese*

Manner of articulation	Place of articulation							
	Bilabial	*Alveolar*	*Alveo-palatal*	*Palatal*	*Velar*	*Uvular*	*Glottal*
Stops	p b	t d			k g		
Fricatives	ɸ	s z	ʃ	ç			h
Affricates		ts dz	tʃ dʒ				
Nasals	m	n			ŋ	N	
Liquids		ɾ					
Glides				j	w		

1.2   Vocal tract

1.2.1   Structure of vocal tract

Speech sounds are formed in the **vocal tract**, a cavity through which the airstream passes (Figure 1.1). The vocal tract consists of two cavities: the **oral cavity** (Figure 1.1, no. 2), which refers to the mouth, and the **nasal cavity** (Figure 1.1, no. 1), which refers to the nose.

Figure 1.1 *Vocal tract*

1.2.2   Oral cavity versus nasal cavity

Most speech sounds are formed in the oral cavity, which consists of articulators – organs in the mouth (often called 'speech organs') – used to articulate sounds. Figures 1.2 and 1.3 show the names of the main articulators on the upper and lower surface of the vocal tract. Nasal sounds are formed

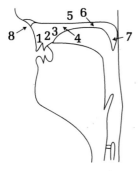

1 Upper lip
2 Upper teeth
3 Alveolar ridge
4 Hard palate
5 Nasal cavity (nose)
6 Soft palate (velum)
7 Appendage (uvula)
8 Nostrils

Figure 1.2 *Upper articulators*

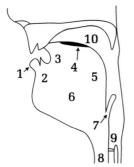

1 Lower lip
2 Lower teeth
3 Tongue tip
4 Middle of the tongue
5 Back of the tongue
6 The tongue body
7 Epiglottis
8 The larynx
9 The vocal cords
10 Oral cavity (mouth)

Figure 1.3 *Lower articulators*

in the nasal cavity, which does not contain articulators because its parts are not flexible or able to move, unlike those of the oral cavity.

1.2.3 Articulators

The production of speech sounds is usually characterized by the movement of a lower articulator against an upper articulator. This movement may achieve a complete or partial closure of the oral cavity. The modified size and shape of the vocal tract resulting from the movement between articulators gives rise to a speech sound. For example, when you say با *ba*, you may notice that the upper and lower lips come into contact (i.e., both lips are active) in the oral cavity (Figure 1.4) causing the complete closure of the oral cavity. When you say نَ *na*, the lower articulator, the tongue, comes into contact with the upper articulator, the alveolar ridge (i.e.,

3

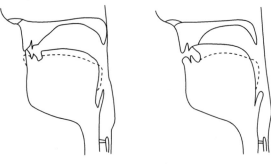

Figure 1.4 ば   **Figure 1.5** な

only the tongue is active), causing a complete closure in the oral cavity (Figure 1.5). You can see that the closure of the oral cavity is achieved differently. The interrupted lines indicate the position of the tongue for the vowel あ *a*. When あ is pronounced, the lips are open.

When you say あい *ai*, you may notice that the tongue first forms a low position when あ is pronounced (Figure 1.6), then rises for the pronunciation of い (Figure 1.7). Unlike ば or な, the movement of the lips is irrelevant, that is, they remain in almost the same position, and there is no closure of the oral cavity.

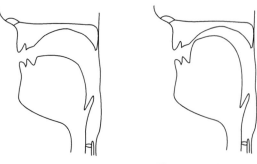

Figure 1.6 あ   **Figure 1.7** い

1.2.4 *Phonetic transcription*

Sounds shown in Table 1.1 are presented in square brackets [ ]. あい or バイ are presented as [ai] or [bai], respectively. We call this presentation of speech sounds **phonetic transcription**.

1.3 Classifications of speech sounds

1.3.1 Voiced versus voiceless

Speech sounds can be classified according to different articulatory (= concerning the production of sounds) criteria. The first classification is the distinction between **voiced** and **voiceless sounds**. This distinction depends on the degree of opening of the **vocal cords** (Figure 1.3, no. 9; Figures 1.8 and 1.9), which are housed in the larynx (Figure 1.3, no. 8). The larynx is a cartilaginous and muscular organ in the throat, more precisely, where the Adam's apple (more technically, the thyroid cartilage – the part located at the front part of the vocal cords) protrudes. The vocal cords comprise two small muscular folds (= vocal folds). When the folds are apart, the air passes through without obstruction, and the folds do not vibrate, resulting in what are called voiceless sounds (Figure 1.8). The first sound [s] in さる *saru* is a voiceless sound. When the folds are adjusted, a narrow passage forms between them. The air passes through under pressure, causing the vocal cords to vibrate, and voiced sounds (Figure 1.9) are created. The first sound [z] in ざる *zaru* is a voiced sound. Place your finger against your throat or Adam's apple and pronounce [s] and [z] for three seconds – you can feel the difference in that the latter creates vibration, while the former does not.

 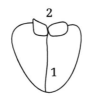

1 Vocal folds
2 The glottis

Figures 1.8 and 1.9

1.3.2 Consonants versus vowels

In addition to the distinction between voiced and voiceless sounds, sounds are divided into **consonants** and **vowels** based on the presence or absence of friction in the vocal tract. Consonants are produced when the airstream passing through the vocal tract is **obstructed** in differing degrees by the position of two articulators. When you pronounce the first consonant [s] in すき *suki*, you may notice that the tongue comes into close contact with the alveolar ridge. At the moment of this contact, air is hindered from passing smoothly in the oral cavity, causing friction or obstruction in the vocal tract. Vowels, by contrast, are produced without contact between

5

articulators; the passage of the airstream is thus relatively **unobstructed**. Note that both consonants and vowels are also characterized as either voiced or voiceless. While consonants in Japanese are either voiced or voiceless (see Table 1.1), vowels in Japanese are normally voiced (see section 2.2.2 for cases where vowels become voiceless). You can feel the vibration of the vocal cords when Japanese vowels (i.e., あ *a*, い *i*, う *u*, え *e* and お *o*) are pronounced.

1.3.3 Place of articulation

Consonants are further sub-classified by identifying **place** and **manner of articulation**. The formation of [p] is, for instance, represented as 'bilabial (place) and stop (manner)' and [h] as 'glottal (place) and fricative (manner)'. Place of articulation indicates where in the oral cavity consonants are made. The following seven places of articulation are identified in Japanese.

Bilabial sounds are produced when the upper and lower lips come into contact. Say バリ *bari* 'Bali', パパ *papa* 'dad, papa', ふろ *furo* 'bath', まり *mari* 'ball'. You may notice that the first sound (i.e., [b], [p], [ɸ], [m]) of these words is produced with both lips. Special attention is needed for the first sound [ɸ] of ふろ. The contact of two lips is much weaker than that of the other bilabial sounds.

Alveolar sounds are created when the tongue tip touches the alveolar ridge, the place just behind the upper teeth. Try saying だれ *dare* 'who', たれ *tare* 'sauce, soup', 風 *kaze* 'wind', さる *saru* 'ape', 図画 *zuga* 'drawing', 月 *tsuki* 'moon', 何 *nani* 'what', らく *raku* 'easiness'. When the first sound (i.e., [d], [t], [z], [s], [dz], [ts], [n], [ɾ]) of these words is pronounced (except for [kaze]), you may notice that the tip of your tongue is placed behind the upper teeth.[1]

Alveo-palatal describes the area just behind the alveolar ridge. When the tongue blade (not the tongue tip)[2] touches this area, the tongue tip may be up near the alveolar ridge. The first sound of 社会 *shakai* 'society', 事故 *jiko* 'accident', 地理 *chiri* 'geography' (i.e., [ʃ], [dʒ], [tʃ]) are all created at this place of articulation.

Palatal refers to the area of the hard palate. Palatal sounds are created when the middle of the tongue rises towards the hard palate (but does not necessarily touch it). When you pronounce the first consonant [ç] in 費用 *hiyō* 'costs, expenses' or [j] in 山 *yama* 'mountain', you may feel the middle of your tongue rise towards the hard palate.

Velar sounds are produced when the back of the tongue touches the soft palate. When you pronounce the first sound [g] in 軍 *gun* 'army' or [k] in 訓 *kun* 'Japanese pronunciation', you may feel that the back of the tongue is raised towards the soft palate. The second sound of the first

6

character in 参観 *sankan* 'visit, inspection' and the first sound of 私 *watashi* 'I' also contain a velar sound, [ŋ] and [w], respectively.

Uvular sounds are produced when the appendage hanging down from the back of the oral cavity is in contact with the back of the tongue. There is only one uvular sound in Japanese, that is [N] in 四 *yon* 'four' or 山 *san* 'mountain'.

Glottal sounds are produced when the vocal cords are slightly apart – forming the glottis (space between the vocal cords by close approximation) – and the airstream passes through accompanied by some weak friction (i.e., turbulent airflow) at the cords. There is only one glottal sound in Japanese, that is [h] in the first sound of 八 *hachi* 'eight' or 恥 *haji* 'shame, disgrace'.

1.3.4 Manner of articulation

Manner of articulation indicates the manner in which two articulators achieve contact in the oral tract when consonants are formed and let the air go out of it. There are six manners of articulation in Japanese.

Stops are created by the combination of the complete closure of the airflow in the oral cavity and its release through either the oral or nasal cavity. In Japanese there are three types of stops: (i) the closure created by two lips (i.e., [p], [b] in パパ *papa* 'dad, papa', バリ *bari* 'Bali'), (ii) the closure created by the contact of the tongue tip with the alveolar ridge (i.e., [t], [d] in たれ *tare* 'sauce, soup', だれ *dare* 'who'), and (iii) the closure created by the contact of the back of the tongue with the soft palate (i.e., [k], [g] in 訓 *kun* 'Japanese pronunciation', 軍 *gun* 'army').

Fricatives are created by the close approximation of two articulators (= two articulators come very close to each other, creating a narrow gap between them). Since the closure is not as complete as with stops, the airstream is only partially obstructed and turbulent airflow is produced. In Japanese there is only one voiced fricative [z] as in 禅 *zen* 'Zen-Buddhism' created by the contact of the tongue blade with the alveolar ridge, while there are five voiceless fricatives (i.e., [ɸ], [s], [ʃ], [ç], [h]). The first consonant of the word 坂 *saka* 'hill, slope' contains the voiceless alveolar fricative [s].

Affricates are sounds that involve a combination of a stop closure followed by a fricative release. A word such as 頭痛 *zutsū* 'headache' contains voiced and voiceless alveolar affricates (i.e., [dz] and [ts]). The first consonant of the word 地理 *chiri* 'geography' contains a voiceless alveolar-palatal affricate [tʃ], while 時間 *jikan* 'time' contains a voiced alveolar-palatal affricate [dʒ] as its first consonant.

Nasals are a kind of stop; they are created in the nasal cavity by the complete closure of the airstream by two articulators in the oral cavity, followed by release through the nasal cavity. When you say ま *ma*, な *na*, or ん *n*, you can feel closure in three different places. For [m], closure is caused by the contact of the upper and lower lips (= bilabial). For [n], closure is at the alveolar ridge (= alveolar), and for [N], closure is created by the contact of the tongue with the appendage (= uvular), which hangs down at the back of the oral cavity. Another velar sound [ŋ] is also written as ん (e.g., 漫画 *manga* 'comic strip') but it is only created when followed by [k] and [g]. The closure is at the soft palate.

Liquids are produced when the central part of the tongue comes into quick contact with the alveolar ridge of the mouth, but the sides remain open so that air can exit freely over the sides of the tongue without inducing friction, unlike obstruents. Japanese has the liquid [ɾ] in the first sounds of らくだ *rakuda* 'camel' and 理解 *rikai* 'understanding'.

Glides are also called semivowels since they share the properties of vowels in that they are produced without obstructions in the oral cavity. Japanese has [j] and [w] glides in the first sounds of 山 *yama* 'mountain' and 私 *watashi* 'I'.

1.3.5 Rounded versus unrounded

Since **vowels** are produced by movements of the tongue but not by contact between two articulators, they are characterized by the following: (i) roundedness of the lips, (ii) horizontal positions (= front or back) of the tongue, and (iii) vertical positions (= height) of the tongue. Let us first look at lip rounding. Vowels are rounded when the lips are curved in shape, while they are unrounded when the lips are spread. There is only one **rounded** vowel [o] in Japanese, as in お. **Unrounded** vowels are [a], [e], [i], and [ɯ] as in あ, え, い and う. Note that English [u] or Chinese [ü] are rounded vowels. The use of the special phonetic symbol [ɯ] signals the unroundedness of /u/ in Japanese. Try saying the five vowels in Japanese in front of the mirror and observe the shape of your lips.

1.3.6 Front/back

Vowels are also classified according to whether the front or back of the tongue is used as an articulator. When the body of the tongue moves towards the hard palate, the vowels produced are classified as **front vowels**. Try saying い *i* and え *e*. When the back of the tongue articulates against the soft palate, the vowels produced are described as **back vowels**. When you say あ *a*, う *u*, and お *o*, the back part of the tongue moves towards the soft palate.

1.3.7 High/mid/low

The final classification of vowels is according to the height of the tongue. When the tongue comes as close as possible to the roof of the mouth, the vowels produced are **high vowels**. い *i* and う *u* are high vowels in Japanese. When the tongue does not rise as much as in high vowels, **mid vowels** are created. Try saying いえ *ie* or うえ *ue*; you will probably feel your tongue lower when the second vowel え *e* is pronounced. Aside from え, お *o* is another mid vowel. Try saying いお *io* or えお *eo*; you may notice that the tongue position lowers again when お *o* is pronounced. あ *a* is a **low vowel** because the tongue is placed low or flat in the mouth. Try saying あお *ao*; your tongue rises when お is pronounced. Finally, you can observe your tongue rise to three different heights when you say 青い *aoi* 'to be blue'. Figure 1.10 depicts the places of the tongue when the five vowels in Japanese are articulated. Remember that the pronunciation of お is accompanied by the rounding of lips.

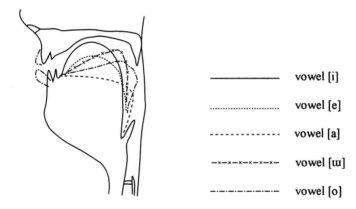

————————	vowel [i]
....	vowel [e]
- - - - - - - - - -	vowel [a]
–x–x–x–x–x–x–	vowel [ɯ]
–·–·–·–·–·–·–	vowel [o]

Figure 1.10 *Vowels*

Activity 1

This activity is provided with answers.

Identify the manner of articulation for the consonants shown in Figures 1.11 to 1.16. Explain the important articulatory features for each sound. The place of articulation for each figure is as follows. Figures 1.11, 1.12 and 1.13 are all alveolar sounds. Figures 1.14 and 1.15 are velar sounds. Figure 1.16 is a bilabial sound. Consult Table 1.1 and sections 1.3.3 and 1.3.4 to check your answers.

9

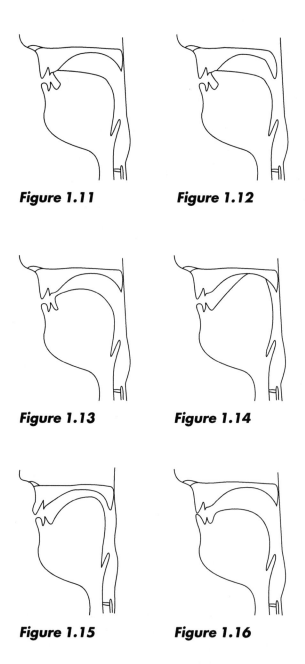

Figure 1.11   **Figure 1.12**

Figure 1.13   **Figure 1.14**

Figure 1.15   **Figure 1.16**

Answers for each consonant are as follows (these figures do not show the differentiation between voiced and voiceless sounds):

Figure 1.11 [t] [d] alveolar, stop
Figure 1.12 [n] alveolar, nasal
Figure 1.13 [s] [z] alveolar, fricative
Figure 1.14 [k] [g] velar, stop
Figure 1.15 [w] velar, glide
Figure 1.16 [m] bilabial, nasal

Activity 2

One important trait of Japanese sounds is that consonants are normally followed by vowels. When you pronounce さくら *sakura*, notice that each consonant ([s], [k], [ɾ]) is followed by a vowel ([a], [ɯ], [a]). This unit of sound is called a 'mora' (see Chapter 2, section 2.4 for the concept). For this special property of Japanese sounds, some figures below contain interrupted lines corresponding to the position of the tongue for the articulation of a vowel. The Figures 1.17 to 1.26 illustrate sounds in the columns of た and は. Assign *hiragana* with a phonetic transcription to each figure.

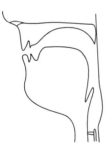

Figure 1.17

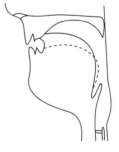

Figure 1.18

Figure 1.19

Figure 1.20

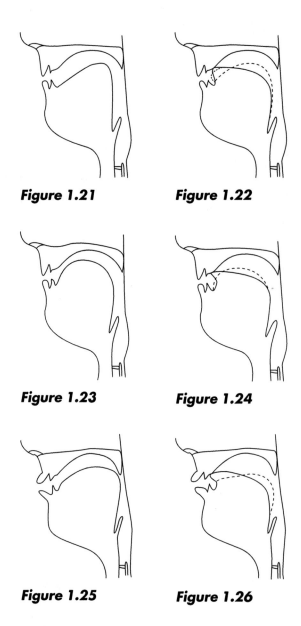

Figure 1.21 **Figure 1.22**

Figure 1.23 **Figure 1.24**

Figure 1.25 **Figure 1.26**

Commentary

Tables 1.2 and 1.3 summarize the sounds indicated by each figure. In the た column of Table 1.3, there is a clear difference between the positions of the tongue for consonants and vowels, while in the は column of Table 1.2

there are virtually no salient positional differences of the tongue for consonants and vowels. The absence of an interrupted line means the pronunciation of a consonant is practically the same as that of a vowel. This is because [h] (glottal, fricative), [ç] (palatal, fricative) and [ɸ] (bilabial, fricative) are produced without causing friction in the oral cavity. As you have learned in section 1.3.5, vowels are produced only by tongue movement without any contact between articulators. The interrupted lines in Figure 1.19 draw your attention to the slightly greater opening in the oral cavity when the vowel [i] is produced (″ means 'the same as above').

Table 1.2

Figures	Sounds	Consonants		Remarks
		Place	*Manner*	
17	は [ha]	glottal	fricative	
19	ひ 嗣[çi]	palatal	″	
21	ふ [ɸɯ]	bilabial	″	Lips come closer
23	へ [he]	glottal	″	
25	ほ [ho]	″	″	Lips are protruded

Table 1.3

Figures	Sounds	Consonants		Remarks
		Place	*Manner*	
18	た [ta]	alveolar	stop	
20	ち [tʃi]	~~palatal~~ alveo-palatal	affricate	The dotted line is the position of a fricative [ʃ]
22	つ [tsɯ]	alveolar	affricate	The dotted line is the position of a fricative [s]
24	て [te]	″	stop	
26	と [to]	″	″	

Exercise

After you have finished Activity 2, try to draw figures for other ひらがな *hiragana*-columns and create a summary in a table similar to Tables 1.2 and 1.3 above. It is recommended that you work in a group.

Notes

1   As mentioned in Tsujimura (1996: 14), [z] and [dz] do not clearly contrast in many cases. That is, the pronunciation of these two sounds varies depending on individual words. Tsujimura claims that /z/ in 貧しい *mazushī* 'poor' and みかづき *mikazuki* 'crescent moon' alternates between [z] and [dz], while many speakers of Japanese pronounce 地図 *chizu* 'map' invariably as [z].

2   'Tongue blade' refers to the surface of the tongue and its margins. This part of the tongue is particularly important when fricatives are articulated. Because the tongue blade is three-dimensional, it cannot be indicated in Figure 1.3 in section 1.2.2.

2 Sound structure

The study of **sound structure** is called **phonology**, or 音韻論 *on-inron*. This describes a set of principles that apply to when we speak. When speakers of a given language produce speech sounds, they unconsciously follow these principles. In the previous chapter, speech sounds were examined by exploring how and where they are articulated. The focus now will be the topic of 'how' speech sounds are organized in Japanese; to put it more simply, those factors that govern the production of speech sounds in Japanese. Two pivotal concepts will be covered: **assimilation** and **moraic structure**. Assimilation refers to a situation in which sounds change their quality in response to their environment (section 2.2), while moraic structure indicates how Japanese uses timing to organize sounds (or more precisely, phonemes) (section 2.4). These concepts and other basic terms (e.g., phonemes in section 2.1) may appear 'abstract' first time they are encountered. However, a good knowledge of sound structure is an integral part of the overall understanding of the language.

It is important to remark that it is virtually impossible to discuss the sound structure of Japanese without recourse to notions from other areas of linguistics – particularly from vocabulary (Chapter 3) such as 'Sino-Japanese', 'native Japanese', or 'foreign loans', and from word structure (Chapter 5) such as 'morphology', 'compounds', 'ideograms', 'affixes', 'prefixes' or 'suffixes'. All these notions are explained in detail in their respective chapters.

2.1 Phonemes

Phonemes are the smallest units of phonology and represent distinctive speech sounds. 'Distinctive' means that phonemes distinguish similar words. Phonemes are presented with two slashes / /. We call this presentation of sounds **phonemic transcription**, as opposed to phonetic transcription (see Chapter 1, section 1.2.4). When we have two words of similar pronunciation such as 坂 /saka/ 'slope' and 鷹 /taka/ 'hawk', what makes these two words different are the phonemes /s/ and /t/. The presence of these phonemes helps to identify the words by showing that they differ in meaning. When /saka/ is contrasted with 鹿 /sika/ 'deer', what distinguishes the meaning of the two words is the presence of the phonemes /i/ and /a/. The identification of phonemes is a useful medium for differentiating words. Each language has its own inventory of phonemes. The Japanese phonemic inventory consists of twelve consonants, two special consonants, five vowels, two semivowels and one special vowel.

Table 2.1   *Japanese Phonemic Inventory*

consonants	/p, t, k, b, d, g, s, h, z, r, m, n/
special consonants	/N, Q/
vowels	/i, e, a, o, u/
semivowels	/j, w/
special vowel	/R/

It makes sense to treat a special sound /N/ separately from /n/ because of its distinct allophonic realizations (see Table 2.3). /N/ is treated as 撥音 *hatsuon* in Japanese phonology and written as ん, as in まんざい (漫才) /maNzai/ 'cross-talk', or かんぱい (乾杯) /kaNpai/ 'cheers'. Another special sound /Q/ is the initial sound of a geminate (= doubled, lengthened) consonant. In Japanese phonology this sound is called 促音 *sokuon* and is represented by a small written っ, as in がっこう (学校) /gaQkou/ 'school' or いっぱい /iQpai/ 'full'. These two sounds are 'special' because they can form an independent sound (= one mora). As will be shown in section 2.4, Japanese consonants cannot stand alone and are normally accompanied by a vowel. However, /N/ and /Q/ do not need accompaniment by a vowel, meaning that their realization is influenced by a following consonant. /N/ thus assimilates into a consonant such as /b/ by sharing the same place of articulation (e.g., /siNbuN/ becomes [ʃimbuN] because of the voiced stop /b/). Likewise, when /Q/ is realized, it has the same place and manner of articulation as the following sound (e.g., /iQpai/ is articulated as [ipːai] because of the presence of the voiceless stop /p/). The realization of other consonants (e.g., /t/, /d/) is influenced by the vowel that follows them.

Semivowels are often referred to as 'glides' in phonetics (see Chapter 1, section 1.3.4). Semivowels are so-called because their articulation does not produce obstructions between articulators, but they remain distinct from vowels in that they share the consonantal feature of being followed by a vowel. For example, the first consonant /y/ of 山 /yama/ 'mountain' is a semivowel, followed by a vowel /a/. /R/ is a special vowel and is called 引く音 *hiku oto* in Japanese phonology. This refers to the second part of the geminated vowel. For example, 映画 /eRga/ 'movie' or 応援 /oReN/ 'support' contain /R/, indicating that the preceding vowel /e/ or /o/ is prolonged. This sound is treated as 'special' since its actual sound becomes more like the vowel that precedes it and it counts as an independent sound unit (or one mora).[1]

Note that the concept that phonemes serve to differentiate meaning is not unproblematic when we encounter **homonyms** (see Chapter 6, section 6.1.1) such as 桃 /momo/ 'peach' and 腿 /momo/ 'thigh'. What this means is that Japanese has words whose meanings are not distinguishable by phonemes but by their pitch accent, which is dealt with in section 2.5.

Activity 1

In this activity, you will practise how to identify phonemes. First, be certain of the pronunciation of each word, and then try to find pairs of words distinguishable by a single phoneme.

時　森　月　土器　赤　都市　秋　軒　餅　敵

Commentary

Table 2.2 summarizes word pairs with distinguishable phonemes.

Table 2.2

Word pairs		Distinguishable phonemes
時 /toki/ 'time'	都市 /tosi/ 'city'	/k/ versus /s/
森 /mori/ 'forest'	餅 /moti/ 'Japanese rice cake'	/r/ versus /t/
土器 /doki/ 'earthenware'	軒 /noki/ 'eaves'	/d/ versus /n/
月 /tuki/ 'moon'	敵 /teki/ 'enemy'	/u/ versus /e/
赤 /aka/ 'red'	秋 /aki/ 'autumn'	/a/ versus /i/

2.2　Assimilations

2.2.1　Allophones

As said in 2.1, phonemes are units at an abstract level, which means that the inventory (Table 2.1) does not take into account the actual realization of phonemes. In reality, phonemes are realized as **allophones** when pronounced by the speaker. The occurrence of allophones is often influenced by the quality of another sound in their vicinity. Note that languages do not have the same inventory of allophones at their disposal; that is, allophonic realizations of phonemes are language-specific. The same sound therefore can be an allophone in one language and a phoneme in another. For instance, while [ts] is an allophone in Japanese that occurs only before /u/, [ts] in Chinese is a phoneme, since it can occur in all environments.

The process of modifying a sound dependent on its neighbouring sound is known as **assimilation**. Assimilation facilitates the task of speaking; in this respect it is germane not only to Japanese but also to other languages. What differs among languages are the conditions under which assimilation occurs. When neighbouring sounds become similar, the transition from one sound to the next becomes smoother and more economical, and, as a result, speaking becomes effortless. There are two types of assimilation. When a sound is modified to make it similar to its preceding sound, this is called **regressive assimilation**. When a sound is modified to make it similar to its following sound, it is called **progressive assimilation**.

There are phonemes that have only one realization, or, to put it differently, some phonemes do not have allophonic realizations. Because they are realized independently of their environment, the same symbol is used (e.g., /p/ versus [p]). If the phoneme is realized as more than two allophones, these are presented by different phonetic symbols (e.g., /s/ versus [s] and [ʃ]). This means that phoneme /s/ has two allophones depending on the type of vowel that follows it. When /s/ is followed by the vowels /a, u, e, o/, it is realized as a fricative alveolar [s]. When it is followed by a high front vowel /i/, it is realized as a fricative alveo-palatal [ʃ]. [ʃ] is produced in a slightly higher (i.e., palatalized) position than [s]. The distribution of [ʃ] and [s] shows that allophones are distributed complementarily; that is, their distributions do not overlap. Table 2.3 illustrates the inventory of allophones in Japanese with their environments and examples (based on Iwasaki 2002: 20).[1]

Table 2.3 *Phonemes and their allophonic realizations in Japanese*

Phonemes	Realization of allophones	Examples with a phonetic transcription
/p/	[p] in all environments	[paɴ] パン 'bread'
/t/	[t] before /a, e, o/	[take] 竹 'bamboo'
	[tʃ] before /i/	[tʃi] 血 'blood'
	[ts] before /u/	[tsɯkɯe] 机 'desk'
/k/	[k] in all environments	[kaki] 柿 'persimmon'
/b/	[b] in all environments	[bɯki] 武器 'weapon'
/d/	[d] before /a, e, o/	[daʃi] だし 'broth, soup stock'
	[dʒ] before /i/	[dʒikaɴ] 時間 'time'
	[dz] before /u/	[dzɯga] 図画 'drawing'
/g/	[g] in all environments	[gakɯ] 額 'tablet'
/s/	[s] before /a, u, e, o/	[saka] 坂 'slope'
	[ʃ] before /i/	[ʃika] 鹿 'deer'
/h/	[h] before /a, e, o/	[haʃi] 橋 'bridge'
	[ç] before /i/	[çima] 暇 'free time'
	[ɸ] before /u/	[ɸɯne] 船 'ship'

Phonemes	Realization of allophones	Examples with a phonetic transcription
/z/	[dz] word initial	[dzak:a] 雑貨 'sundries'
	[z] intervocalic	[kaze] 風 'wind'
/r/	[ɾ] in all environments	[ɾika] 理科 'science' [haɾe] 晴れ 'fine'
/m/	[m] in all environments	[matʃi] 街 'city centre' [mɯra] 村 'village'
/n/	[n] in all environments	[natsɯ] 夏 'summer' [mono] 物 'thing'
/ɴ/	[n] before [t, d, n]	[kanda] 神田 (place name in Tokyo)
	[m] before [p, b, m]	[kombɯ] 昆布 'sea tangle'
	[ŋ] before [k,g]	[keŋka] 喧嘩 'row' [maŋga] 漫画 'comic strip'
	[ɴ] elsewhere	[daɴwa] 談話 'discourse'
/Q/	[k] before [k]	[gak:o:] 学校 'school'
	[s] before [s]	[kis:a] 喫茶 'tea drinking'
	[ʃ] before [ʃ]	[saʃ:i] 冊子 'booklet'
	[t] before [t]	[zat:a] 雑多 'miscellaneous'
	[tʃ] before [tʃ]	[matʃ:i] マッチ 'match'
	[ts] before [ts]	[its:u:] 一通 'a copy of'
	[p] before [p]	[rap:a] ラッパ 'trumpet'

Table 2.3 is divided into two sub-parts. As briefly mentioned in section 2.1, this division shows you how each phoneme is influenced by the following sound. Most phonemes presented in the upper division acquire a vowel feature of the following sound. Special phonemes presented in the lower division acquire a consonant feature of the following sound. Note that assimilation of /ɴ/ occurs only before stops, and /Q/ occurs before certain types of consonants. Vance (1987: 148) claims that /Q/ does not normally appear before /h/ or /r/ except in recent foreign loanwords such as /waQhuru/ ([waɸ:ɯrɯ]) 'waffle'.

2.2.2 Vowel devoicing

Vowel devoicing concerns the devoicing of high vowels and represents both progressive and regressive assimilation. It is also an example of **voice assimilation**. All five vowels in Japanese are voiced sounds, but the high vowels /i/ and /u/ can become devoiced in the following two environments: (i) when /i/ or /u/ appears between voiceless consonants, and (ii) when /i/ or /u/ is preceded by a voiceless consonant and appears at the end of the word. Some examples are given below. Voiceless consonants are marked in boldface in both phonemic and phonetic transcriptions, and the devoiced vowels that appear immediately after them are marked by a diacritic placed below the phonetic symbol. As stated in Chapter 1 (p. 5), 'devoiced' means that voiced sounds become voiceless, which happens when the vocal cords stop vibrating. When placing your fingers against your throat or

Adam's apple, you should not feel any vibration when pronouncing the high vowels in the following words:

Between voiceless consonants:
まきこ /makiko/ → [maki̥ko]
焼き鳥 /yakitori/ → [yaki̥tori]
四季 /siki/ → [ʃi̥ki]
佃煮 /tukudani/ → [tsɯ̥kɯdani]
服地 /hukuji/ → [ɸɯ̥kɯdʒi]

Word final preceded by a voiceless consonant:
道 /miti/ → [mitʃi̥]
柿 /kaki/ → [kaki̥]
岸 /kisi/ → [kiʃi̥]
書く /kaku/ → [kakɯ̥]
待つ /matu/ → [matsɯ̥]

2.2.3 Vowel gemination

High vowels undergo another type of assimilation in two environments in which the vowel becomes more like the vowel preceding it. One environment is when /i/ is preceded by /e/, and the other is when /u/ is preceded by /o/. In both cases, high vowels become identical to the preceding vowel. This phonological process is an example of regressive assimilation. Note, however, that /i/ does not undergo assimilation when it is preceded by /o/ (e.g., 甥 /oi/ 'nephew') or when /u/ is preceded by /e/ (e.g., 稀有 /keu/ 'unique'). That is to say, gemination of /e/ and /o/ only applies in the two environments mentioned above. Examples are given below:

{/e + i/ becomes [e:]} せんせい /senseR/ → [sense:] 'teacher'
{/o + u/ becomes [o:]} おとうさん /otoRsan/ → [oto:san] 'father'

It is important to note that vowel gemination does not always occur, for example, in speech situations such as lectures or sermons, since these types of speech require a certain level of formality (see Inazuka and Inazuka 2003: 105). Furthermore, as mentioned by Vance (1987: 13), vowel gemination occurs within the morphological structure of a word. Consider 講師 *kōshi* 'lecturer' and 子牛 *koushi* 'calf'. Only the first word undergoes gemination since the first *kanji* or 'ideogram' in 講師 (see Chapter 5, section 5.2 for the notion) contains both /o/ and /u/, whereas the first ideogram in 子牛 contains only /o/.

2.2.4 Sequential voicing

Sequential voicing (SV) or 連濁 *rendaku* causes the initial voiceless consonant of the second element of a compound to become voiced. This phonological process is an example of regressive assimilation in that a voiced sound causes a following sound to change its voice quality. Because the voicedness of the preceding segment is carried over to the following segment of the compound, this assimilation process can also be referred to as voice assimilation (see section 2.2.2). Since you will learn about compounds in Chapter 5, it suffices to say for now that compounds are words consisting of two (or more) independent words.

{/t/ → /d/} 本 /hoɴ/ + 棚 /tana/ → 本棚 /hondana/ 'book shelf'
{/k/ → /g/} 和 /wa/ + 菓子 /kasi/ → 和菓子 /wagasi/ 'Japanese-style confection'
{/s/ → /z/} 青 /ao/ + 空 /sora/ → 青空 /aozora/ 'blue sky'
{/t/ → /z/} 頬 /hoR/ + 杖 /tue/ → 頬杖 /hoRdue/ 'resting one's chin on one's hands'

The examples above show that SV occurs within the same place and manner of articulation, but what changes is the quality of voice. One exception to this rule is the alteration between /h/ and /b/. This contradicts the phoneme inventory in which /b/ is contrasted to /p/ in terms of voicing (see Table 1.1 in Chapter 1). It has been claimed in Japanese linguistics literature that the rise of the glottal fricative /h/ is descended from a voiceless bilabial stop /p/, and that the alteration between /h/ and /b/ is reminiscent of the old pair /p/ and /b/ (see Iwasaki 2002: 22; Vance 1987: 134).

{/h/ → /b/} 薬 /kusuri/ + 箱 /hako/ → 薬箱 /kusuribako/ 'a medicine chest'

Note that SV should not be considered a regular phonological process, since there are many exceptions that are governed by at least two conditions. The first is that SV is inhibited when the second member of a compound contains a voiced sound (stop or fricative). This inhibiting effect is called **Lyman's Law**, named after the scholar who first recognized it in the nineteenth century. In the case of 大風, the initial consonant /k/ does not undergo SV because of the presence of the voiced fricative /z/ in the second part of the compound.

大 /oR/ + 風 /kaze/ → 大風 /oRkaze/ 'heavy wind'

The second condition is that SV does not occur when the second member of the compound is of foreign origin, be it Sino-Japanese or Western.

Sino-Japanese:
安 /yasu/ + 建築 /kentiku/ → 安建築 /yasukentiku/ (×/yasugentiku/) 'cheap architecture'
和風 /wafuR/ + 建築 /kentiku/ → 和風建築 /wafuRkentiku/ (×/wafuRgentiku/) 'Japanese-style architecture'

21

Western:
安 /yasu/ + ホテル /hoteru/ → 安ホテル /yasuhoteru/ (×/yasuboteru/)
'cheap hotel'
和風 /wafuR/ + スパゲッティ /supageQti/ → 和風スパゲッティ
/wafuR supageQti/ (×/wafuRzupageQti/) 'Japanese-style spaghetti'

Native Japanese:
(SV occurs here because the second element is native Japanese.)
{/t/ → /d/} 安作り 安 /yasu/ + 作り /tukuri/ → /yasudukuri/ 'being
cheaply made'
{/s/ → /z/} 和風皿 和風 /wafuR/ + 皿 /sara/ → /wafuRzara/ 'Japanese-
style plate'

Finally, there are those compounds that exhibit irregularities. Apparently
no convincing explanation has yet been given for these cases. In some
cases, such as the ones below, the second element is of native-Japanese
origin but SV is not permitted.

芝刈り /siba + kari/ (×/sibagari/) 'firewood gathering'
味噌汁 /miso + siru/ (×/misoziru/) 'miso soup'
赤土 /aka + tuti/ (×/akazuti/) 'red earth'
カタカナ /kata + kana/ (×/katagana/) 'Japanese script'
(versus ひらがな /hira + kana/ → /hiragana/)

There are also cases where the second element is of Sino-Japanese origin
but does permit SV.

{/s/ → /z/} 生醤油 /ki + syoRyu/ → /kizyoRyu/ (×/kisyoRyu/) 'pure soy
sauce'

Some cases containing 甘 /ama/ 'sweet' as their first element demonstrate two possibilities. All the second elements are of native-Japanese
origin.

SV is applied:
{/s/ → /z/} 甘酒 /ama + sake/ → /amazake/ 'sweet drink made from a
fermented rice'
{/k/ → /g/} 甘栗 /ama + kuri/ → /amaguri/ 'sweet chestnuts'

SV is not applied:
甘口 /ama + kuti/ → /ama + kuti/ (×/amaguti/) 'sweet tooth'
甘皮 /ama + kawa/ → /ama + kawa/ (×/amagawa/) 'scarfskin'

Activity 2

You have now learned that sequential voicing (SV) is not applied to all
compounds. Below is a list of compounds that may or may not undergo
SV. First provide the reading of each compound and then sort them out by
referring to the principles highlighted in 2.2.4.

三日月 'crescent moon'　毎月 'every month'　水玉 'drop of water' シャボン玉 'soap bubble' 離れ島 'solitary island'　大島 'Ōshima Island'　横縞 'lateral strips' 雨合羽 'raincoat' 巻き煙草 'cigarette'

Commentary

Words that undergo or do not undergo SV are given below. Their readings and their phonemic changes are provided on the right.

SV is applied:

三日月	みかづき	($/t/ \rightarrow /d/$)
シャボン玉	しゃぼんだま	($/t/ \rightarrow /d/$)
離れ島	はなれじま	($/s/ \rightarrow /z/$)
横縞	よこじま	($/s/ \rightarrow /z/$)
雨合羽	あまがっぱ	($/k/ \rightarrow /g/$)

SV is not applied:

毎月	まいつき
水玉	みずたま
大島	おおしま
巻き煙草	まきたばこ

Consider first the words that do not undergo SV. They look quite similar to those that do undergo SV. For example, how would you explain that 毎月 *maitsuki* does not undergo SV, while 三日月 *mikazuki* does, although both contain the same character 月 *tsuki* 'month, moon'? 水玉 *mizutama* and シャボン玉 *shabondama* both contain a character 玉 *tama* 'ball', while only the latter undergoes SV. Similarly, 離れ島 *hanarejima* and 大島 *ōshima* both have the same character 島 'island', but SV is only applied to the former. The second element of 横縞 *yokojima* reads as /sima/ on its own, in the same way as 島, but is voiced when compounded. In all these examples, the second element is native Japanese.

The irregularities we have just observed indicate that we have to consider other factors that go beyond the etymologies of these words (i.e., the question of whether they are Sino-Japanese, native, or foreign loans). We can raise the question of whether the pairs (三日月 versus 毎月, シャボン玉 versus 水玉, 横縞 versus 大島) are linguistically analysable in the same way. Because the first element of 毎月 can be attached to other characters such as 日 *hi* 'day', 週 *shū* 'week' and 年 *toshi* 'year' (e.g., 毎日 *mainichi* 'every day', 毎週 *maishū* 'every week', 毎年 *maitoshi* 'every year'), it can be treated as an affix (see Chapter 5, section 5.6). By contrast, 三日 in 三日月 'crescent moon' is not an affix; it is employed only when referring to the crescent moon, that is, this word is part of a compound and contributes to form a special meaning. This different morphological process is worthy of mention.

Consider the difference between シャボン玉 'soap bubble' and 水玉 'a drop of water, polka dot'. A similar explanation to the above may be applicable to this pair. In the former, シャボン can only be used when 玉 follows it (シャボン is a loanword from Portuguese *sabão* 'soap'), while 水 'water' in 水玉 can be attached to other words such as 溜まり 'pool of liquid' or 鳥 'bird', resulting in 水溜まり *mizutamari* 'puddle' and 水鳥 *mizutori* 'water bird', respectively. It seems that 水 *mizu* behaves in much the same way as 毎 *mai*. We are tempted to say that while シャボン forms a compound, 水 does not but instead functions as a prefix. An affix is an element that does not stand by itself (Chapter 5, section 5.6). However, 水 with the meaning of 'water, liquid' can stand as an independent word (e.g., 水が飲みたい 'I want to drink **water**'). This may show that the difference between シャボン玉 and 水玉 is not as distinct as that between 毎月 and 三日月.

What would be your explanation for 島 *shima* and 縞 *shima*? One explanation is that 大島 *Ōshima* is the name of an island located southeast of the Izu Peninsula (伊豆半島 *Izu-hantō*) and the first element does not carry its own meaning; it does not mean 'a big island'. SV is allowed when the word is a composite of two independent parts; that is, the meaning of the parts reflects that of the entire word in some way. 離れ島 *hanarejima* 'a solitary island' is a composite of 離れ 'detached, isolated' and 島 'island', and it therefore undergoes SV. The same line of thinking also explains why /s/ of 縞 in 横縞 *yokojima* 'lateral stripe' is voiced – this word is a composite of 横 'lateral' and 縞 'stripe'.

Finally, the pair between 雨合羽 *amagappa* 'raincoat' and 巻き煙草 *makitabako* 'cigarette' may remind you of foreign loanwords (see Chapter 3, section 3.3); they are in fact derived from Portuguese words. What is interesting here is that although the second element is a loanword, 雨合羽 undergoes SV but 巻き煙草 does not. You will learn in Chapter 3 that loanwords, especially from Portuguese, were assimilated into Japanese vocabulary because of their early adoption (in the sixteenth century). As a result, Japanese people nowadays do not recognize that these are originally foreign words. This explains why 雨合羽 permits SV. Both words have the same history, but why is 煙草 inconsistent with SV? Recall that 大風 *ōkaze* 'heavy wind' disallows SV (p. 21). The same account is applied to 煙草, which contains a voiced stop /b/.

24

Activity 3

The following passage is taken from *Calling You*. The occurrence of SV is not very frequent in this text. After this activity you will be in a position to explain why sequential voicing rarely occurs in this text.

Text 2.1

```
 1  下校途中、バスの中でだれかの携帯電話が鳴りだした。目覚時計のよ
    うな音。わたしの前に座っていた男の子が慌てて鞄を探った。電話を
    耳にあて、そのまま会話をはじめた。暖房のせいで窓は曇り、外の風
    景は見えない。わたしはとりとめのない空想をしながら、ぼんやり車
 5  内を見回した。乗客は他に、通路をはさんで買い物袋を抱えたおばさ
    んがいるだけだった。携帯電話で話をする男の子に、彼女はそれとな
    く迷惑そうな顔を むけた。複雑な気持ちだった。乗り物や店内で携帯
    電話を使用するのは人の迷惑になるかもしれないが、一方でそういっ
    た状況に対してあこがれにも似た気持ちを抱いていた。男の子が電話
10  を切ると、運転手がスピーカーを通して言った。「他のお客様のご迷
    惑になりますので、車内での電話は控えるようにお願いします」ただ
    それだけの、何でもない出来事だった。それから十分ほど静かにバス
    は走り続けた。暖かい空気が気持ちよく、わたしは半分、眠りかけて
    いた。
```

© 2003 Otsu, Ichi / *Calling You* (p. 12), Kadokawa

Commentary

There are three compounds that have undergone SV: 目覚時計 *mezamashi-dokei* 'alarm clock' (line 1), 買い物袋 *kaimono-bukuro* 'shopping bag' (line 5), and 出来事 *deki-goto* 'event' (line 12). 運転手 *unten-shu* 'driver' (line 10) does not undergo SV, the reason being that the second element 手 is a suffix (see Chapter 5, section 5.6 for an exploration of affixation). お客様 *okyaku-sama* 'guest' (line 10) does not undergo SV either. The reason might be either that 様 *sama* is a suffix or that it contains a voiced /m/ (see 横縞 *yokojima* in Activity 2). There are two reasons why ご迷惑 *gomēwaku* 'trouble, annoyance' (lines 10–11) is insensitive to SV: (i) ご is an affix (more precisely, politeness prefix) and (ii) 迷惑 *mēwaku* is Sino-

Japanese. 下校途中 *gekōtochū* 'on the way home' (line 1) does not undergo SV because its second element 途中 *tochū* is Sino-Japanese.

SV does not occur as frequently in this passage as we might expect, mainly because although the passage exhibits many compound words, their second elements are not native-Japanese words. Between lines 1 and 10, for example, you can find words consisting of two characters such as 電話 *denwa* (line 2), 会話 *kaiwa* (line 3), 暖房 *danbō* (line 3), 風景 *fūkē* (lines 3–4), 空想 *kūsō* (line 4), 通路 *tsūro* (line 5), 複雑 *fukuzatsu* (line 7), 店内 *ten-nai* (line 7), 使用 *shiyō* (line 8), 一方 *ippō* (line 8) and 状況 *jōkyō* (line 9). These words are all Sino-Japanese. In other words, the number of hybrid compounds is rare (see Chapter 3, section 3.4).

2.3 Alterations

This section is concerned with sound alterations. **Alterations** have to be treated separately from assimilations (section 2.2) because they do not deal with the modification of a sound becoming similar to its neighbouring sound. Sound alterations alter a sound by inserting an extra sound (e.g., /i/ or /s/) or by simply changing the quality of the sound (e.g., /n/ → /ɴ/ or /e/ → /a/) regardless of its neighbouring environment. The distinction between assimilation and alteration is not always clear-cut, however. Patterns V and VI in section 2.3.1 may fall under assimilation in that the final consonant of the verb turns into a /t/ through which the sound becomes identical to the influencing sound. Sound alterations are subsumed under the **morphophonological** process because the phonological realization of words is dependent on their morphological structure. Section 2.3 looks at 'sandhi' and other minor alterations. **Sandhi**, originally from *samdhi* in Sanskrit, meaning 'to put together' (*The New Oxford Dictionary of English* 1998: 1646), is an ancient Indian term referring to the process by which 'the sound of a word is modified or fused at or across word boundaries' (Matthews 1997: 327).

2.3.1 Sandhi

Sandhi is called 音便 *onbin* in Japanese linguistics. Unlike sequential voicing, sandhi does not apply to compounds (see Activity 4, p. 28) but occurs only when the second element is a suffix. The occurrence of sandhi is restricted to certain morphophonological environments in which a verbal suffix beginning with /t/ (た (past marker), て (linking marker), たら (conditional marker) or たり (coordinating marker)) is attached to the preceding verb. Sandhi is considered a historical residue and apparently first occurred as early as the ninth century when a massive number of Chinese loanwords entered the Japanese lexicon. When Chinese words started entering Japanese vocabulary, the process began compelling changes in the Japanese sound system (Vance 1987: 56). Students of Japanese encounter sandhi when they are taught changes of the final consonant of the past tense verb into Ø, /N/ or /Q/. When the verb root ends in a vowel (Pattern I) or /s/ (Pattern II), sandhi does not occur. The insertion of /i/ is required in some cases (Patterns II and III), but alteration only occurs in Pattern III. In other cases, the final consonant of the verb alters to a special consonant, /N/ or /Q/ (Patterns IV, V and VI). If the final consonant is voiced, /t/ becomes /d/.

Pattern I
When the final sound of the root is a vowel, no sandhi occurs:
見る　mi-ru → mi-**ta**
見える mie-ru → mie-**ta**

Pattern II
When the final sound of the root is /s/, it becomes /si/ before /t/:
増す mas-u → mas-i-**ta**

Pattern III
When the final consonant is /k/ or /g/, it is deleted before /i/ followed by /t/ or /d/:
抜く　nuk-u → nuk-i- **ta** → nu-i-**ta**
脱ぐ nug-u → nug-i-**da** → nu-i-**da**

Pattern IV
When the final consonant is /n/, /m/ or /b/, it becomes /N/ before /d/:
死ぬ sin-u → siN-**da**
編む am-u → aN-**da**
運ぶ hakob-u → hakoN-**da**

Pattern V
When the final consonant is /t/, /r/ or /w/, it becomes /Q/ before /t/:
待つ matu → maQ-**ta**
降る furu → fuQ-**ta**
洗う ara(w)u → araQ-**ta**

Pattern VI
The verb 行く is an exception. Although its root ends in /k/ (see Pattern III), it becomes /Q/ before /t/:
行く ik-u → iQ-**ta**

2.3.2　Other alterations

Three minor alterations need to be mentioned here. The first alteration occurs between two vowels: (i) /e/ → /a/, (ii) /i/ → /o/ and (iii) /o/ → /a/. These occur when two characters are conjoined, changing the final vowel of the first element into /a/ or /o/. As shown in 目蓋 *mabuta* 'eyelid', this alteration concurs with sequential voicing. Examples are based on the list

27

provided by Vance (1987: 149–153). We can observe certain irregularities. For example, 雨風 *amekaze* 'rain with wind' is not pronounced as /amakaze/. Similarly, 白糸 *shiroito* 'white thread' does not become /siraito/. According to Vance, these three vowel alterations are, similarly to sandhi, historical residues; they may signal that old Japanese used to have eight vowels.

> {/ame/ → /ama/} 雨 *ame* + 合羽 *kappa* → 雨合羽 *amagappa* 'raincoat'
> {/ame/ → /ama/} 雨 *ame* + 水 *mizu* → 雨水 *amamizu* 'rainwater'
> {/koe/ → /kowa/} 声 *koe* + 色 *iro* → 声色 *kowairo* 'a tone of voice'
> {/me/ → /ma/} 目 *me* + 蓋 *futa* → 目蓋 *mabuta* 'eyelid'
> {/ki/ → /ko/} 木 *ki* + 陰 *kage* → 木陰 *kokage* 'the shade of a tree'
> {/siro/ → /sira/} 白 *shiro* + 雲 *kumo* → 白雲 *shirakumo* 'white clouds'

The next alteration is the insertion of a sound when words are combined. All examples contain a character 雨 *ame* 'rain' as their second element. The first vowel /a/ becomes /sa/ as a result of the insertion of an alveolar fricative /s/. One presumes that this, too, is a historical residue. Not all words containing 雨 as the second element read as /same/, as shown in 大雨 *ōame* (× *ōsame*) 'heavy rain' or 長雨 *nagaame* 'long lasting rain' (× *nagasame*) (see also Table 3.2 in Chapter 3).

> {E1 + /ame/ → E2 + /same/}
> 春 *haru* + 雨 *ame* → 春雨 *harusame* 'spring rain'
> 秋 *aki* + 雨 *ame* → 秋雨 *akisame* 'autumn rain'
> 小 *ko* + 雨 *ame* → 小雨 *kosame* 'light rain'
> 霧 *kiri* + 雨 *ame* → 霧雨 *kirisame* 'drizzle'

The third alteration concerns two types of adjectives, な-adjective and い-adjective, when they are used in past tense. A cluster of sounds is inserted between the root of both adjectives (/sizuka/ and /utukusi/) and the past tense marker た: /daQ/ for な-adjective and /kaQ/ for い-adjective.

> 静か → 静かだった {/sizuka/ → /sizukadaQ + ta/}
> 美し → 美しかった {/utukusi/ → /utukusikaQ + ta/}

Activity 4

Your task in this activity is to identify sound alterations in Text 2.1 (p. 25). List all the verbs that are attached by a suffix beginning with /t/, and try to explain what triggers the alteration.

Commentary

Table 2.4 summarizes the occurrences of morphologically complex verbs that demonstrate two types of sound change, one being sandhi and the

Table 2.4

Lines	Examples	Phonological representation	Sound change patterns
1	鳴り出した	naridas-i-ta	II
2	座って	suwaQ-te	V
2	いた	i-ta	I
2	慌てて	awate-te	I
2	探った	saguQ-ta	V
3	はじめた	hajime-ta	I
5	見回した	mimawas-i-ta	II
5	はさんで	hasaɴ-de	IV
5	抱えた	kakae-ta	I
6	だった	daQ-ta	Addition of /Q/
7	むけた	muke-ta	I
7	だった	daQ-ta	Addition of /Q/
8–9	いった	iQ-ta	V
9	似た	ni-ta	I
9	抱いて	ida-i-te	III
9	いた	i-ta	I
10	通して	toRs-i-te	II
10	言った	iQ-ta	V
12	だった	daQ-ta	Addition of /Q/
13	走り続けた	hasirituzuke-ta	I
13	眠りかけて	nemurikake-te	I
14	いた	i-ta	I

other the insertion of a special consonant /Q/. It is intriguing that a compound verb 走り続けた 'continued to run' (line 13) whose second element begins with /t/ is not subject to the alteration. This substantiates the observation that sandhi occurs only when the first element precedes a suffix but not when the word forms a compound.

Activity 5

Look at Text 2.1 again. You were asked to find cases of sequential voicing (Activity 3, p. 25) and sound alterations (Activity 4, p. 28). Now you are asked to identify examples for each of the following assimilation processes. Try to find one example for each case and include your concise explanations.

- Progressive assimilation
- Regressive assimilation
- Palatalization assimilation
- Voice assimilation
- Place of articulation assimilation.

29

Commentary

An instance of progressive assimilation is that /s/ is realized as [s] in はさんで (line 5) and as [ʃ] in しれない (line 8), respectively.

Regressive assimilation is found in 買い物袋 *kaimono-bukuro* 'shopping bag' (line 5), in which the first segment of the compound (買い /kai/) makes the initial consonant /h/ of the second segment (袋 /hukuro/) voiced (/kaimonobukuro/). Vowel gemination pertains to regressive assimilation: /ou/ (or /oR/) becomes [o:] because of the preceding /o/ in ような /yoRna/ (lines 1–2), そう /soR/ (line 8), and ように /yoRni/ (line 11).

Palatalization assimilation takes place when, for example, the glottal fricative /h/ is followed by a high vowel /i/; it is realized as the palatal fricative [ç], as in 控える *hikaeru* 'refrain' (line 11).

Vowel devoicing is an example of voice assimilation. For example, 通して (line 10) undergoes devoicing because /i/ is surrounded by voiceless consonants: /toRsite/ → [to:ʃi̥te].

When /N/ becomes like the sound that follows it, this assimilation changes the place of articulation of the preceding sound. For example, /N/ in 何でも /naNdemo/ (line 12) and 半分 /haNbuN/ (line 13) are modified depending on the place of articulation of the following consonant. In the former, /N/ becomes /n/ (i.e., [nandemo]) because of the alveolar [d], while in the latter /N/ changes to /m/ (i.e., [hambun]) due to the bilabial /b/. The manner of articulation of these sounds (i.e., nasal) remains unchanged.

2.4 Mora

Another important trait of Japanese sound structure is the putting together of phonemes according to **moraic structure**. A mora is a unit that organizes the way in which phonemes are ordered. How does it do this? The answer is that the time needed to pronounce each mora is supposed to have approximately the same length or duration. This means that phonemes are organized according to a temporal unit whose duration of pronunciation is approximately the same. As shown below, the moraic unit is formed following one of six combinations of sounds, each unit requiring roughly the same duration when pronounced. No single consonant except the special consonants /N/ and /Q/ can form a moraic unit (see 2.1), while each vowel (i.e., /a, e, i, o, u/) and a special vowel /R/ comprise one moraic unit.

```
I     V
II    C V
III   Cy V
IV    N
V     Q
VI    R
```

For instance, 坂 'slope' consists of two morae, that is, /sa.ka/, and each mora, /sa/ and /ka/, is supposed to be constant in its duration. When /N/ is in the middle, we get 参加 /sa.N.ka/ 'participation' with three morae. As these two examples show, one mora corresponds to one item in the *kana* syllabary (e.g., さ, ん, か).

Let us look at the meaning of each combination of moraic structure. Combination I refers to items in the *kana* syllabary of the あ column (i.e., あ,い,う,え,お), where one vowel forms one mora. Thus, 愛 /a.i/ 'love' consists of two morae, and 家 /i.e/ 'house, home' likewise has two morae.

Combination II is where one consonant is followed by one vowel such as 蚊 /ka/ 'mosquito' or 歯 /ha/ 'teeth'; this refers to all items of the *kana* syllabary except the あ column, the palatalized consonants (e.g., きゃ, きゅ, きょ), and the special consonant ん.

Combination III refers to palatalized consonants. Consonants such as a velar consonant /k/ are occasionally palatalized when articulated with the rising of the tongue towards the hard palate (see Figure 1.2 in Chapter 1, section 1.2.2). Palatalization is indicated in writing by adding small ゃ, ゅ, ょ symbols to the preceding *kana* syllabary. Thus, きゃく (客) /kya.ku/ 'guest' consists of two morae; ひゃく (百) /hya.ku/ 'hundred' also contains two morae. ひゃくしょう (百姓) /hya.ku.syo.R/ 'farmer, peasant' has four morae.

Combination IV shows that one mora consists of one consonant /N/ or ん. Thus, 三 /sa.N/ 'three' has two morae, while 安心 /a.N.si.N/ 'relief' has four morae.

Combination V concerns geminate consonants such as 学校 /ga.Q.ko.R/ 'school' or バッタ /ba.Q.ta/ 'grasshopper'. The former consists of four morae, the latter three.

Combination VI involves geminate vowels (i.e., /aR/, /iR/, /uR/, /eR/, /oR/) such as 名画 /me.R.ga/ 'noted film, masterpiece of painting' or 解答 /ka.i.to.R/ 'answer'. They are written in Japanese in two ways: (i) by repeating the initial vowel in *hiragana* (e.g., /ra.R.me.N/ らあめん 'Chinese noodles'), and (ii) by using a dash (–) in *katakana* (e.g., /ra.R.me.N/ ラーメン).

31

The perception of mora in Japanese is important for several reasons. First, the presence of mora can explain why the pronunciations of 谷 /ta.ni/ 'valley' and 単位 /ta.N.i/ 'unit' are different. In the former, /n/ forms a mora when combined with /i/, while in the latter, /N/ constitutes a mora by itself. In other words, /N/ in 単位 belongs to the first segment of a compound (i.e., 単), whereas 谷 forms a morphologically simple word, in other words, not segmentable. The pair 蟹 /ka.ni/ 'crab' and 簡易 /ka.N.i/ 'simplicity' illustrates the same morphophonological processes.

Second, speech errors seem to occur in accordance with moraic structure. In Japanese, consonants are often replaced by vowels or vice versa. In the example below, /n/ is replaced by /i/ (Tsujimura 1996: 69):

da.n.ga.i.sa.i.ba.n.syo　弾劾裁判所　'Court of Impeachment'　→
da.i.ga.n.sa.i.ba.n.syo

This speech error can occur because the substitution is sensitive to two morae, and this fact extends beyond the qualitative difference between consonant and vowel. In English or other languages whose basic organization is not moraic, this type of substitution would hardly occur.

Third, when foreign loanwords enter the Japanese lexicon, they undergo a phonological change based on moraic structure. The English word *dessert* /dɪsə:rt/, which consists of two syllabic units, becomes デザート /de.za.a.to/, which contains four moraic units. Another English word *skin* /skɪn/ has one syllabic unit, which becomes スキン /su.ki.N/ with three morae. When foreign words end with a consonant or a schwa /ə/, one of the five vowels is employed to fulfil the moraic structure. Table 2.5 illustrates some examples. *May Day* ends with a diphthong /eɪ/, but its Japanese equivalent triggers the prolongation of /e/.

When the foreign loanword is a long word such as *department store*, it normally shortens to four or five morae. We say デパート *depāto* 'department store' and スーパー *sūpā* 'supermarket', both of which have four morae. There are more examples of foreign loanwords in section 3 of Chapter 3. When young people coin their young people's language,

Table 2.5 *Pronunciation of English loanwords in Japanese*

Examples	English	Word-final vowel in Japanese
データ	data /deɪtə/	a
ケーキ	cake /keɪk/	i
デスク	desk /desk/	u
メーデー	May Day /meɪ deɪ/	e
デート	date /deɪt/	o

the same phonological alteration seems to be at work. A word such as 気持ち悪い *kimochi-warui* 'feel unwell, sick' turns into a three-moraic word キモい *kimoi* (see JLU: Chapter 4, section 4.5.1)

Activity 6

No commentary is provided for this activity.

This activity involves practice in identifying different morae. First look at the examples and then use the presentations demonstrated in section 2.4. Words are taken from Text 2.1 (p. 25). The list includes four additional words.

Example: a.ka. two morae (V.CV).

3 下校 げこう	2 音 おと	4 空想 くうそう
3 途中 とちゅう	3 単位 たんい	2 蟹 かに
3 簡易 かんい	4 探った さぐった	3 車内 しゃない
2 バス	4 風景 ふうけい	4 乗客 じょうきゃく
2 谷 たに	4 おばさん	2 顔 かお

2.5 Pitch accent

Pitch accent is a type of accent specific to Japanese (apart from 'stress accent' as in English, and 'tone accent' as in Chinese) and is identified through the pitch patterns assigned to the entire word. Pitch is a physical property of sounds and is characterized by lowness and highness of the sound. High pitch is produced when, for example, women squeal, while low pitch is produced when we speak softly and quietly. These different qualities of sound are applied to the speech sounds in Japanese. Japanese has four basic pitch patterns: (i) L (Low), (ii) HL (HighLow), (iii) LH (LowHigh) and (iv) LHL (LowHighLow). These patterns are associated with morae, that is, each mora is assigned one pitch (low or high), and the pronunciation of the entire word is accompanied by a combination of pitch patterns. You may recall six patterns of moraic structure demonstrated in section 2.4. Each moraic pattern is assigned one pitch accent. Taken this way, 桃 /momo/ comprises two morae, having a low and high accent, while 股 /momo/ likewise comprises two morae, having a high and low accent. In short, this homonym is differentiated by two pitch accent patterns. It is important to note that basic textbooks for Japanese introduce, as a rule, Tokyo pitch accent, as it is considered standard in education. In reality, people from different dialectal backgrounds use different

33

pitch accents. To illustrate, local residents in Fukushima City in Tohoku do not normally make a clear accentual distinction between 桃 and 腿 (see Map II in *Japanese Pronunciation and Accent Dictionary* 1985).

An understanding of pitch accent is especially important when dealing with homonyms. The list below contains six such words. The first three have the same order of phonemes, as do the next three. Each word is indicated by the patterns of pitch accent. In *Japanese Pronunciation and Accent Dictionary* (1985: 710), 鉢 and 八 are assigned the same pitch accent. The prime symbol (') is inserted in the locus of accent – the place where high pitch falls to low pitch. Words such as 端 (3) and 蜂 (6), in which high pitch is not followed by low pitch, are not marked by the prime symbol.

箸　橋　端　鉢　八　蜂

(1) 箸 /ha'si/ 'chopsticks' HighLow
(2) 橋 /hasi'/ 'bridge' LowHighLow
(3) 端 /hasi/ 'corner' LowHigh
(4) 鉢 /hati'/ 'flower pot' LowHighLow
(5) 八 /hati'/ 'eight' LowHighLow
(6) 蜂 /hati/ 'bee' LowHigh

Bear in mind that homonyms such as 町 *machi* versus 街, 始め *hajime* versus 初め, 関心 *kanshin* versus 感心 and 意志 *ishi* versus 意思 are pronounced with the same pitch accent and their meanings are quite similar. These words are distinguished by the context (see JLU: Chapter 2, section 2.3) in which they are used or the co-text (see JLU: Chapter 2, section 2.2) with which they co-occur.

Activity 7

Manga, or comic strips, contain quite a few expressions that represent spoken Japanese. At first glance, spoken expressions strike us as 'deviant' from standard expressions (that we normally learn in language tutorials). The important thing is that phonological processes often give rise to spoken expressions. The five texts below are taken from 陽あたり良好 *Hiatari Ryōkō* 'Full of Sunshine' and いつも美空 *Itsumo Misora* 'Always Misora' (personal name). Each drawing contains a spoken expression that represents a phonological process. Your task is to identify the phonological process and then explain what this process is.

Text 2.2

© 1996 Adachi, Mitsuru / *Hiatari Ryōkō* (p. 298), Shogakukan

Text 2.3

© 2001 Adachi, Mitsuru / *Itsumo Misora* (p. 172), Shogakukan

Text 2.4

© 1996 Adachi, Mitsuru / *Hiatari Ryōkō* (p. 18), Shogakukan

35

Text 2.5

© 1996 Adachi, Mitsuru / *Hiatari Ryōkō* (p. 320), Shogakukan

Text 2.6

© 1996 Adachi, Mitsuru / *Hiatari Ryōkō* (p. 50), Shogakukan

Commentary

Text 2.2 contains an expression 行くぞォ /i.ku.zo.R/ 'We're leaving!'. This expression is created by a geminated vowel. The vowel ォ is a repetition of the second part of the preceding CV mora (/zo/). In spoken Japanese, the final vowel is often prolonged to underline the meaning of the word, and it is, needless to say, a frequently occurring technique in most *manga*.

Text 2.3 has an expression だっけ /da.Q.ke/. っけ is reminiscent of an auxiliary けり *keri* in old Japanese and is used in spoken modern Japanese to express uncertainty. In modern Japanese it is categorized as a sentence-final particle and occurs exclusively in informal talks among close friends or kinships regardless of gender. A copula /da/ is combined with /k/, whereby /k/ influences the preceding sound, resulting in the insertion of the geminate consonant. In section 2.3.2, we dealt with a similar case with だった /da.Q.ta/, which also contains the gemination of /t/ when the past marker た is attached to the copula だ.

Text 2.4 deals with a special consonant /N/. The key expression is なにしてんの /na.ni.si.te.N.no/. Here /N/ replaces る /ru/. The equivalent expressions you may have learned in a classroom should be なにしているの 'What are you doing?' or its shortened, more colloquial form なにしてるの (い is deleted). The alteration from /ru/ to /N/ sounds most colloquial, and it occurs in conversations between friends or family members, signalling their closeness and familiarity. The two people in Text 2.4 know each other well, and this circumstance gives rise to the phonological alteration. おばさん literally means 'aunt' but is also used as a form of address for a lady who is middle aged.

Text 2.5 contains an exclamation わっ with a small っ at the end. This symbol is used when the utterance is emphatic (see also Vance 1987: 32–33). わっ expresses the speaker's heightened emotions or excitement, for example, when something happens unexpectedly. In Text 2.5, かすみ *Kasumi* and 高杉くん *Takasugi-kun* 'Mr Takasugi' are excited about the fact that the fish they caught looks big. We have learned that the small っ represents the first part of a geminate (see Text 2:3), but in Text 2.5 this symbol refers to **glottalization**. This means that the second sound of the final mora (i.e., V) is pronounced with the closure of the vocal cords. This phonological process results in the simultaneous articulation of two successive sounds (or more technically, coarticulation). This closure of the vocal cords is transcribed using the symbol [ʔ] in the following way: わっ [waʔ]. Ō (1996: 24–25) claim that あっ is an example of glottalization to express happiness or delight. It is plain to see the similarity between this example and ours. Vance (1987: 43) treats utterance-final glottal as an allophone of /Q/.

「あっ、あった!」 'Oh, I've found it!'

Finally, Text 2.6 depicts the deletion of the first mora of a word. ったく is a shortened form of まったく /ma.Q.ta.ku/. Similar to Texts 2:2 and 2:4, this shortened form is used in emphatic utterances. In Text 2.6, かすみ *Kasumi* speaks this way to intensify her disapproval of 高杉くん's *Takasugi-kun's* carelessness: he went on skiing down the hill without turning in the opposite direction despite her earnest advice. Saying ったく shows her annoyance to be excessive. You may certainly have come across the expression まったく during your study of Japanese. It is normally used in its 'basic' senses. *Kodansha's Furigana Japanese-English Dictionary*

37

(1995: 457) provides English translations such as 'quite, really, completely, absolutely, at all' for まったく. ったく cannot be used here, as it is an exclamation to convey the speaker's emotions but does not function as an adverb.

> それはまったく (×ったく) 別の事だよ。
> *Sore wa mattaku betsu no koto da yo.*
> That's a completely different matter.

The discussion above demonstrates that *manga* utilize particular phonological processes, and these processes are employed efficiently to create effective spoken text. Looked at in this way, phonological variations mirror in one way or another emotions (e.g., anger, irritation, surprise, disappointment, joy, expectation) assigned to the protagonists in a given story. This phenomenon can be seen to represent aspects of **meta-language** – a language, expressed verbally or non-verbally, that comments on the meaning of the utterance (see Mey 2001: 173–175). To take an example, ったく in Text 2.6 can be interpreted as the metalanguage saying 'I am annoyed'. The use of mimetic words in *manga* (see Chapter 3, Activity 8, pp. 67–70) can also be subsumed within this concept. It may be worthwhile to bear in mind that some metalinguistic statements in *manga* are often exaggerated and may not always parallel real speech situations in contemporary Japan. Although *manga* have recently gained popularity as teaching materials considered to represent Japanese colloquialism (Mangajin 1998; Katō et al. 2003), we should remember that some, if not all, *manga* employ frivolous and fanciful styles of writing and descriptions. In this regard, special styles we observe in Japanese *manga* could be seen as the emotive voices of the authors themselves.

Let us briefly look at the daily column in the 11 June 2002 edition of the *Mainichi Newspaper*. It highlights the same point: when Japanese cheer their national team at the world cup soccer game, they do not say ニホンコール /ni.ho.N/ but ニッポンコール /ni.Q.po.N/ with a geminate. The reason is straightforward: the latter with a phonological change is more expressive and adequate. The insertion of a geminate occurs when an utterance is carried out with an emphasis. The addition of /Q/ has been interpreted as 'colloquialism', 'slang', or 'vulgarism' in traditional Japanese linguistics literature (cited in Vance 1987: 148), but colloquialism should not be treated simply as 'deviant' from the standard language; rather it elaborates on the reality of everyday communication in Japanese society.

Text 2.7

> ニッポンコールはあるがニホンコールはあまり聞かない。日本語でも
>
> 「とても」が「とっても」、「やはり」が「やっぱり」になるように、
>
> 促音が入ると意味が強調される。ワールドカップも「ニッポン」でなけ
>
> ればやっぱり力が入らないとみえる。

© 2002 *Mainichi Newspaper* 11 June

Translation:
We hear 'Nippon-kōru' but do not often hear 'Nihon-kōru'. In the same way as 'totemo' becomes 'tottemo' and 'yahari' becomes 'yappari' in Japanese, the insertion of geminates emphasizes the meaning. The cheering seems to lose its efficacy without 'nippon' in the world cup.

Note

1. Consult *New Concise Japanese Accent Dictionary* (2006: 24–5) for more elaboration of geminate vowels.
2. 拗音 *yō-on* are the sounds produced by the combination of the palatalized consonant and the vowel. It is important to note that the transcription of three subclasses of 拗音 (i.e., (i) しゃ [ʃa], しゅ [ʃɯ], しょ [ʃo], (ii) じゃ [dʒa], じゅ [dʒɯ], じょ [dʒo] and (iii) ちゃ [tʃa], ちゅ [tʃɯ], ちょ [tʃo]) contain [ʃ], [dʒ] and [tʃ], respectively. These sounds are presented as allophones in Table 2.3. However, it is more likely that they are phonemes here, since they occur freely in three environments (before the vowel [a], [ɯ] or [o]), that is, their occurrences are not complementary.

3 Vocabulary

Vocabulary, or 語彙 *goi*, is used in two different but interrelated senses. The first sense refers to the words individual speakers know in a given language (e.g., Japanese), while the second sense refers to the total number of words encoded in a given language. In the first sense, we say 'His vocabulary is limited' or 'She has a wide vocabulary' to refer to the differing capacities of individuals to deal with words. This chapter is concerned with the second sense and provides an overview of three vocabulary strata that have played an important role in the construction of the modern Japanese lexicon. These three strata (語種 *goshu*) include **native-Japanese words** (和語 *wago*), **Sino-Japanese words** (漢語 *kango*) and **foreign loanwords** (外来語 *gairaigo*). According to scholars, basic concepts in our everyday life often fall under native-Japanese words (Ōno 1974: 6), while Sino-Japanese words tend to be used to express abstract or scientific concepts because of their precision (Maynard 1998: 15). Sections 3.1 to 3.4 take a closer look at the characterizations of each stratum. Sections 3.5 to 3.7 examine Japanese vocabulary from three perspectives: (i) how choice of vocabulary and text type interrelate (3.5), (ii) how new vocabulary comes into existence (3.6) and (iii) how mimetic words enrich the vocabulary (3.7).

3.1 Native-Japanese words

3.1.1 General

Native-Japanese words (NJ, henceforth), or 和語 *wago*, are those words that existed before the active borrowing of Chinese words took place at about the sixth century. The first character 和 *wa* is an ancient name for Japan before the modern name 日本 *nihon* (read as /riben/ in Mandarin) came to be used at about the seventh century. The character 和 is still used to refer to Japan in some expressions of modern Japanese; compounds such as 和洋折衷 *wayō-setchū* 'blending of Japanese and Western styles', 和式 *washiki* 'Japanese style', 和歌 *waka* 'Japanese poems', 英和辞典 *ēwa-jiten* 'English-Japanese dictionary' or 和英辞典 *waē-jiten* 'Japanese-English dictionary' are some examples. What characterizes 和語 is that they are read in *kun*-reading (訓読み *kunyomi*), which is an original reading of NJ words. The *kun*-reading of words such as 雨 *ame*, 山 *yama*, or 水 *mizu* indicates that they are originally NJ words; the fact that they are written in Chinese characters goes back to that ancient time when NJ words were assigned appropriate Chinese characters, or 漢字 *kanji*. This historical event took place after Sino-Japanese words were introduced into Japan. For example, the Chinese character 雨 (read as /yü/ in Mandarin) meaning 'rain' was assigned to the Japanese word pronounced /ame/, which means 'rain'.

Activity 1

Now that you have learned that NJ words are written in Chinese characters, it is useful for you to distinguish NJ words from Sino-Japanese words. The distinction between the two coincides with *kun* and *on* readings (訓読み *kun-yomi* and 音読み *on-yomi*, respectively). *Kun*-reading is a Japanese reading (e.g., 雨 *ame*), while *on* reading is the Chinese way of reading *kanji* (e.g., 雨 *u*) derived from the pronunciation of original Chinese words. Look at an extract below, the beginning of a daily column 天声人語 *tensē-jingo* 'Heaven's Voice and Men's Words' in the *Asahi Newspaper*. This column describes a ward in a hospital where seriously handicapped children are treated and accommodated. List the words written in *kanji* and indicate whether they are NJ or Sino-Japanese. Consult a dictionary (e.g., 漢和辞典 *kanwa-jiten*) when you have concerns about the readings.

Text 3.1

スプーンを口に近づけられると、いやいやをする。舌が飛び出してくる。いったん口に入れた食べものをプーと吐き出す子もいる。国立病院機構・千葉東病院 の 重症 心身障害児の病棟である。ここの子どもたちは、一人では食べることも飲むこともできない。その訓練を見せてもらう機会があった。看護婦さんらがやさしく声をかけて緊張をほぐす。子どもたちのあごに手を当てて、口をゆっくり閉じる。そうすれば、もぐもぐできるようになる。

© 2005 *Asahi Newspaper* 2 May

Translation:
When children are given a spoon closer to their mouth, they utterly refuse it. They stick out their tongue. Some vomit the food they already had in their mouth. Here is a ward in the Higashi Hospital, Chiba, which accommodates severely handicapped children. It belongs to a national hospital organization. Children here can neither eat nor drink alone. I had a chance to observe the training of these children. Nurses speak to them gently and relax their tension. They touch their hand on the children's jaws and get their mouths to close slowly. This training helps the children to chew the food.

Commentary

The total number of expressions (segmented according to meaningful units) with *kanji* is 31 (口 appears three times and 子どもたち appears twice). Words with *kun* reading (= NJ words) are used 19 times, while words with *on* reading (= Sino-Japanese words) are used 11 times. It is interesting to note that more NJ words are used in this passage than Sino-Japanese. The clue to identifying the two readings is that *kun* is often accompanied by *hiragana* to complete the meaning of the entire word. For example, 近づける has the *kanji* part 近 supplemented by *hiragana* づける to mean 'to approach'. Sino-Japanese words consist merely of *kanji*. There is one compound (千葉, the name of a prefecture in Kanto District) consisting of 千 *chi* (Sino-Japanese) 'thousand' and 葉 *ha* (NJ) 'leaf'. There is also one foreign loanword (スプーン *supūn* 'spoon'). This last type will be dealt with in Section 3.3.

> *Kun* reading (NJ):
> 口 (3), 近づける, 舌, 飛び出す, 食べもの, 吐き出す, 東,
> 子どもたち (2),
> 一人, 食べる, 飲む, 見せる, 声, 手, 当てる, 閉じる
>
> *On* reading (Sino-Japanese):
> 国立病院, 機構, 病院, 重症, 心身, 障害児, 病棟, 訓練, 機会, 看護婦,
> 緊張
>
> Hybrids (*on* + *kun*):
> 千葉

3.1.2 Expressions for body parts

Ōno states (1974: 6) that the **basic vocabulary** often consists of NJ words. 'Basic' means vocabulary words essential to our everyday life. According to Ōno (ibid.), words such as 月 *tsuki* 'moon', 風 *kaze* 'wind' and 水 *mizu* 'water' are basic words because they represent basic components of nature.

In a similar vein, Trask (1996: 23) refers to basic vocabulary in English. According to him, basic vocabulary comprises classes of words less likely to be borrowed because they refer to items of high frequency that we can expect to find in every language. In other words, borrowing tends to occur when speakers of the borrowing language are unfamiliar with the concepts of new things that exist in the lending language (ibid.: 18). He (ibid.: 23) mentions the following classes of words that are basic to every language and are therefore rarely borrowed: kinship terms, names of body parts, simple verbs (e.g., *go, be, have, want, see, eat* and *die*), simple adjectives (e.g., *big, small, good, bad* and *old*) and names of natural phenomena (e.g., *sun, moon, star, fire, rain, river, snow, day* and *night*).

In Japanese, many words designating **body parts** are NJ (see also Hoshino 1976: 167), as shown below.

> 足 *ashi* 'foot', 脚 *ashi* 'leg', 歯 *ha* 'teeth', 肘 *hiji* 'elbow', 膝 *hiza* 'knee', 顔 *kao* 'face', 肩 *kata* 'shoulder', 髪 *kami* 'hair', 口 *kuchi* 'mouth', 首 *kubi* 'neck', 腰 *koshi* 'waist', 毛 *ke* 'hair', 背 *se* 'height', 手 *te* 'hand', 目 *me* 'eye', 耳 *mimi* 'ear', 腿 *momo* 'thigh', 指 *yubi* 'finger'

The following list of verbs is composed of NJ words; every action they denote makes use of one or two parts of our body. Interestingly, basic activities in our human life such as speaking, seeing, eating, hearing or sleeping are all expressed in NJ words.

> 歩く *aruku* 'walk', 走る *hashiru* 'run', 蹴る *keru* 'kick', 聞く *kiku* 'hear, listen to', 見る *miru* 'see, watch, look at', なめる *nameru* 'lick', 殴る *naguru* 'hit, knock', 眠る *nemuru* 'sleep', 飲む *nomu*, 'drink', 押す *osu* 'push', 触る *sawaru* 'touch', 吸う *sū* 'inhale, smoke', 叩く *tataku* 'knock', 立つ *tatsu* 'stand', 食べる *taberu* 'eat', 打つ *utsu* 'hit', 休む *yasumu* 'rest'

Table 3.1 classifies verbs according to the major body parts each action denotes.

Table 3.1

Verbs	Body parts used
吸う, なめる	lips
見る	eyes
聞く	ears
食べる, 飲む	mouth, fingers and hands
歩く, 走る, 蹴る	legs
休む, 眠る, 触る, 押す, 叩く, 殴る, 打つ	the body in general

3.1.3 Weather expressions

NJ words are particularly rich in **weather expressions** (Shibatani 1990: 140–141). This reflects traditional Japanese society in which farming has been an important activity, the success of which depends on weather conditions. The association of NJ words with weather also substantiates their basic function as expressions of basic terms in everyday life. As Table 3.2 demonstrates, each word refers to one of the four seasons. Note, however, that not all words are NJ words. Words such as 南風 *nanpū* 'south wind' or 台風 *taifū* 'typhoon' are read in a Chinese manner and are indicators of summer and autumn, respectively.

Table 3.2

Seasons	Weather expressions	
	雨	風
春 *haru*	春雨 *harusame* 'spring rain' 五月雨 *samidare* 'early summer rain'	春風 *harukaze* 'spring breeze/wind' 春一番 *haruichiban* 'the first storm in the spring'
夏 *natsu*	梅雨 *tsuyu* 'the rainy season' にわか雨 *niwakaame* 'shower'	やませ *yamase* 'cold dry wind blowing down from over the mountains'
秋 *aki*	秋雨 *akisame* 'autumn rain'	秋風 *akikaze* 'autumn wind/breeze' 涼風 *ryōfū* 'cool/refreshing breeze' 野分 *nowake* 'a typhoon of early autumn'
冬 *fuyu*	時雨 *shigure* 'shower in early winter' 氷雨 *hisame* 'chill rain'	木枯らし *kogarashi* 'cold wintry wind' 北風 *kitakaze* 'north wind' 空っ風 *karakkaze* 'dry wind'

Some weather expressions are related to the parts of the day. The reason 夕露 *yūtsuyu* 'evening dew' (intended reading and meaning) is absent is simply that the dew normally falls during the night or early in the morning. This shows that whatever does not occur as a natural phenomenon is absent from linguistic expressions.

Table 3.3

Parts of a day	Weather expressions	
	露 *tsuyu*	風 *kaze*
朝 *asa*	朝露 *asatsuyu* 'the morning dew'	朝風 *asakaze* 'morning breeze'
夕 *yū*	–	夕風 *yūkaze* 'evening breeze'
夜 *yoru*	夜露 *yotsuyu* 'night dew'	夜風 *yokaze* 'night wind'

Weather expressions also penetrate into the literary world. 短歌 *tanka* 'Japanese verse with thirty-one morae' or 俳句 *haiku* 'poem with seventeen morae' often contain weather expressions (e.g., 春雨 'spring rain' and 木枯らし 'cold wintry wind') that have the effect of evoking images of the natural world, and accordingly of the writer's sentimentality (see Chapter 2, section 2.4 for the notion of 'mora'). The following are two famous examples from 短歌 and 俳句, respectively.

くれなゐの二尺のびたる薔薇の芽の針やはらかに**春雨**のふる
Kurenaino nishaku nobitaru bara no me no hari yawarakani harusame no furu
A rose in bright red has grown as high as 60 cm. Spring rain falls gently on the surface of a soft and tiny bud of this rose.

海に出て**木枯らし**帰るところなし
Umi ni dete kogarashi kaeru tokoro nashi
A strong, wintry wind blows into the sea and it never returns to the land.

3.2 Sino-Japanese words

3.2.1 General

Sino-Japanese words (SJ, henceforth), or 漢語 *kango*, arrived in Japan through Korea when Buddhism (仏教 *bukkyō*) was brought to Japan in the middle of the sixth century (AD 538). It is generally stated that from the third century onward the state of Yamato (大和朝廷 *Yamato-chōtei*) already had contact with the Continent and possessed knowledge of Chinese words. However, Chinese words did not begin to spread widely in Japan until Japanese people started reading books about Buddhism. Before the introduction of Chinese words, Japanese had no means of written expression. After this important historical event, Japanese people not only adopted Chinese words but also invented new words by assigning new meanings to existing Chinese words (2) or by combining Chinese characters differently (3). Some Japan-made words were even reimported to China (4). We can characterize the adoption of Chinese words and characters by Japanese in the four ways below.[1] Simplified Chinese characters are not considered here when their old forms correspond to current Japanese characters.

(1) Words that exist in both Japanese and Chinese and have the same meaning:

45

	Meaning
夜景 *yakei*	scene by night
秘密 *himitsu*	secret
調和 *chōwa*	harmony
時間 *jikan*	time
娯楽 *goraku*	leisure
肥料 *hiryō*	fertilizer
花瓶 *kabin*	vase
国民 *kokumin*	nation
困難 *kon-nan*	difficulty
早退 *sōtai*	leave school early

(2) Words that exist in both Japanese and Chinese, but that can have a different meaning in Chinese:

	Japanese	Chinese
野菜 *yasai*	vegetable	wild vegetables
汽車 *kisha*	train	bus, car
医院 *īn*	doctor's office	hospital
勉強 *benkyō*	study, learn	achieve something with difficulty
工作 *kōsaku*	handicraft	work
試験 *shiken*	exam	experiment
露骨 *rokotsu*	direct, blunt	projected bone
新聞 *shinbun*	newspaper	news
残業 *zangyō*	overtime work	cruel work
左右 *sayū*	influence	left and right
大変 *taihen*	very	change largely
交通 *kōtsū*	traffic	communication
愛人 *aijin*	mistress	husband/wife
便宜 *bengi*	convenient	cheap

(3) Words that exist only in Japanese:

	Meaning
非常口 *hijōguchi*	emergency exit
財布 *saifu*	wallet, purse
映画 *ēga*	movie
運転 *unten*	drive
土足 *dosoku*	bare foot
女体 *nyotai*	female body
自転車 *jitensha*	bicycle
度胸 *dokyō*	courage
挨拶 *aisatsu*	greeting

(4) Japan-made words (words originated in Japan) reimported into Chinese (see Kindaichi 1998: 52). Most were coined when Western words were introduced into Japanese society during the Meiji Period. Since Japanese vocabulary was insufficient for translating the newly arrived words, new words were coined using Chinese characters. These words are often called 和製漢語 *wasē-kango* 'Japan-made Sino-Japanese' (see also 和製英語 *wasē-eigo* in section 3.3.2).

		Japanese/Chinese
哲学	*tetsugaku*	philosophy
放送	*hōsō*	broadcast
社会	*shakai*	society
科学	*kagaku*	science
文学	*bungaku*	literature
心理	*shinri*	psychology
自然	*shizen*	nature
工業	*kōgyō*	industry

Sections (2) to (4) are essentially Japan-made words, but they pertain to the category of SJ vocabulary in that they are read in *on*-reading and written in *kanji*. Thus, not all Sino-Japanese words are, strictly speaking, of Chinese origin. Because SJ vocabulary has been used since ancient times and has made important contributions to the creation of Japanese vocabulary, native speakers of Japanese do not feel that these are foreign loanwords.

Activity 2

At the outset of this chapter, we mentioned that SJ words are suitable for expressing abstract thoughts because of their precise and analytical quality. This activity will help increase your understanding of the nature of SJ words. Let us take a pair, 寝る *neru* and 就寝する *shūshin-suru*. These are considered synonymous because both express the activity of sleeping (see Chapter 6, section 6.1.2 for synonyms). Explain how these words differ in meaning and to what extent 就寝する is a more accurate expression. Consult a dictionary, if necessary.

Commentary

The basic meaning of 寝る is to lie somewhere. Thus, we can say 草の上に寝た *Kusa no ue ni neta* 'We lay on the grass'. When it comes to the activity of sleeping (e.g., 夜8時に寝た 'I went to bed at 8 pm'), it connotes that the person lies in a place such as a bed. By contrast, 就寝 is a 'compound' (see Chapter 5, section 5.5. for the notion) that combines 寝 with 就. By adding 就, the whole expression has a narrower, more specific meaning. Instead of meaning 'lying', it explicitly indicates that someone goes to bed and sleeps. The basic meaning of 就 is that one comes to be engaged in something. There are related compounds: 就職 *shūshoku* means that one comes to hold a post in a new workplace, while 就学 *shūgaku* means that children begin elementary education and 就任 *shūnin* refers to the commencement of a higher post resulting from promotion. 就寝 thus means that someone comes to sleep in bed. Thus a more specific meaning encoded in Sino-Japanese promotes the accuracy of the word meaning.

Activity 3

This activity is not provided with commentary.

Japanese has groups of words whose meanings differ depending on how they are read, *on* or *kun*. Examples are given in Table 3.4. Write an appropriate meaning for each word. Consult a dictionary, if necessary.

Table 3.4

Words	Native-Japanese	Meaning	Sino-Japanese	Meaning
風車	かざぐるま	pinwheel	ふうしゃ	windmill
色紙	いろがみ	colored paper	しきし	autograph paper
人気	ひとけ	signs of life	にんき	popular
細目	ほそめ	narrow eyes	さいもく	details
訳	わけ	reason	やく	translation
干物	ほしもの	hang out to dry clothes	ひもの	dried fish
一月	ひとつき	one month	いちがつ	January

3.2.2 Multiple readings

A notorious problem that students of Japanese encounter during their learning is that *kanji* have many *on*-readings. This variation reflects the historical fact that SJ words arrived in Japan at different times and from different regions in China, presumably via Korea. The fact that the characters used in present-day Japanese are called 漢字 *kanji* (*hanzi* in Chinese) has a historical explanation, since most of these characters arrived in Japan during the Han (written as 漢) Dynasty (206 BC to AD 9), the most influential in the history of China. We say 漢音 *kan-on* for the readings associated with this period. Chinese characters were also imported to Japan in three other periods. Readings associated with the Wu Dynasty (AD 222–280) are called 呉音 *go-on*,[2] readings associated with the Song Dynasty (AD 960–1279) are called 宋音 *sō-on*, and readings associated with the Tang Dynasty (AD 618–907) are called 唐音 *tō-on* (see also Kess and Miyamoto 1999: 14–16). For example, 行 exhibits three readings: (i) 漢音 (e.g., 旅行 *ryokō* 'trip'), (ii) 呉音 (e.g., 行政 *gyōsei* 'administration') and (iii) 唐音 (e.g., 行脚 *angya* 'pilgrimage'). Note that many *kanji* do not have all four readings. The most common *on*-reading is 漢音. 呉音 is the second most frequent reading, which came in with Buddhist terminology and spread into other domains (ibid.: 15). 唐音 and

宋音 are the least frequent readings and are also called 唐宋音 *tōsō-on* as a jointed name (e.g., 提灯 *chōchin* 'paper lantern', 椅子 *isu* 'chair', 蒲団 *futon* 'thick bed quilt'). Some examples are given in Table 3.5. Many of you may be familiar with 漢音 but may not be with 呉音.

Table 3.5

	Kanji	漢音 *kan-on*	呉音 *go-on*
1	仕	し (**仕**事 *shigoto* 'job')	じ （給**仕** *kyūji* 'waiter'）
2	目	もく (**目**的 *mokuteki* 'purpose')	ぼく （面**目** *menboku* 'face'）
3	食	しょく (**食**事 *shokuji* 'meal')	じき （断**食** *danjiki* 'fasten'）
4	若	じゃく (**若**年 *jakunen* 'younger generation')	にゃく （老**若** *rōnyaku* 'old and young people'）
5	遠	えん (**遠**足 *ensoku* 'excursion')	おん （久**遠** *kuon* 'eternity'）

老若男女　all people
ろう にゃく だんにょ

Activity 4

This activity is not provided with commentary.
The following sentences contain the same *kanji* with different *on*-readings. Give the appropriate reading for each word and indicate which *on*-reading it is. Do you think there are clues to different readings? State your opinions.

---

1. 中学校の入学祝いに人形をもらった。

2. 無理な試みだったが、無事にプロジェクトが終了した。

3. お正月なのに、校正の仕事を頼まれた。

4. 容易な方法で諸外国と貿易をしたい。

5. 暴力団の住み家が暴露された。

6. 信仰深い人でしたので、ニュースに仰天した。

7. 土砂降りの雨で道路の砂利が流れた。

8. あの柔和なKさんが柔道をしているとは驚きだ。

9. 効率よく勉強するように先生は率直な説明をした。

10. 体育施設が昨日施工された。

Translations:
1. I received a doll as a celebration of my entrance into the junior high school.
2. We completed the project safely although it was a tough attempt.
3. I was asked to do proofreading although it was New Year's Day.
4. I would like to trade with foreign countries in an easy way.
5. The location of the gangster's organization was disclosed.
6. We were astonished at the news because he was a man of deep faith.
7. A pouring rain washed away gravels on the road.
8. It is a surprise that Mr K, a gentle person, is practising judo.
9. The teacher gave us a straightforward explanation so that we can study efficiently.
10. The construction of the health and sports building started yesterday.

Exercise

After you have finished Activity 4, try to collect similar examples of pairs of *kanji*. Some kanji have the same writing but differ only in pronunciation (e.g., 明確 *mēkaku* versus 明後日 *myōgonichi*, 明星 *myōjō* versus 明星 *mēsē*, and 関西 *kansē* versus 関西 *kansai*).

3.3 Foreign loanwords

3.3.1 General

Foreign loanwords, or 外来語 *gairaigo*, entered Japanese at the beginning of the sixteenth century when Portuguese traders set foot on an island called 種子島 *Tanegashima*, south of 九州 *Kyūshū* in 1543. Unlike SJ words, foreign loanwords (FL, henceforth) are classified as loanwords because the borrowing took place much later than the introduction of SJ words. As mentioned earlier, upon the arrival of SJ words, Japanese underwent a period in which it intermingled with the Chinese language. Some scholars perceive that when FL words flowed into Japan, the Japanese language already had a well-established Japanese lexicon based on NJ and SJ words.

FL words were introduced to Japanese society when Japan came into direct contact with European civilization. The adoption of foreign words took place in three phases. The first occurred during the sixteenth century when the activities of European traders and Catholic missionaries brought a new cosmopolitan flavour to Japan. Since the Portuguese were the first European traders, Portuguese words such as *carta*, *tabaco*, *pão de Castella*, *castella* and *tutanaga* were adopted as かるた *karuta* 'Japanese-style play-ing card', たばこ *tabako* 'tobacco', かすてら *kasutera* 'sponge cake' and トタン *totan* 'corrugated iron'. Loanwords from these early periods are often written in *kanji*, as shown in (1) and (2) below. We see two ways of assigning *kanji*: *kanji* correspond to either the pronunciation of the word (1) or the meaning of the word (2). For example, the pronunciation of three characters in 加留多 in (1) imitates the way the original word is pronounced (= /ka.ru.ta/), while 煙草 in (2) reflects the meaning of cigar-ettes by combining characters meaning 煙 'smoke' and 草 'grass', thereby leaving pronunciation out of account.

(1) 羅紗 *rasha* 'woollen cloth', 襦袢 *juban* 'undergarment', 加留多 *karuta* 'Japanese syllabary cards', 天麩羅 *tenpura* 'deep-fat-fried food', 金平糖 *konpētō* 'sweets'.
(2) 煙草 *tabako* 'cigarette', 南瓜 *kabocha* 'pumpkin', 煙管 *kiseru* 'pipe'.[3]

The second phase of borrowing occurred during the Edo period (1600–1868). Only the Dutch and Chinese were allowed to trade at 長崎 *Nagasaki* in Kyushu. Consequently, words from Dutch such as *kop*, *ransel*, *schop* and *pek* entered the Japanese language as コップ *koppu* 'cup', ランドセル *randoseru* 'school satchel', スコップ *sukoppu* 'scoop, shovel' and ペンキ *penki* 'paint'. These words were no longer written in *kanji*; instead *katakana* started to be widely applied.

The third phase took place after the Meiji Restoration (1868) in which Japan resumed foreign trade. Foreign words from different European nations and the United States surged into Japanese vocabulary. The influence of English, whether British or American, is particularly noteworthy in modern Japanese. The following list gives some idea of English loanwords classified according to everyday routines.

Food
アイスクリーム *aisukurīmu* 'ice cream'
ウイスキー *uisukī* 'whisky'
サラダ *sarada* 'salad'
ドレッシング *doressingu* 'dressing'
ジャム *jamu* 'jam'
バター *batā* 'butter'
マーガリン *māgarin* 'margarine'
ホットドッグ *hottodoggu* 'hot dog'
ハンバーガー *hanbāgā* 'hamburger'
サンドイッチ *sandoitchi* 'sandwich'

51

Dresses and ornaments
エプロン *epuron* 'apron'
セーター *sētā* 'sweater'
ジーンズ *jīnzu* 'jeans'
シャツ *shatsu* 'shirt'
アクセサリー *akusesarī* 'accessory'
イヤリング *iyaringu* 'earring'

Sports
ゴルフ *gorufu* 'golf'
スキー *sukī* 'ski'
バトミントン *batominton* 'badminton'
サッカー *sakkā* 'soccer'
スケート *sukēto* 'skate'
テニス *tenisu* 'tennis'

News
ニュース *nyūsu* 'news'
アナウンサー *anaunsā* 'announcer'
コラム *koramu* 'column'
インタビュー *intabyū* 'interview'
レポーター *repōtā* 'reporter'

Others
コンディション *kondishon* 'condition'
チャンス *chansu* 'chance'
スリル *suriru* 'thrill'
スタミナ *sutamina* 'stamina'
メッセージ *messēji* 'message'
リスク *risuku* 'risk'

3.3.2 Patterns of adoption

Foreign words did not enter Japanese vocabulary randomly; instead they were adopted in association with Japanese grammar and socio-cultural conventions.

3.3.2.1 Direct transfer

Direct transfer means that FL words are used without changing their meaning. These words entered the Japanese lexicon partly because Japanese vocabulary had no equivalents at that time. For example, people did not use forks or knives before the introduction of Western cuisine, and fruits such as bananas, melons and kiwis were introduced from countries outside Japan. Bear in mind that when foreign words enter Japanese vocabulary, their writing is modified to fit the moraic structure of Japanese (see Chapter 2, section 2.4 for the concept of 'mora'). Long vowels are expressed by the dash written in *katakana* (see also Chapter 2, section 2.2.3 and Chapter 4, section 4.2.2).

banana バナナ *banana*	ski スキー *sukī*
melon メロン *meron*	fork フォーク *fōku*
kiwi キーウィ *kīwi*	knife ナイフ *naifu*
shampoo シャンプー *shanpū*	spoon スプーン *supūn*
steak ステーキ *sutēki*	table テーブル *tēburu*
skirt スカート *sukāto*	rent-a-car レンタカー *rentakā*

3.3.2.2 Shortened forms

FL words are sometimes **shortened** when they enter Japanese vocabulary. The italic parts of the words have remained and the resulting words consist of either four or five morae. Not all FL words are shortened, however. One example is ファッションモデル *fasshon-moderu* 'fashion model', which falls under direct transfer.

*depart*ment store デパート *depāto*
*apart*ment アパート *apāto*
*televi*sion テレビ *terebi*
*fami*ly *rest*aurant ファミレス *famiresu*
*conveni*ence store コンビニ *konbini*
omelette rice オムレツ *omuretsu* オムライス
*ball*point *pen* ボールペン *bōrupen*
*pla*stic *model* プラモデル *puramoderu*

3.3.2.3 Grammatical reduction

When FL words are introduced into Japanese vocabulary, the grammar of the original language is **reduced** to fit that of the target language. Plural markers, markers for present and past participles, and conjunctions are often omitted, as shown below. Italic parts have remained in Japanese. Note, however, that not all FL words reduce their grammar when entering the Japanese lexicon. For example, 'shoes' is accepted as シューズ *shūzu*, retaining its plural form. You may also have encountered the name of a bookstore such as ブックスハセガワ *bukkusu Hasegawa* 'Hasegawa Bookstore'.

*slipper*s スリッパ *surippa* (deletion of a plural marker *s*)
*fry*ing *pan* フライパン *furaipan* (deletion of a present participle *ing*)
*corn*ed *beef* コーンビーフ *kōnbīfu* (deletion of a past participle *ed*)
ham and *egg*s ハムエッグ *hamueggu* (deletion of a conjunction *and* as well as a plural marker *s*)

3.3.2.4 Semantic narrowing

When FL words enter the Japanese lexicon, they do not always maintain their original meaning. The original meaning often becomes either **narrowed** (i.e., more specific) or **broadened** (i.e., more general). We encounter narrowing more often than broadening; it often means that an FL word has retained one or two senses of the meanings of the original word in the source language. For example, ヒ ー タ ー *hītā* in Japanese means a piece of equipment used to raise the air temperature, while in English, the source language, a *heater* can be used to heat not only air but also water. Similarly, ス ト ー ブ *sutōbu* in Japanese refers to an apparatus that provides heat for heating a room, while *stove* in English is used for both heating a room and cooking. In both cases, the meaning of the loanwords corresponds to only one sense of their original word in English. Can you tackle the other examples in the box?

Exercise 1

heater ヒ ー タ ー

stove ス ト ー ブ

cooler ク ー ラ ー

stick ス テ ッ キ

bargain バ ー ゲ ン

sex セ ッ ク ス

3.3.2.5 Semantic broadening

Examples of **broadening** are not as common as narrowing. As observed in Shibatani (1990: 151), expressions containing the personal pronoun *my* often have an extended meaning in Japanese; that is, both マ イ ホ ー ム *maihōmu* and マ イ カ ー *maikā* do not refer to a specific entity but to any house or car that is under ownership, while in English *my home* or *my car* means a specific house or car that I own (e.g., Mr Smith is interested in 'my home').

> my home マ イ ホ ー ム *maihōmu*
> my car マ イ カ ー *maikā*

Some names of professions are a result of semantic broadening. Someone who works at the front desk of a hotel may write in his curriculum vitae that his type of job is フ ロ ン ト *furonto* or ホ テ ル の フ ロ ン ト *hoteru no furonto*, just like 'teacher' or 'engineer'. The word 'front' is a shortened form of 'front desk', but in English it does not mean a job category. Thus, フ ロ ン ト is an example of semantic broadening in that its original meaning (= a place at which work is carried out) comes to mean a profession. レジ *reji* is another example of semantic broadening. This word refers to people (mostly female) who work at a cash desk where customers pay money for their purchases in shops (particularly in supermarkets). レジ is a shortened form of the English word 'cash register'. This English word refers to a machine that has a drawer for keeping money for the amount of sales for the day. While レジ in Japanese still indicates the place this machine is located, it also refers to a person who handles payments. Similar to フロント, レジ is used as a job category.

3.3.2.6 Japan-made Western words

Japan-made Western words, or 和製英語 *wasē-eigo*, (see also 和製漢語 *wasē-kango* in section 3.2.1) are created by the Japanese and are often unintelligible at first glance to non-Japanese. Look at the box below. The first group of words (1 to 7) are compounds in which the second element is the core element. The first element provides information that elaborates on the second element. The core element of ペーパードライバー *pēpā-doraibā* is ドライバー 'driver' because ペーパードライバー is a kind of driver. ペーパー, which comes from 'paper' in English, refers to a driver's licence. The reference to paper indicates that the licence has not been used in practice; the person has not driven a car despite the licence he has obtained. Words in the second group (8 to 10) differ in that the second element is not always present.

You may already be familiar with some of the words in the box. Can you work out the meaning of the rest of the words and explain why they are coined the way they are?

Exercise 2

> 1. ペーパードライバー *pēpādoraibā*
> 2. サインペン *sainpen*
> 3. シャープペンシル *shāpupensiru*
> 4. テーブルスピーチ *tēburusupīchi*
> 5. オールドミス *ōrudomisu*
> 6. ショートケーキ *shōtokēki*
> 7. カップヌードル *kappunūdoru*
> 8. ナイター *naitā* night game
> 9. コーポラス *kōporasu*
> 10. ベースアップ *bēsuappu* (often shortened as ベア *bea*) raise minimum wage

3.3.2.7 Adopting an alternative

Some FL words may stand in complementary distribution to existing Japanese words. This is partly because FL words came to represent specific socio-cultural conventions in Japan. For example, the meaning of ランチ (from *lunch*) is not entirely synonymous with that of the existing word 昼食 *chūshoku* 'lunch'. The use of ランチ is associated with the socio-cultural trend in present-day Japan where people eat a light meal for lunch in a restaurant; this type of meal is customarily offered as a set menu at a reasonable price. This shows that at least two categories exist for the concept of the meal that Japanese people have in the middle of the day: (i) 'lunch' we order in a restaurant, and (ii) 'lunch' we do not order (e.g., we eat at home, school, or workplace). While an FL word ランチ has a specific meaning, the original word 昼食 retains its traditional meaning. Consider Text 3.2 where ランチ cannot be replaced by 昼食 (see also JLU: Chapter 2, Activity 3). The reason is clear: lunch here refers to a set menu that costs ¥1050 offered by a pension in 都路村 *Miyakoji-mura* in Fukushima Prefecture.

Text 3.2 ランチ

都路村古道の小高い丘に建つペンションで９２年に営業開始。和室と洋室が２部屋ずつあり、１５人程度利用できる。１泊２食付きで１人１万円（税、サービス料込み）。日中は正午から午後１時半まで、ランチサービス（１０５０円）もしている。宴会なども受け付けている。予約は０２４７・７５・３３２９へ。

© 2004 *Asahi Newspaper* 7 January

Activity 5

Examine the pairs of words below. Although they are synonymous, they are not always interchangeable (see also Chapter 6, section 6.1.2 for the notion of 'synonym'). State how they differ in meaning and try to explain in light of real texts.[4]

> 季節 *kisetsu* versus シーズン *sīzun* 'season'
> 面接 *mensetsu* versus インタビュー *intabyū* 'interview'
> ごはん *gohan* versus ライス *raisu* 'rice'
> 運転 *unten* versus ドライブ *doraibu* 'drive'
> 台所 *daidokoro* versus キッチン *kitchin* 'kitchen'

3.4 Hybrids

Vocabulary expands its scope by combining different classes of words.
Hybrids, or 混種語 *konshugo*, are good examples of this phenomenon.
These words arise from combining NJ, SJ or FL words (see McClure 2000:
64–65 for further examples).

> NJ and SJ: 赤字 *akaji* 'deficit', 紙粘土 *kami-nendo* 'paper clay'.
>
> SJ and NJ: 台所 *daidokoro* 'kitchen', 筋肉 *kin-niku* 'muscle',
> 中華そば *chūka-soba* 'Chinese-style noodles'.
>
> FL and NJ: タバコ屋 *tabakoya* 'tobacco shop', シャボン玉 *shabon-dama* 'soap bubble', ジャグジー風呂 *jagujī-buro* 'jacuzzi'.
>
> NJ and FL: 板チョコ *itachoko* 'slab of chocolate', 鳥インフルエンザ
> *tori-infuruenza* 'bird flu', いちごケーキ *ichigo-kēki* 'strawberry
> cake'.
>
> SJ and FL: 自主トレ *jishutore* 'independent training', 完熟トマト
> *kanjuku-tomato* 'fully ripened tomato', 学カテスト *gakuryoku-tesuto* 'achievement test', 筆記ミス *hikki-misu* 'writing error'.
>
> FL and SJ: ジンクス対策 *jinkusu-taisaku* 'a measure to counter a
> jinx', レッカー車 *rekkāsha* 'a car carrying wrecked cars or cars
> illegally parked', ヒロイン像 *hiroinzō* 'an image of a heroine',
> バス停留所 *basu-tēryūjo* 'bus stop', ドライブ旅行 *doraibu-ryokō*
> 'travelling by car'.

新型

Activity 6

This activity tests your overall understanding of the three strata you have
learned in the previous sections. Look at Text 3.3 from a newspaper article.
Pick out nominal hybrids and state how they are characterized according to
the three word strata.

Example: 東アジア hybrid (東: NJ + アジア: FL)

Text 3.3 鳥インフルエンザ

---

1 日本を含む東アジアで鳥インフルエンザの発生が相次いでいます。
このウイルスが、爆発的に人から人へ感染する「新型インフルエン
ザウイルス」に変異するのではないか、と心配されています。その
一方で、今ある人のインフルエンザも、死者が国内だけで千人を超
5 える年があり、警戒が必要です。今シーズンの流行状況と、気をつ
けたい病状やワクチンの効果などについて紹介します。

© 2004 *Asahi Newspaper* 29 January

Commentary

The following is a suggested answer to Activity 6. As indicated by Table 3.6, SJ words are used most productively (they are shaded). This passage has only four hybrids. Note that the second element of 新型 *shingata* (line 2) has undergone sequential voicing (see Chapter 2, section 2.2.4). What happens to 心配 *shinpai* 'worry' (line 3) and 一方 *ippō* 'on the other hand' (line 4) is that the first consonant of the second element /h/ becomes /p/ when combined. When /h/ appears in the first element (発生 *hassei* 'birth' [line 1]) or the first element contains a voiced sound (爆発 'explosion' [line 2]), this does not happen. This alternation might be related to the historical fact that /h/ descended from /p/ in old Japanese (see Chapter 2, p. 21). When SJ words are in discussion, the table gives their readings according to the different dynasties they belong to (based on the information provided by the dictionary *Gendai Kango Reikai Jiten* ('Modern Chinese-Reading Dictionary with Examples' (1992)). Note that some *kanji* are given 漢 and 呉 when they pertain to both Han and Wu dynasties (see

Table 3.6

Example	Reading	Hybrid	(1) Element	(2) · (3) Element
日本	*nihon*		呉	漢呉
東アジア	*higashi-ajia*	hybrid	NJ	FL
鳥インフルエンザ	*tori-infuruenza*	hybrid	NJ	FL
発生	*hassei*		漢	漢
爆発的	*bakuhatsuteki*		⊗	漢・漢
感染	*kansen*		漢呉	⊗
新型	*shingata*	hybrid	漢呉	NJ
変異	*hen-i*		漢呉	漢呉
心配	*shinpai*		漢呉	漢呉
一方	*ippō*		漢	漢呉
死者	*shisha*		漢呉	漢呉
国内	*kokunai*		漢呉	呉
千人	*sen-nin*		漢呉	呉
警戒	*keikai*		漢	漢呉
必要	*hitsuyō*		漢	漢呉
今シーズン	*kon-sīzun*	hybrid	呉	FL
流行	*ryūkō*		漢	漢
状況	*jōkyō*		呉	漢呉
病状	*byōjō*		呉	呉
効果	*kōka*		漢	漢呉
紹介	*shōkai*		漢	漢

section 3.2.2). ⊗ signals that the origin of the *kanji* is unknown. Only one example contains the third element (爆発的).

3.5 Vocabulary and text

The type of text can influence the distribution of vocabulary. Shibatani (1990: 143) claims, based on a survey by the National Language Research Center (国立国語研究所 *Kokuritsu Kokugo Kenkyūjo*) from the 1960s, that SJ words are used more frequently in newspapers and scientific magazines, while FL words are more popular in women's magazines. This generalization may be refined such that the choice of vocabulary depends on the information the writer intends to convey in a text. For example, even within a newspaper, articles describing facts differ from the letters of readers, depending on the writer's perspective. Texts 3.4 and 3.5 demonstrate two different types of text: one is an extract from a newspaper article, and the other is a personal letter (which resembles the above-mentioned type of letter). They exhibit an interesting contrast with respect to the use of vocabulary.

Text 3.4 Newspaper article

こうめいとう　　　　　　　　　　　　にち　とうけんぽうちょうさかい　　　けんぽう　　こんかん　　　　　　　　　へいわしゅぎ　さだ
公明党は２８日の党憲法調査会で、憲法の根幹である平和主義を定めた

がつ　　とうたいかい　　　　　　じょう　あつか　　ぎろん　たいしょう　　　　ほうしん　き
１１月の党大会で「９条の扱いも議論の対象とする方針を決めた。

じょうけんじ　　　　き　　　　　　　　じみん　みんしゅりょうとう　かいけんろんぎ　かそく
０２年９条堅持」を決めたが、自民、民主両党が会見論議を加速させ、

しゅうさんりょういん　けんぽうちょうさかい　さいしゅうほうこく　ねんない　　　よてい
衆参両院の憲法調査会の最終報告が年内にも予定されていることから、

ぎろんじたい　さ　　　　　　　　　はんだん
議論自体は避けられないと判断した。

© 2004 *Asahi Newspaper* 29 January

Translation:
In the meeting of the Research Commission on the Constitution on the 28th, the Komeito [the Clean Government Party] put forward the policy that they will also discuss the treatment of Article 9 that deals with Pacifism. Although the Party decided to firmly maintain Article 9 in the November meeting in 2002, they judged that further discussion will be unavoidable. This judgement was influenced by the fact that both parties, Jimin [the Liberal Democratic Party] and Minshu [the Democratic Party], accelerated the debate and that the final report from the Research

59

Commission on the Constitution in the Upper and Lower Houses is planned to be held within the year.

Text 3.5 Personal letter

その後おかわりありませんか。疲れなどなかったでしょうか。きちょう
な滞在で私に会ってくれて本当にありがとう。心づかいのはがきもあな
たらしい気くばりでうれしかったですヨ。お気に入りのパソコンはみつ
かりましたか？イギリスで再会したり日本で再会したり何か不思議なめ
ぐり会いの気がしました。一生けんめいに自分の道を歩んでいるあなた
を見ていると、自分の今までに歩んできたのがこれで本当に良かったの
かと思えてしまうくらい感動をしてしまう。

Translation:
How have you since been? Didn't you get tired? Thank you for meeting me during your important stay [in Japan]. I was also pleased to receive your postcard that was so thoughtful, which reflects your noble being. Have you found a personal computer you like? I can see a strange fate whenever I recall our reunion in England and Japan. When looking at you, who have been paving your own way, I'm deeply impressed such that I can't help asking myself if the path I have followed has really been the best thing.

Text 3.4 appears on the front page of the *Asahi Newspaper* describing the plans proposed by the Komei Party, while Text 3.5 is a letter from a woman aged 45, who writes to her close friend and describes her pleasant and enjoyable reunion in Japan with her former classmate. Text 3.4 uses SJ words for most of its **content words** except for three NJ words (定めた *sadameta*, 扱い *atsukai*, 決めた *kimeta*), while Text 3.5 contains a higher percentage of NJ content words. The crucial difference between the two texts lies in the authors' purpose for writing. Text 3.4 conveys the plain facts, whereby the emphasis is laid on the accuracy of the information (date, purpose and consequence of the meeting), while the latter adopts a casual style of writing whose main focus is on expressing the author's personal feelings and avoiding being too direct. Note that the author's feelings are conveyed by expressions such as ありがとう *arigatō* 'Thank you', 心づかいの *kokoro-zukai no* 'thoughtful', あなたらしい気くばりで

anatarashii kikubari de 'your special care', うれしかった *ureshikatta* 'was pleased', 不思議なめぐり会い *fushigina meguriai* 'miraculous coincidence', 感動 *kandō* 'fascination', and that all except 感動 and 不思議 are NJ words (or NJ-based). Aside from serving as basic vocabulary (see 3.1.2 above), NJ words are preferred for expressing feelings in an everyday context. This may also account for the frequent use of NJ words in poetry (see section 3.1.3, p. 45). In addition, the uses of と思えてしまう *to omoete shimau* 'I wonder if' and 気がしました *kiga shimashita* 'I felt that' help the author avoid being direct when describing her opinions (see JLU: Chapter 1, section 1.2.5).

3.6 Old and new newspaper articles

When we look at old newspapers, for example, from 1940, we notice the following three characteristics: (i) SJ words appear more frequently, (ii) SJ words are used differently (i.e., they would not be used in the same contexts as present-day Japanese) and (iii) more NJ words are written in *kanji*.

Text 3.6 Newspaper article from 1940

このやうに①鋏はただ②玩具である③許りでなく④教具でもあり子供が

生活するための一つの⑤道具でもあります。⑥手技玩具としては、

粘土、色紙、千代紙、⑦糊などもよいでせう。

© 1940 *Asahi Newspaper* 2 July

In present-day Japanese, ②玩具 *gangu* 'toy' (see Table 3.7) might not be used in this context, as it refers to specific objects such as dolls, model cars or stuffed toys – all of which are made specifically for playing. By contrast, 玩具 in this passage simply refers to 'tool' and 'instrument'. Children in the 1940s probably did not have 'specially made toys' at their disposal but played with scissors and enjoyed cutting a piece of paper into different features or shapes. An equivalent for this word in present Japanese vocabulary would be 遊び道具 *asobi-dōgu* 'tools for playing'. Present-day Japanese has a synonymous word おもちゃ *omocha* 'toy'. As pointed out in Asano (1981: 96), the difference between these two words in present-day Japanese may lie in formality: 玩具 is a formal expression, while おもちゃ is an informal expression.

④教具 *kyōgu* in present-day Japanese refers to objects used for teaching in a classroom. Scissors in the above text refer not to the teaching material but to the tools from which children can learn. The SJ compound ⑥手技玩具 *shugi-gangu*, consisting of two independent words (手技+玩具), may hardly be used in present-day Japanese. Both 教具 and 手技玩具 can thus be replaced by different words (see Text 3.7 below). Finally, ①鋏 *hasami* and ⑦糊 *nori* would be written in *hiragana* in present-day Japanese. Both *kanji* do not pertain to 常用漢字 *jōyō-kanji* – a selected list of *kanji* (total of 1,945) used in the educational system (see also Kess and Miyamoto 1999: 17). Although the character 許 is listed as 常用漢字, it is normally written in *hiragana* when it serves as a function word, as in ③.

This discussion suggests that the usage of SJ and NJ words in an old newspaper reveals some interesting aspects of language change. This change reflects the extent to which people used and understood scissors in a children's context in the 1940s. The scope of vocabulary continues to change while being used by members of a society. Text 3.6 shows us that no word meaning is static, that is, no word retains the same meaning over time. Table 3.7 summarizes the above discussion. For the sake of clarity, the table is organized by two criteria.

Table 3.7   *Summary of the discussion*

Examples	Criteria	
	1	2
① 鋏		○
② 玩具	○	
③ 許り		○
④ 教具	○	
⑤ 道具	○	
⑥ 手技玩具	○	
⑦ 糊		○

Note:
1 Words existing in modern Japanese that do not have exactly the same reference.
2 Words existing in modern Japanese with the same reference but written in *hiragana*.

Text 3.7 Modern version

Text 3.7 is a modern version of Text 3.6 suggested by the author. Two forms, よう *yō* and しょう *shō* shown in bold, replace their old alternatives. This replacement occurred as a result of the orthographical reform that followed World War Two.

> このようにはさみはただ遊び道具であるばかりでなく勉強道具でもあり
>
> 子供がが生活するための一つの生活用具でもあります。手を使った遊び
>
> 道具としては、粘土、色紙、千代紙、のりなどもよいでしょう。

3.7 Vocabulary and mimetic words

This section demonstrates how Japanese vocabulary is enriched by **mimetic words**. 'Mimetic' means the imitation of sounds or the depiction of situations or human feelings by the form of words. For example, when a vase falls from a shelf to the ground, it breaks into pieces and makes a noise. Japanese perceives this sound as がちゃん *gachan*. We thus say that 花瓶ががちゃんと床に落ちた *Kabin ga* **gachanto** *yuka ni ochita* 'The vase crashed to the floor'. The mimetic word がちゃんと functions as an adverb and describes how the falling of the vase happens. When someone knocks at the door, this noise can be reproduced as とんとん. We say that だれかがドアをとんとん叩いた *Dareka ga doa o* **tonton** *tataita* 'Someone tapped at the door'. The mimetic word とんとん imitates the sound produced by the knocking of the door. If someone pounds the door, we then say だれかがドアをどんどん叩いた, whereby /t/ in とんとん becomes voiced as /d/ in どんどん. When a young woman gets surprised in the dark, she makes a noise similar to きゃあ. We may say that 女の人がきゃあと声をあげた *On-na no hito ga* **kyāto** *koe o ageta* 'A woman screamed'. These mimetic words are called **onomatopoeia** or, more technically, **phonomimes** (擬音語 *giongo*), as they reproduce or imitate the sounds.

Japanese has two other types of mimetic words: one is **phenomimes** (擬態語 *gitaigo*), describing the manner in which something occurs or someone acts, and the other is **psychomimes** (擬情語 *gijōgo*), describing the way we feel internally. When seagulls fly lightly in the sky, we say that 海鳥がすいすい飛んだ *umidori ga suisui tonda*. The phenomime すいすい depicts the way the seagulls fly. When a Japanese business-man is afraid of being sacked, we might say that 彼は首になるのではないかとびくびくしている *kare wa kubi ni naru node wa naika to* **bikubiku** *shite iru*. The psychomime びくびく depicts the feeling of fear in this man. Morphologically, mimetic words are easily differentiated from non-mimetic words in that they are often dupli-cated (e.g., とんとん, びくびく) or can be accompanied by an adverbial indicator と (e.g., がちゃんと, きゃあと). Semantically, they serve to describe speech events more expressively and vividly. Mimetic words are found frequently in *manga* (see Activity 8, pp. 67–70). Some children's books also make ample use of the effects of mimetic words, as in the example of Activity 7.

Activity 7

Text 3.8 is the beginning part of a children's story entitled くまの子ウーフ *Kuma no Ko Ūfu* 'A Bear Cub Ufu'. In this passage a bear cub ウーフ meets bees, *medaka* (= killifish) and carps, and is fascinated by their skills in flying or swimming. Find mimetic words and list them according to the three classifications. [. . .] in the text indicates an omission of sentences.

Text 3.8　くまの子ウーフ

1　ぶなの木の下で、ひるねをしていたくまの子ウーフは、目をさまし
　　て、木をみあげました。ぶなの木は、みどりの葉をつけて、さもき
　　もちよさそうに風にふかれていました。
　　「木はいいなあ。木になりたいなあ。」と、ウーフは思いました。
5　「こんなもしゃもしゃの毛皮のかわりに、みどりの葉っぱをつけて、
　　すずしそうに立っているんだ。そしてさ、じっとたっていたら、み
　　つばちがきて、すをつくるかもしれないね。そしたら、ぼく、きの
　　ぼりしなくてもはちみつがなめられるよ。だって、ぼくが木なんだ
　　もの。」ウーフははちみつのことをかんがえて、ごくんとつばをの
10　みこみました。それから、
　　「でも ……」と、くびをふりました。
　　「木は、はちみつをなめないのかな。そんならぼくは、みつばちに
　　なろう。そしたら、すごいぞ。ぼくのうちにはいつだって、はちみ
　　つがいっぱいあるんだ。」ウーフは、たまらなくなりました。
15　けれど、いったい、どうやったら、みつばちになれるのでしょう。
　　ウーフは両手をひろげました。みつばちはいつだって、こんなふう
　　にして、ぶーんととんでくるのです。

ぶーん　ぶうぅーん

ウーフがうなっていたら、ほんとに、ぶーんと小さなうなり声がし

20 て、金いろのみつばちがやってきました。目のまえのつりがねそう

の花にとまって、羽をふるわせています。

「あ、みつばち。ぼくね、きみみたいなはちになりたいの。どうや

ってとぶか、教えてよ。」ウーフは、両手をひろげていいました。

「みてて！いま、とんでみるからね。」

25 ウーフはぶーんとうなって、とびあがり、すぐに、ずてんところび

ました。

そのとたんに、みつばちは、つりがねそうの花から、まいあがりま

した。ぶーんとうなって、あいさつもしないでとんでいきました。

「おーい。まってよ。みつばちーー」

30 ウーフはおいかけました。みつばちは野原をこえて、小川をこえて、

いってしまいました。

じゃぶじゃぶじゃぶ

ウーフは川の中までおいかけてから、こぶしをふりあげました。

「うー、みつばちのやつ！」

35 すると、ウーフの二ほんの足のあいだを、めだかのむれが、つーつー

泳いでいきました。

「や、さかなだ。」ウーフは、めだかをみていいました。

「さかなはいいなあ。」ウーフはためいきをつきました。[...]

「おい、きみたち、どうしてそんなにうまく、泳げるの。」ウーフ

40 は、たずねました。そのとたんに、足がつるりとすべって、ころび

そうになりました。

「あっぷっぷっ。たすけてえーー」

水をぱしゃぱしゃさせて、やっとおきあがったときです。

「おう、くまこう、なにしにきたんだ。」

45 川の中からふなが、かおをつきだしました。

「おまえ、わしたちをつかまえにきたな。」

「ちがうよ、ちがうよ。」

ウーフは、びっくりしていいました。

「ぼく、さかなになりたいの。ねえ、さかなは手も足もないくせに、

50 どうして泳げるの。」

すると、ふなは目玉をぎょろっとさせて、いばりました。

「わしらは生まれたときからおよげるんだ。おまえもさかなになり

たけりゃ、そのけむくじゃらな手と足をすてちゃいな。」

「えっ？」[. . .]

55 「そうともさ。まだあるぞ。いいか、昼でも夜でも、おきていても

ねていても、その二つの目だまは、ぱっちりあけていなくちゃなら

ん。まばたきひとつ、してはならんのだ。」

「ねてても目をあけてるんだって？」

ウーフは目をまるくしました。[. . .]

60 「いいというまでまばたきするなよ。わしがテストしてやるから

な。一、二、三、四、五、六. . . . .」[. . .]

ああ、くるしい、目がひりひりします。

「百！」と、ふながどなったとき、ウーフは、もう、たまらなくな

って、つづけさまにぱちぱちとまばたきをしました。なみだがぼろ

65 ぼろこぼれました。

「はっはっはっ。らくだいだ。おまえはさかなにゃなれんぞ。」

ふなは、きもちよさそうにわらいました。

「どうだ、くまこう。からだは小さくとも、さかなさまはえらいだ

ろう。わかったら、これからわしらをつかまえるなよ。」

70 ふなは口をぱくぱくあけて、いいました。

Commentary

The majority of mimetic words are either phonomimes or phenomimes. There is only one instance of a psychomime. Since Japanese is a **head-final language** (i.e., the main part comes after the part that modifies it), the mimetic word provides an additional explanation of the content of the word that follows it within a sentence. For example, もしゃもしゃ (line 5) is a phenomime that modifies the word 毛皮 *kegawa* 'fur'; it makes explicit how the bearskin looks. Likewise, a phonomime, ぶーんと (line 17), modifies the word とんでくるのです 'fly'; it makes explicit which sounds bees make when they fly. Sentences without mimetic words are still acceptable, but the addition of these words enriches their information (see Table 3.8).

Table 3.8 *Mimetic words in Text 3.8*

Line	Examples	Phono-mimes	Pheno-mimes	Psycho-mimes	English translations
5	もしゃもしゃ		○		shaggy, bushy
6	じっと		○		still
9	ごくん		○		the way one swallows
17	ぶーんと	○			buzz, hum
18	ぶううーん	○			buzz, hum
25	ずてんと		○		tumble down heavily
32	じゃぶじゃぶじゃぶ	○			dabble, splash
35	つーつー		○		swim smoothly
40	つるりと		○		slip, slide
42	あっぶっぶっ	○			flounder in water
43	ばしゃばしゃ	○			splash, babble
51	ぎょろっと		○		glare at
56	ばっちり		○		open one's eyes widely
62	ひりひり			○	feeling of pain due to injury
64	ぱちぱちと		○		blink one's eyes
64–65	ぼろぼろ		○		shed big drops of tears
66	はっはっはっ	○			sound of laughing
70	ぱくぱく		○		open and close one's mouth repeatedly

Activity 8

Look at the extracts taken from いいひと。*Ī hito* 'a good-natured person' from Texts 3.9 to 3.12. This time you will find more instances of psycho-mimes. Identify mimetic words and classify them the way you did in Activity 7.

Text 3.9 ビクッ

© 2004 Takahashi, Shin / *Ī Hito* (p. 204), Shogakukan

Text 3.10 ギク

© 2004 Takahashi, Shin / *Ī Hito* (p. 47), Shogakukan

Text 3.11 ゾゾ—

© 2004 Takahashi, Shin / *Ī Hito* (p. 277), Shogakukan

Text 3.12 し — ん

© 2004 Takahashi, Shin / *Ī Hito* (p. 99), Shogakukan

Commentary

The first three texts deal with cases of psychomimes. Words such as ビクッ *biku* (Text 3.9), ギク *giku* (Text 3.10) and ゾゾー *zozō* (Text 3.11) all depict the protagonist's inner emotions in response to an external stimulus. In Text 3.9, the man with a higher position in a company is greatly surprised at the presence of a young employee, 北野 *Kitano*, who he was not expecting. In Text 3.10, a female employee, 小鴨 *Kogamo*, is startled because her colleague witnessed a scene in which she secretly gave a man from another company a free one-day ticket to get into her company's sports club. In Text 3.11 a female employee, 小鴨, is horrified at the thought of obeying the ideas of another company, 金丸繊維 *Kanemaru Sen-i* 'Kanemaru textile company', which plans to sell odd swimming costumes. Text 3.12 differs from the other texts in two ways. First, it is a phenomime, since it depicts what is happening in a swimming pool (i.e., the characters do not say anything), and second, this silent situation indicates the awkwardness caused by 真理子's *Mariko*'s inability to swim. Thus, the silence that overwhelms the atmosphere reflects the participants' psychology; the description of the situation parallels the mental reality of the participants. We conclude that Text 3.12 represents a phenomime co-existing with a psychomime. You may notice that two other psychomimes, namely ビクッ and ギク, can be considered phenomimes. This overlap may occur when the word serves to explain the protagonist's external facial expression. 'Face' is an important part of our body that communicates our inner feelings. As shown below, the fact that psychomimes in Texts 3.9 and 3.10 can occur with the word 顔 *kao* 'face' means that what we feel inside can also show overtly on our face. This substantiates the overlap of psychomimes with phenomimes.

> びくっとした顔 *bikutto shita kao* 'a startled face'
> ぎくっとした顔 *gikutto shita kao* 'startled face'

It is important to note that ゾゾー (which is an emphatic form of
ゾッとする *zotto suru*) in Text 3.11 is not felicitous with 顔 *kao*, indicating
that it only expresses the protagonist's fear or horror. In other words, not
all psychomimes overlap with phenomimes.

A similar interpretation is applicable to phonomimes. Recall the
phonomime ばしゃばしゃ *pasha pasha* in Activity 7 once again (line 43 in
Text 3.8). This word can be treated as a phenomime in that the sound of
splashing can be conceived of as how ウーフ hits the water. In other
words, sounds perceived and the body movements that originate the
sounds are conceptually intertwined and therefore not separable.

Figure 3.1 is a diagram that summarizes the main points of our discussions above. The borderlines between the three classifications are not
clear-cut; some portions of phonomimes and psychomimes enter the
domain of phenomimes, while phonomimes and psychomimes never
overlap.

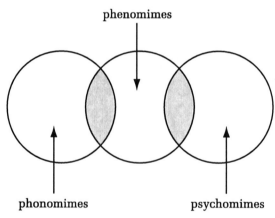

Figure 3.1 *Distribution of phonomimes, phenomimes and psychomimes*

Notes

1 This list is not only based on the author's knowledge of Mandarin
   but also supported by people in Singapore and Malaysia who are
   speakers of Cantonese, Hokkien or Mandarin. The author expresses
   gratitude to them for spending time answering questions.
2 *Go-on* reading was introduced to Japan via 百済 *Kudara* in Korea.
   This ancient state, in the southwest of the Korean Peninsula, had a
   trade with the area, roughly present-day Shanghai, at the downstream
   of the River 長江 *Chōkō* (presently called 揚子江 Yōsukō in Japanese
   or the Yangtze in Chinese). In this region, a variation of Chinese was
   spoken from which *go-on* reading descended.

3   The last two words in (2) are borrowed from Cambodian.
4   Interested readers are advised to consult *Basic Japanese Vocabulary*: *An Explanation of Usage* (Yamaguchi 2005), since this book deals with the word pairs presented here.

4 The writing system

The main purpose of this chapter is to examine the ways in which modern Japanese is written. In the final section (4.5), we take a brief look at some historical changes that have occurred in the writing system by examining some newspaper excerpts.

In Japanese, 表記のしくみ *hyōki no shikumi* is used for the **writing system**, in which 表記 *hyōki* is a special expression for writing on a piece of paper using scripts, numbers, or symbols. The central scripts in the Japanese writing system are ひらがな *hiragana*, カタカナ *katakana* and 漢字 *kanji*. As mentioned in the previous chapter, 漢字 is the oldest Japanese writing system, adopted in the sixth century when Buddhism was first introduced to Japan from the Continent; before its adoption there was no means of writing. In the Heian Period (平安時代 *Heian-jidai* (794–1185)), when ひらがな and カタカナ were invented based on the shape of *kanji*, literary work was written with ひらがな, specifically by female writers. Two important types of narrative prevailed in this era: the tale (物語 *monogatari*) and the diary (日記 *nikki*). A well-known work of the former is 源氏物語 *Genji-monogatari* by 紫式部 *Murasaki Shikibu*, while 土佐日記 *Tosa-nikki* by 紀貫之 *Kino Tsurayuki* marks the beginning of the latter. Another well-known work is 枕草子 *Makura no Sōshi* by 清少納言 *Seishō Nagon,* which pioneered the popular genre of essays (随筆 *zuihitsu*). It is rarely the case, however, that modern Japanese texts consist of a single script alone unless a text is written for a specific purpose (e.g., a children's book). As a rule, scripts in modern texts are mixed and sentences are accompanied by symbols such as commas (読点 *tōten*) and full stops (句点 *kuten*). Different writing systems are chosen according to their functions. The scripts most frequently used in everyday communication are a combination of ひらがな and 漢字. When students take an exam or write an essay at school in Japan, ひらがな and 漢字 are the basic scripts they use. The main function of カタカナ, as shown in Chapter 3, is to write foreign loanwords. This chapter will introduce other functions of カタカナ in terms of a writer's rhetorical intentions. Apart from the scripts mentioned above, Roman letters (ローマ字 *rōmaji*) (section 4.3), numerals (数字 *sūji*) and symbols (符号 *fugō*) (section 4.4) will also be examined.

4.1 *Kanji* and *Hiragana*

Text 4.1 is the first sentence of the preface to *Kanji in Context*. This sentence is written in both *kanji* and *hiragana*. The crucial difference between these two scripts is that each *kanji* functions as **content words**, which stand in opposition to **grammatical words**. Content words are words that possess their own semantic content or lexical meanings, while grammatical words refer to words that function as morphological elements in words or syntactic elements in sentences, and hence possess grammatical meanings. For example, the word 書いた *kaita* 'wrote' consists of two elements, 書い and た. 書い is a content word because it possesses a lexical meaning of 'writing'. As a lexical word, its meaning stays consistent regardless of the environment in which it occurs. For example, 書い in both 順子が本を書いた *Junko ga hon o kaita* 'Junko wrote a book' and 順子が書いた本 *Junko ga kaita hon* 'A book Junko wrote' has the same meaning although it appears in different syntactic environments. By contrast, た is a grammatical word whose meaning is decided by its relation to other elements. While 順子が本を書いた refers to the action of Junko's writing that took place in the past, 順子が書いた本 is not always associated with a past event; た rather expresses the completion of writing because of its syntactic function as a noun-modifier (see Chapter 7, section 7.7). It can be used in a context in which a speaker is referring to a future event; for instance, a situation in which a teacher, Mr A, is talking about the book Junko is writing. When he says 順子さんが書いた本を教室で使いたいと思っております *Junko-san ga kaita hon o kyōshitsu de tsukaitai to omotte orimasu* 'We would like to use the book Junko will have written in a classroom', 書いた refers to an event that will be completed in the future.

Consider Table 4.1, which organizes Text 4.1 according to content and grammatical words. Content words are expressed either with *kanji* alone or with *kanji* and *hiragana*. In the latter, *hiragana* serves to provide 送りがな *okurigana* 'root kana ending' to supplement the content part. It is easy to see from the table that *hiragana* – except for its function as 送りがな – is used to express grammatical functions. 送りがな is often contained in inflected words such as verbs (e.g., 始まる) and adjectives (e.g., 難しい *muzukashii*). As you may notice, an abstract noun 難しさ *muzukashisa* 'difficulty' contains し followed by its inflection さ. Note that some uninflected words such as nouns (後ろ *ushiro* 'behind' or 祭り *matsuri* 'festival') also contain *hiragana* (this example does not occur in Text 4.1) (see Backhouse 1993: 51–52). Not all content words are written in *kanji*, however. むずかしさ is a good example that could be presented as 難しさ. Japanese notions used in the table have the following English equivalents: inflection (活用 *katsuyō*), particle (助詞 *joshi*), linking (接続詞

73

setsuzokushi), auxiliary verb 助動詞 *jodōshi*) nominalization (名詞化 *meishika*) and copula (コピュラ *kopyura*).

Text 4.1

漢字習得のむずかしさは、日本語教育が始まって以来一貫して指摘されてきたことです。

© 1994 Inter-University Center for Japanese Language Studies, The Japan Times

Translation:
Ever since the beginning of Japanese language education for foreigners, the task of learning *kanji* has been one of the major challenges for learners.

Table 4.1

Content words		活用	助詞	接続詞	助動詞	名詞化	コピュラ
漢字 ひらがな	送り がな			Grammatical words			
漢字習得			の				
*むずか	し	さ	は				
日本語 教育			が				
始	まっ			て			
以来							
一貫		し		て			
指摘		され		て	きた	こと	です

Activity 1

The following passage is a follow-up to Text 4.1. Analyse the sentence based on the sample in Table 4.1.

Text 4.2

アメリカ・カナダ大学連合日本研究センターでは過去３０年にわたって、日本研究を専攻する北米の大学院生に対して上級及び専門的な日本語教育を行ってきましたが、本校でも漢字の指導は長い間教育上の問題となっていました。

© 1994 Inter-University Center for Japanese Language Studies, The Japan Times

Translation:
The Inter-University Center for Japanese Language has been offering advanced and specialized Japanese language courses for postgraduate students majoring in Japan-related fields in North America over the last 30 years. Teaching *kanji* has been a long-standing pedagogical problem in this school, too.

Commentary

My suggestion is summarized in the table below (p. 76). There are words such as わたって *watatte* or きました *kimashita* that have an alternative writing using *kanji* (亘って, 来ました). Unlike むずかしさ in Text 4.1, 亘る *wataru* is not frequently used because it is not included in 常用漢字 *jōyō-kanji* 'Chinese characters of common use' adopted in public writings (such as newspapers) and the educational system. When 来る is written in *kanji*, it accommodates the meaning of motion, which is not the case here since it is an auxiliary verb (see also section 4.5 below).

4.2 Katakana

4.2.1 Expressing foreign loanwords

The major function of *katakana* is writing foreign loanwords (see Chapter 3, section 3.3). When loanwords entered Japanese through Portuguese traders, they were customarily assigned *kanji* (e.g., 金平糖 *konpētō* (from Portuguese *confeito*) 'sweets' or 合羽 *kappa* (from Portuguese *capa*) 'raincoat'), though this practice did not persist in the Meiji Period (明治時代 *Meiji-jidai*) (1868–1912), in which quite a few foreign loanwords were adopted. In present-day Japan, the preference is to use *katakana* when adopting loanwords. The following words are written in *katakana* in the preface of *Kanji in Context* (1994). Not only loanwords but also proper names (countries, companies) as well as personal names are in *katakana*.[1]

4.2.2 Insufficiency of traditional katakana scripts

Katakana scripts alone do not reproduce the totality of loanwords. Some symbols and scripts are required to supplement them. First, when a word contains long vowels (see Chapter 2, section 2.2.3), the dash (–) is used instead of repeating the vowel. ブーム in 日本語教育ブーム *nihongo kyōiku būmu* (see Table 4.3) comes from *boom* /bu:m/ in English. Here the long /u:/ is indicated by (–), not by ウウ. A word of caution is in order here: English diphthongs such as [eɪ] or [ou] become long vowels in

75

Table 4.2

Content words		Grammatical words			
漢字 ひらがな カタカナ	送り仮名	助詞	コピュラ	活用	接続詞
アメリカ					
カナダ					
大学連合					
日本研究					
センター		では			
過去３０年		に			
わた	っ				て
日本研究		を			
専攻				する	
北米		の			
大学生		に			
対	して				
上級					
及	び				
専門的				な	
日本語教育		を			
行	っ				て
き				ました	が
本校		でも			
漢字		の			
指導		は			
長	い				
間					
教育上		の			
問題			でし	た	

Japanese. Examples are テーブル (from table [teɪbəl]) or ノート (from note [nout]).

Second, when writing personal names, the symbol (・) is used to separate the given name from the family name (e.g., トム・ジョーンズ *Tomu Jōnzu*) (see Table 4.3).

Third, eleven sounds, as shown in Table 4.4, were added to *katakana* scripts to accommodate Western sounds that were originally absent in the Japanese sound system. These sounds combine a consonant and a vowel. Vowels are written in small letters. To take an English word *party*, /tɪ/ in

Table 4.3

Loanwords:	
日本語教育ブーム	Japanese education boom
日本研究センター	Centre for Japanese Studies
コンピューター	computer
プロジェクト	project
Country names:	
アメリカ	America
カナダ	Canada
Company name:	
ジャパンタイムズ	The Japan Times
Personal name:	
ジョン・スミス	John Smith

English and チ in Japanese are not the same sound. By inventing a new *katakana* script ティ (counting as one mora (see Chapter 2, section 2.4)), Japanese registers *party* as パーティー. Otherwise, this would be written as パーチー and its resulting pronunciation would be [pa:tʃi:]. However, this convention does not always appear to be regular. チケット or チップ correspond to the English words *ticket* [tɪkit] and *tip* [tɪp], respectively. These words should be written as ティケット and ティップ if the writing of ティ is applied across the board.

Table 4.4 *Eleven extra katakana scripts*

Pronunciation	カタカナ	Examples
ʃe	シェ	シェフ chef
ʒe	ジェ	ジェスチャー gesture
tʃe	チェ	チェス chess
ti	ティ	パーティー party
di	ディ	ディック Dick
dʃɯ	デュ	デュエット duetto(Italian)
ɸa	ファ	ファイト fight
ɸi	フィ	フィアンセ fiancé(French)
ɸe	フェ	フェリー ferry
ɸo	フォ	フォト photo
ɯo	ウォ	ウォーター water

Table 4.5 shows additional minor *katakana* scripts which may be used to present foreign loanwords in Japanese. Note that their use may vary depending on the users. For example, 'violin' can be represented as バイオイン or ヴァイオリン.

Table 4.5   *Minor Katakana scripts*

	イェ			
	ウィ		ウェ	ウォ
クァ	クィ		クェ	クォ
	スィ			
ツァ	ツィ		ツェ	ツォ
		トゥ		
		ドゥ		
ヴァ	ヴィ	ヴ	ヴェ	ヴォ
グァ				
			ヒェ	

Activity 2

Analyse the following sentences based on what you have learned so far. The texts are extracted from *Newsweek* magazine (in Japanese translation) from May 1–8, 2002.

Text 4.3

時間と勇気がある旅行者にとって、カリフォルニアの海岸線はドラマテ

ィックな景色と歴史と多様な文化が交鎖する魅惑的なドライビングロー

ドといえる。

© Newsweek Japan 1–8 May (p. 69), 2002

Translation:
For travellers who have the time and courage, the coastline roads of California, where dramatic sceneries, history, and different cultures intersect, can be fascinating to drive.

Text 4.4

欧米の主要空港のそばには、たいてい大手レンタカーチェーンの看板が

ある。市内に向かうタクシーやリムジンバスからその看板を見て、外国

でのドライブ旅行を夢見た経験はないだろうか。

© Newsweek Japan 1–8 May (p. 64), 2002

Translation:
Close to the main airports of Europe and America, there are as a rule signposts for major car rental companies. When you see such signposts from the window of a taxi or a limousine on your way to the city centre, have you ever dreamt about renting a car and travelling in a foreign country?

Commentary

The texts consist of three scripts, 漢字 *kanji*, ひらがな *hiragana*, and カタカナ *katakana*. Expressions written in カタカナ are all derived from English (カリフォルニア *kariforunia*, ドラマティック *doramatikku*, ドライビングロード *doraibingu-rōdo*, レンタカーチェーン *rentakā-chēn*, タクシー *takushī*, リムジンバス *rimujin-basu*, ドライブ *doraibu*). ドラマティック and カリフォルニア contain special *katakana* scripts ティ and フォ, respectively. The use of dash for ロード and チェーン is because of the diphthong /ou/ in *road* and /eɪ/ in *chain*. Expressions written in *kanji* are all content words referring to abstract (勇気 *yūki* 'courage') and concrete (海岸線 *kaigansen* 'coastline') entities. Only a few content words are written in *hiragana* (ある *aru* 'exist', そば *soba* 'nearby', たいてい *taitei* 'usually'). にとって is a postposition (後置詞 *kōchishi*) that corresponds to 'for' or 'to' in English. The verb いえる, following the quotative と, is not written in *kanji* (言える *ieru*) because the quotation here is not a 'real' quotation (= uttered by a real person) but instead refers to the writer's opinion (i.e., the coastline roads of California are worth driving). Finally, ドライブ 'drive' is not interchangeable with 運転 *unten* 'drive', since driving here not only means 'operating a car' but also 'a journey' in a car. Thus, the use of ドライブ adds an extra meaning; it refers not only to 'driving a car' but also to one's enjoyment associated with travelling by car. Note that ドライブ does not necessarily mean that the person operates a car but that he or she can also sit next to the driver. ドライブ旅行 *doraibu-ryokō* is a hybrid consisting of a loanword and a Sino-Japanese word (see Chapter 3, section 3.2).

4.2.3 Providing the pronunciation of words

The third function of *katakana* is to indicate the pronunciation of words. As mentioned in 4.2.2, *katakana* acquired additional scripts because of the phonological gaps between the Japanese and Western (mostly English) sound systems. Accordingly, this practice enriched the size of *katakana* scripts. In this regard, *katakana* is a convenient means for displaying the complex quality of sounds. Text 4.5 is an example (やさしい日本語指導

Yasashī Nihongo Shidō 'An Easy Guide to Japanese' Ikeda 2000: 18) that illustrates the assumption that two types of sound changes might have occurred to the pronunciation of the さ column before the establishment of the present pronunciation of サシスセソ *sa, shi, su, se, so*.

Text 4.5

> たとえば、「シャ　シュ　シェ　ショ　ジャ　ジ　ジュ　ジェ　ジョ」
> と発音したか、はたまた、「サ　スィ　ス　シェ　ソ」であったかについては明らかではありません。

4.2.4 Accentuating words

The accentuation of words is the fourth function of the use of *katakana*. Accentuation involves the emphasis of words. The writer uses *katakana* for words that can otherwise be written in *hiragana* or *kanji*. This use of *katakana* is clearly associated with the writer's inner feelings with respect to what he or she writes. By emphasizing a particular word, he or she attracts the reader's attention. Texts 4.6 to 4.9 are extracted from Asahi.com and demonstrate two different writings of イライラ *iraira*: one is in *katakana*, and the other is in *hiragana*. Close examination of each extract shows that *katakana* is employed when an actual irritation growing in the writer is talked about, while *hiragana* is used when the irritation mentioned does not belong to a particular person. In Text 4.6, the journalist, who now resides in Yamagata, describes his experience in Tokyo. Texts 4.7 to 4.9 all use *hiragana* for irritation. An important point is that none of these extracts, unlike Text 4.6, talks about the irritation of a specific person. Text 4.7 is concerned with the results of a survey after the arrest of a high school student. 'Irritation' is mentioned as one category (among others) in this survey. Text 4.8 reports the profit-oriented research atmosphere at universities in Japan. While young researchers need, somewhat reluctantly, to adapt themselves to this new system, a relaxed atmosphere among the older generation awaiting their upcoming retirement is regarded as a source of irritation. Text 4.9 describes how irritated the citizens in Kitami city were when the city was affected by the heavy snowfall of January 2004 and the removal of snow did not proceed as fast as they expected.

Text 4.6

東京は人が多い。緑が少ない。面積が広いが、建物や車がいっぱいで
狭苦しい。天気が良くてもスカッと晴れることはなく、高いビルが林立
していて、空が小さい。普段は気にならないが、仕事などで神経がささ
くれ立っていると、我慢できなくなる。故郷の北海道は違う。広くて、
人が少なくて、緑が多くて、何と言っても空が大きい。どうしてこんな
に**イライラ**するんだろう。ああ、今の自分には北海道が足りないんだー。
そして北海道へ行きたくなる。実際には行けず、よけい**イライラ**するの
だが。

© 2004 Asahi.com 19 October

Translation:
Tokyo is full of people. It lacks greenery. It is a large area but it is narrow and cramped as there are many buildings and cars. Even if the weather is fine, the sky never becomes clear and blue. Tall buildings stand next to each other, and the sky looks small. I normally do not care about all this but cannot stand it particularly when I am hypersensitive due to my work. Hokkaido, my home town, is different. It is large, has fewer people and lots of greenery. Needless to say, the sky is big. I wonder why I get so irritated. Ah, I need Hokkaido in me! And I feel like going to Hokkaido. I actually cannot go there, and it makes me more irritated.

Text 4.7

学校のまとめによると、「事件が頭から離れない」と答えた生徒が
72％と最も高く、「なかなか集中できない」が53％、「気持ちが落
ち込む」が50％と続いた。「身体がだるい」た47％、「**いらいら**す
る」が44％、「事件のことを早く忘れてしまいたい」も44％と、
半数近かった。

© 2004 Asahi.com 15 July

Text 4.8

T大学のA助教授は、研究から何らか収益とみなせるものをあげよう、と
必死だ。そうでないと、研究予算の配分からあぶれる恐れがあるからだ。
上司で定年間近のT教授が悠然としているのも、**いらいら**の種になるほど
だ。

© 2003 Asahi.com 25 December

Translation:
Professor A at T University is eager to produce a profit from his research. If he cannot do so, there will be a danger that he may fail to receive research funds. The fact that Professor T, who is approaching his retirement, behaves in a grand manner can be another cause for irritation.

Text 4.9

雪に閉ざされた市内のあちこちで、スコップなどを手にした市民が、
背丈を超える雪と格闘しながら除雪に追われた。しかし、大雪の後遺症
は予想以上にひどく、一向に進まない除・排雪に市民の**いらいら**が募っ
た。

© 2004 Asahi.com 18 January

Translation:
Everywhere in the city heavily covered by snow, citizens with shovels in hand were struggling with the snow higher than their height and were overtasked with its removal. Despite this collective effort, the aftermath of heavy snow was much severer than they had expected. Citizens got irritated as the removing and clearing of the snow did not proceed quickly.

Activity 3

イライラ *iraira* is a mimetic word (see Chapter 3, section 3.7). Not only mimetic words but also nouns such as names of fruits can be written in *katakana*. Similar to Texts 4.6 to 4.9, the accentuated word (リンゴ 'apple') bears a special meaning. Text 4.10 is taken from Asahi.com and relates a peculiar incident in which apples were stolen from trees. リンゴ occurs twice, as does its *hiragana* equivalent りんご. What do you think is the motivation for using *katakana* and *hiragana* for the same word? What effects does the writer intend to achieve?

Text 4.10

県りんご協会によると、収穫したリンゴを入れた箱を畑に積んでおいて

盗まれる事件は以前からあったが、木から大量にもぎとられることはな

かった。[...]県りんご果樹園によると、リンゴの流通経路は主に、農協

に出荷するか、弘前市や板柳町の産地市場に出すか、専門業者に

売るかだ。

© 2003 Asahi.com 24 November

Translation:
According to the Prefecture's Apple Association, apples had never been plucked in large quantity from the trees, but there were several incidents in which boxes of apples, stacked in the field, were stolen. [...] The prefecture's Apple Orchard said that the main routes for distributing apples are the following: (i) consigning them to Nōkyō (= Agricultural Cooperative association), (ii) forwarding them to the local market in Hirosaki city or Itayanagi town, or (iii) selling them to professional traders.

Commentary

The writer of this article alternates りんご *ringo* and リンゴ *ringo*. The theme of this article is the stealing of apples, and throughout the article 'stolen apples' is written in *katakana*. It is the author's strategy to pay special attention to the apples that are being discussed. When you look at the article closely, you may discover that apples when written in *hiragana* do not refer to stolen apples but serve as an attribute to characterize the organization associated with the fruit. りんご in 県りんご協会 *Ken Ringo Kyōkai* specifies the type of association in the prefecture. りんご in 県りんご果樹園 *Ken Ringo Kajuen* likewise specifies the type of orchard in the prefecture. To reiterate, in both cases りんご does not refer to a fruit but to a category that specifies the organization or association concerned.

4.2.5 Euphemisms

Certain words in Japanese vocabulary should not be verbalized directly. In this context, we use loanwords (mostly from English) and present them in *katakana* so that the unpleasantness implied in the original words may not be revealed directly. These words are called **euphemisms**, used in place of more direct words. It is normal not to say 便所 *benjo* 'toilet' (consisting of 便 'stool, excretion' and 所 'place') to mean the toilet because this expression sounds too direct; instead we use トイレ *toire* (from *toilet* in English). 妻 *tsuma* 'wife' may evoke the meaning of a secondary role. This function is probably derived from its second meaning as 'a garnish served with the main dish'. 刺身のつま *sashimi no tsuma* 'garnish served with raw fish', for instance, refers to seaweeds or vegetables that accompany raw fish to embellish the main dish. Hence, some husbands may refer to their wives as ワイフ (from *wife* in English) when they are conscious of this negative connotation associated with 妻. In this way, foreign words are used to replace the original words to avoid unfavourable overtones. Note that not all euphemistic words are derived from foreign languages. Instead of using トイレ there is also an alternative お手洗い *otearai* (consisting of a honorific prefix お, and two nouns, 手 'hand' and 洗い 'washing'). In place of ワイフ, 女房 *nyōbō* or 家内 *kanai* can also be used.

Text 4.11 contains an euphemistic word エンディングノート *endingu-nōto* (literally: 'ending note') to mean a notebook for older people who can make notes expressing their wishes when, for instance, they need help because they are getting old or when the end of their life approaches. For example, they can express how their funeral should be held or how they want to be buried. This notebook is sold by several organizations in Japan, and what is written in the notebook is intended to be forwarded to a person or persons on whom the individual who wrote it relies.

Text 4.11

いざというときに備え、自分の介護や葬儀の希望などを記しておく「エ

ンディングノート」（昨年十二月二十一日）には、全体で一万件近い

反響が寄せられました。

© 2004 *Yomiuri Newspaper* 1 February

4.3 Roman letters

Like *katakana*, **Roman letters** (ローマ字 *rōmaji*) are used to write foreign words. Roman letters are often used particularly for writing acronyms or abbreviations; unlike the cases in section 4.2, they are rarely used for the writer's rhetorical strategies. Table 4.6 illustrates some examples. In Japanese newspapers, all except the final two (WHO and WTO) are not accompanied by their Japanese equivalents (see Text 4.12). This means that readers are expected to understand these English expressions without help in Japanese. Some expressions such as NHK or CM are so widely accepted by the different generations in Japan that people may not even recognize exactly what they mean. Not all English acronyms are written in English, however; AIDS nowadays often appears as エイズ, while a recently coined acronym, SARS, alternates with サーズ *sāzu* or 新型肺炎 *shingata-haien* 'new pneumonia'. Text 4.12 is a segment of a newspaper article in which the expressions 新型肺炎, SARS, and 世界保健機関 *sekai hoken kikan* (WHO) occur. Text 4.13 exemplifies an acronym, CM (see also Backhouse 1993: 56–57).

Table 4.6 *Examples of words in Roman letters*

Roman letters	Reading	Meaning
FM	エフエム *efu-emu*	frequency modulation
SW	エスエム *esu-emu*	short wave
JR	ジェーアール *jē-āru*	Japan Rail
TBS	ティービーエス *tī- bī-esu*	Tokyo Broadcasting System
NHK	エヌエッチケイ *enu-etchi-kei*	Nihon Hōsō Kyōkai 日本放送協会 'Japanese Broadcasting Association'
OL	オーエル *ō-eru*	office lady
CM	シーエム *sī-emu*	commercial message
2LDK	ニーエルデーケイ *nī-eru-dī-kei*	2 living dining kitchen
100g	ヒャクグラム *hyaku-guramu*	100 grams
200m	ニヒャクメートル *nihyaku-mētoru*	200 metres
WHO	ダブルエイチオー *daburu-eichi-ō*	World Health Organization 世界保健機関 *sekai hoken kikan*
WTO	ダブルティーオー *daburu-tī-ō*	World Trade Organization 世界貿易機関 *sekai bōeki kikan*

Text 4.12

昨年春に新型肺炎 (SARS) が流行した時、ベトナムは最初の感染者発生

から2ヶ月で「制圧宣言」をした。制圧には、一党独裁下で徹底した

上意下達や、世界保健機関 (WHO) や日本を含めた手厚い国際支援が欠

かせない要因だった。それでも SARS 制圧がベトナム人の誇りとして

記憶に刻まれたのは間違いなかった。

© 2004 *Asahi Newspaper* 5 February

Translation:
When SARS (Severe Acute Respiratory Syndrome) spread last spring, Vietnam made a 'denial declaration' two months after the first discovery of an affected patient. Factors that facilitated denial were the thorough conveyance of the message from the dictatorial government to the nation and warm international support notably coming from WHO (World Health Organization) and Japan. Yet, the suppression of SARS was surely engraved in their memory with pride.

Text 4.13

4年前に台湾資本の飲料会社が販売を始め、タイの和食チェーンが追随。

「健康志向」のテレビ CM を流すと、日本食ブームもあって人気に火が

ついた。昨年3月、味の素とカルピスの合併会社も参戦し、今は30以上

の企業が競う。

© 2005 Asahi.com 5 April

Translation:
A soft drink company, capital in Taiwan, started to sell (Japanese green tea) four years ago, and, accordingly, Japanese food chains in Thailand began with the sale. When television broadcast CM on 'healthy food', the Japanese tea triumphed in popularity, facilitated by a Japanese food boom that prevailed in the country. Last March two companies, Ajinomoto and Carupis, were merged and joined the competition. At present more than thirty companies are in competition with each other.

4.4 Numerals and symbols

4.4.1 Numerals

Numbers or 数字 *sūji* are written using both Arabic (1, 2, 3, 4, etc.) and Chinese (一, 二, 三, 四, etc.) notations. Although in modern Japanese, Arabic numerals are used more frequently, the use of both types of numerals is not arbitrary but instead displays interesting distributional patterns.

Activity 4

Texts 4.14 and 4.15 comprise two excerpts from a newspaper. The former is part of a report in the main text about a suicide bombing that caused the death of ten civilians, while the latter is an announcement for a talk by the former Mayor of New York City. Numbers are written in Arabic or Chinese. Consider the different uses of these numbers and explain why they are written in this manner.

Text 4.14

首相公邸目前自爆テロ

路線バス標的１０人死亡

エルサレム中心部のガザ通りを走行中の路線バスで二十九日午前九

時 (日本時間同日午後四時) ごろ、自爆テロがあり、イスラエル放送

などによると、乗客ら少なくとも十人死亡、約五十人が負傷した。

© 2004 *Yomiuri Newspaper* 30 January

Translation:
Suicidal Explosion in front of the Prime Minister's House
Targeted Bus Route 10 Dead
There was a suicidal explosion on the bus route on Gaza Street in the centre of Jerusalem around 9 a.m. on the 29th (4 p.m. Japanese time). According to Jerusalem Broadcasting, at least 10 passengers were killed and about 50 were injured.

Text 4.15

ジュリアーニ前NY市長

治安再生・危機管理を語る

3月30日（火）午後2時　東京講演会

3月31日（水）午後1時　大阪講演会

（NHK大阪ホール）

午後2時15分　パネルディスカッション（同）

© 2004 *Yomiuri Newspaper* 30 January

Commentary

The use of numbers reflects the type of articles featured in the *Yomiuri Newspaper*. Text 4.14 is a report, while Text 4.15 is an announcement. 'Report' means news that features up-to-date information about an event, be it political, financial, social, or local, that has just happened. 'Announcement' in this context is a statement about an event that will happen and that is being publicized through the newspaper. Reports are written in a narrative style integrated with the main parts of a newspaper, while announcements contain minimal information in an elliptical style, treated separately from the main news reports. When the article is a report, as in Text 4.14, numbers are written in Chinese, though interestingly, numbers in headlines are in Arabic (10人) . This use of Arabic numerals may serve to catch the reader's attention. In Text 4.15 informing us of a talk by Mr Giuliani, all numbers are in Arabic.

It is worth noticing that *Asahi Newspaper* uses numerals differently; Arabic numerals are used more widely regardless of the type of text. Below is a news report that uses Arabic numerals to inform us of the date of an accident (23 February 2002), the serial number of the bullet train (417), the numbers of cars (16), the age of the driver (43), and the overrun distance (20). Note that all numbers are written in Arabic.

Text 4.16

JR東海道線の神奈川県・小田原駅で**02**年**2**月**23**日、東京発新大阪行き

「こだま**417**号」（**16**両編成）の運転士（**43**）が眠気に襲われ、ホー

ムの停止位置から約**20**メートル行き過ぎ、車掌が緊急停車させていたこ

とが分かった。

© 2004 *Asahi Newspaper* 24 February

Translation:
It was reported that on 23 February 2002 in Odawara Station, Kana-gawa, on the JR Tokaido Line, a locomotive driver (43) became drowsy and stopped Kodama 417 (16 carriages) 20 metres from the normal stopping point. It was discovered that the station guards had this train make an emergency stop.

There are a few exceptions, however, in which Chinese numerals are used in the *Asahi Newspaper*. Examples in Text 4.17 are taken from the same 24 February 2004 edition.

Text 4.17

- アテネ**五輪** The Athens Olympiad

- 鳥取県の**二十世紀梨** 20th Century pears in Tottori prefecture

- **十五**代目片岡仁左衛門の長男に生まれ、女形の若手として
  活躍する X is born as the first son of Nizaemon Kataoka, the 15th generation, and has been acting as a young female actor.

What these exceptions have in common is that Chinese numerals are used when a journalist wants to give information about how things are ordered or classified rather than a specific number. Recall that the reason the journalist uses Arabic numerals in Text 4.16 is clearly to try to provide relevant numerical information about the accident. Look at the examples in Text 4.17. 五 *go* 'five' in 五輪 *gorin* symbolizes the five circles in the Olympiad; the number 'five' refers to five continents, that is, classifications, of the globe. The concern of 'five' is not the number but to point out the mission of the Olympiad. Similarly, 二十 *nijyū* 'twenty' in 二十世紀梨 *nijussēki-nashi* '20th century pears' does not represent the number of pears but instead refers to one type of pears that have this name. Here, Chinese numerals indicate the type but not the number. 十五 *jyūgo* 'fifteen' in 十五代目 *jūgodai-me* represents the order of generations; that is, X is the oldest son of Mr Uzaemon Kataoka, who represents the 15th generation of his family. Texts 4.14 to 4.17 clearly demonstrate that the use of Chinese numerals is more restricted in *Asahi* and more common in *Yomiuri*.

4.4.2 Symbols

The following tables (4.7 and 4.8) summarize two types of **symbols** or 符号 *fugō* used in Japanese text. Table 4.7 demonstrates symbols that are found more frequently in all types of Japanese texts, while the symbols in Table 4.8 are found less frequently.

Table 4.7 *Frequently used symbols*

Symbols	Readings	Functions
。	まる *maru* ・句点 *kuten*	Completion of a sentence
、	てん *ten* ・読点 *tōten*	Division of a sentence
・	なかてん *nakaten* ・ くろまる *kuromaru*	Juxtaposition of nouns
「 」	かぎ *kagi*	Quotations, titles, emphasis
（ ）	かっこ *kakko*	Supplementing information

Table 4.8 *Less frequently used symbols*

Symbols	Readings	Symbols	Readings
〜	なみせん *namisen*	？ ！	疑問符と感嘆符 *gimonfu to kantanfu*
『 』	ふたえかぎ *futaekagi*	" "	二重引用符 *nijūinyōfu*
< >	ひとえかっこ *hitoekakko*	＝	つなぎ *tsunagi*
《 》	ふたえかっこ *futaekakko*	―	ダッシュ *dasshu*
【 】	すみ付きかっこ *sumitsuki-kakko*	――	ぼうせん *bōsen*
？	疑問符 *gimonfu*	. . . . .	てんてん *tenten*
！	感嘆符 *kantanfu*	：	コロン *koron*

Activity 5

Text 4.18 shows that parentheses ( ) are used by journalists for different purposes. Your task is to identify the functions of the parentheses. All citations are taken from the 30 January 2004 *Yomiuri Newspaper*, pages 1 to 5.

Text 4.18

1. 「イラクの子どもたちに毛布をおくる運動」(主催・東京財団) が三
十日から開始される。

2. 毛布の配布は、日本の政府開発援助 (ODA) で建設されたサマワ市内
の病院など、イラク南部から開始する予定だ。

3. 「新しい日本をつくる国民会議」共同代表の佐々木毅 東大学長らは
二十九日、都内で記者会見し、昨年十一月の衆院選で各党が掲げた
政権公約(マニフェスト)をチェックするため、今春をめどに「マニフ
ェスト検証フォーラム」を開催すると発表した。

4. 対象者の大半は企業幹部や資産家で、滞納所得税の総額は約二億五
千万リンギット(一リンギットは約二十八円)にのぼる。

5. BSE(牛海綿状脳症 ＝狂牛病)感染牛が見つかった米国産牛の
輸入停止が続き、牛肉の在庫がそこをついてきた。

6. 各社は、牛丼に代えて豚肉などを使った新メニューを発売している
が、「消費者に受け入れられるかどうか不透明」(アナリスト)との
見方が多い。

7. アルツハイマー病の原因物質が脳内に増加するのを遺伝子で防ぐこと
に、理化学 研究所(理研)と自治医大の共同グループがマウス実験で
成功し、二十九日発表した。

Translation:
1   A charity to send blankets to children in Iraq will start on the 30th (sponsored by the Tokyo Foundation).
2   The distribution of blankets is planned to begin from the South of Iraq, presumably at a hospital in Samawa that was built by Japanese Official Development Assistance (ODA).
3   Tsuyoshi Sasaki, the president of Tokyo University, representative of the national meeting aiming to create a new Japan, attended a press conference in Tokyo on the 29th and stated that there will be a 'Manifest Inspection Forum' by this spring to check the political pledge (manifest) proposed by each party in the election for the House of Representatives last November.
4   The majority of people concerned are executives of companies or wealthy people. The total of unpaid income tax amounts to ca. two hundred fifty million Ringgit (one Ringgit is roughly twenty-eight yen).
5   It was found that native cows in America were affected by BSE (Bovine Spongiform Encephalopathy), and it prohibited the continued import of American cows. A stock of beef bowls has therefore nearly reached the bottom.
6   Each company is selling new menus with pork in place of beef bowls, but in the view of many, it is not evident whether this is being accepted by consumers (analyst).
7   It was made public on the 29th that a joint group from the Institute of Physical and Chemical Research (Riken) and the Jichi Medical College succeeded, based on experiments on mice, in preventing the increase of the substance that causes Alzheimer's disease in the brain by using genes.

Commentary

Parentheses used in these excerpts have six different functions.

First, parentheses serve to give additional/supplementary information for a word or example immediately preceding (1 and 4): (1) tells who organized a charity, while (4) provides further information about the value of Malaysian currency.

Second, parentheses serve to provide an alternative English expression that is normally abbreviated (2): ODA is equivalent to 政府開発援助 *sēfu kaihatsu enjo*.

Third, when an expression is generally known by other wording, parentheses provide a synonymous expression (3): マニフェスト *manifesuto* is derived from *manifest* in English, and its Japanese equivalent is 政権公約 *sēken-kōyaku*.

92

Fourth, when English abbreviations are used (= BSE), parentheses serve to give their Japanese translations (5).

Fifth, parentheses indicate a source of information: (6) indicates that the opinion expressed (消費者に受け入れられるかどうか不透明 *shōhisha ni ukeirerareru ka dōka futōmē*) is derived from an 'analyst', whose exact name is not provided.

Sixth, if the shortened form (理研 *riken*) is known more widely than its unabbreviated form (理化学研究所 *rikagaku kenkyūjo*), it is indicated in parentheses as an alternative (7).

Activity 6

You have learned that the symbol ・ (なかてん *nakaten* or くろまる *kuro-maru*) is used to juxtapose two nouns. However, its exact function varies depending on how these two nouns are juxtaposed. The following texts illustrate two interesting cases. Try to explain the subsystems you find.

Text 4.19

また、市民の負担を減らすため裁判期間を大幅に短くしなければならず、

検察・弁護側と裁判所は連日開廷できる態勢を整える必要もある。

© 2004 *Asahi Newspaper* 14 February

Translation:
In addition, in order to reduce the citizen's burdens, the trial period should be shortened dramatically, and the prosecution, the defence and the court of justice need to get fully prepared to be able to hold a court at any time.

Text 4.20

為替が急落するなどの通貨危機への備えとしては、現在2国間で通貨

交換協定を結ぶネットワーク「チェンマイ・イニシアチブ」構想にもと

づき、アジア域内では16件の2国間協定が結ばれている。

© 2004 *Asahi Newspaper* 14 February

93

Translation:
As for preparing for a currency crisis such as a sharp decline of the exchange rate, 16 cases in Asia have passed a two-country agreement, based on the concept of a network called the 'Chiang Mai-Initiative', under which two countries conclude an agreement on currency exchange.

Commentary

The symbol ・ in Text 4.19 functions as a coordinator. 検察・弁護側 means 検察 *kensatsu* 'prosecution' 'and' 弁護側 *bengogawa* 'defence'. In Text 4.20, this symbol has a different function. It is not a coordinator but instead points to a relationship between チェンマイ *chenmai* as a modifier and イニシアチブ *inishiachibu* 'initiative' as a head noun. Chenmai is a city in the northwest of Thailand, and this network organization named as an 'initiative' has been founded in this city.

Activity 7

Look at the symbols summarized in Table 4.8. The column for their functions is left blank. Based on Texts 4.21 to 4.25, try to complete the table. Think about the journalist's intentions in using these symbols. All texts are taken from the *Asahi Newspaper*. Two are taken from the 2 May 2005 edition and the other are from the 14 February 2004 edition.

Text 4.21

日本の若者が船に乗りたがらなくなった•••••••

高木船長の嘆きが耳にこびりついている。

© 2005 *Asahi Newspaper* 2 May

Text 4.22

次いで「田」が１９８、「山」が１６８で、「大」「野」と続い

た（９７年４月現在、『日本の地名がわかる事典』（日本実業出版社）

© 2004 *Asahi Newspaper* 14 February

Text 4.23

劇作・演出家の坂手洋二が、主宰する新作「だるまさんがころんだ」を

２０日から３月７日まで、東京・下北沢のザ・スズナリで上演する。

過去の二つの作品が今回原点になった。一つは９５年の「反戦自衛官」。

もう一つは、０２年の「屋根裏」。「『屋根裏』の成功に味をしめて、

断片的なエピソードを集めて一つの流れのある芝居がつくれるのではと

思った」。

© 2004 *Asahi Newspaper* 14 February

Text 4.24

海外の調査では、椎間板ヘルニアの発症要因の７割以上は遺伝的な影響

とみられている。５～１０個の遺伝子が発症に関与すると推定。

© 2005 *Asahi Newspaper* 2 May

Text 4.25

【南極支局＝武田剛】夏の間、日が沈まなかった南極の空に夕日が戻っ

てきた。

© 2004 *Asahi Newspaper* 14 February

Commentary

The following table presents suggested answers for the task in Activity 7. If you are of a different opinion, modify or refine the table. Some symbols are left unexplained. Consult other texts and complete the table.

Table 4.9   *new version*

Symbols	Text	Readings	Functions
~	24	なみせん	from X to Y
『　』	22; 23	ふたえかぎ	titles of books or dramas; used when titles appear in citations
< >		ひとえかっこ	
《　》		ふたえかっこ	
【　】	25	すみ付きかっこ	source information
?		疑問符	
!		感嘆符	
? !		疑問符と感嘆符	
" "		二重引用符	
=	25	つなぎ	relationship/equation between X and Y
—		ダッシュ	
____		ぼうせん	
. . . . .	21	てんてん	hesitation
:		コロン	

4.5   Changes in the writing system

Within the last few decades, the Japanese writing system has undergone important changes. This final section takes a brief look at these changes. Texts 4.26 and 4.27 are extracts from the *Asahi Newspaper* in 1940 (2 July). We can observe three interesting characteristics.

The first is that the spelling differs from that of present-day Japanese. This traditional way of using *hiragana* is called 歴史的仮名遣い *rekishiteki-kanazukai* 'historical kana spelling' (用ゐる *mochiiru* in place of 用いる *mochiiru,* and 云ふ *yū* in place of いう *yū*). This historical spelling was used up until the spelling reforms, which attempted to moderate the discrepancies between pronunciation and spelling and were carried out by the Japanese Government after World War Two. According to Komai and Rohlich (1991: 8), this historical spelling corresponds roughly to the pronunciation of the early Heian period (794–1185).

The second characteristic is that auxiliary verbs (置く *oku* in place of おく *oku;* 居る *iru* in place of いる *iru*) and quotative verbs (云ふ in place of いう) are written in *kanji* (see Chapter 3, section 3.6).

Text 4.26

> 室内はいつも乾燥させて置くことが大切で、それには乾布ふきを多く用
>
> ゐることです。一生涯に出来るだけ過労を避けると云ふことが長命法 の
>
> 最大要素となって居る。

The third characteristic is that loanwords are written and used slightly differently. Text 4.27 exhibits six foreign loanwords. There seems to be a general tendency for loanwords to imitate the original spelling as closely as possible. *Shampoo* is written as シャムプー *shanpū* with <m> because of the English spelling (currently シャンプー). Similarly, *television* is not shortened (currently テレビ *terebi*), and the entire expression is given (e.g., テレビジョン *terebijon*). バタ *bata* for *butter* is not accompanied by a dash (currently バター *batā*), showing that the vowel /a/ in /ta/ at the end of the word is not prolonged. バンド *bando* is an older expression of ベルト *beruto* for 'belt' (see Sanada 1989: 16). スカート *sukāto* for *skirt* and アンテナ *antena* for *antenna* maintain the same form as in present-day Japanese.

Text 4.27

> ★ バンドを用いず吊りスカートにしてお腹を締めない。
>
> ★ 少量のお湯に塩、バタ、砂糖を入れて軟らかくゆでます。
>
> ★ シャムプーにはいろいろ市販の品もありますが、[...]
>
> ★ テレビジョンを遠方まで送るにはアンテナが高ければ高い程よいの
>
> だが、[...]

Exercise

If old newspapers or magazines (before 1970, for example) are available to you, select some articles and examine whether the writing systems are different and, if so, discuss how they have been changed or modified.

Note

1 This name is a pseudonym different from the real name that appears in the text cited.

5 Word structure

This chapter examines how Japanese words (e.g., nouns and verbs) are structured. The study of the structure of words is called **morphology**, or 形態論 *keitairon*, in Japanese linguistics. The topics we will deal with are as follows: (i) morphemes, (ii) the difference between morphemes and ideograms, (iii) nominal compounds, (iv) affixation and (v) verbal compounds. It is important to know that words are not always single units but are often a composite of two (or more) smaller elements. When two elements are conjoined, there is, more often than not, a semantic relationship between them. After illustrating the rudiments of Japanese morphology (sections 5.1 to 5.4), we will look closely at how the study of morphology is related to the meaning encoded in the language (sections 5.5 to 5.7).

5.1 Meaningful units

Chapter 2 stated that the smallest unit of sound structure is the phoneme, and that meaning is one criterion used to find phonemes. Word structure also has a basic unit called the **morpheme**, which is a meaningful unit of a word. What we generally call 'words' are not necessarily the smallest parts of a sentence; these parts may consist of morphemes. Look at sentence (1) and try to identify meaningful units.

> (1) 学生たちは日本語で修士論文を書いた。
> *Gakusē-tachi wa nihongo-de shūshi-ronbun o kaita*
> The students wrote a master's thesis in Japanese.

In order to find meaningful units, you may ask such questions as in (2) to (7).

> (2) What did the students do?
> (3) What did they write?
> (4) What thesis did they write?
> (5) When did they write it?
> (6) How did they write it?
> (7) How many students were involved?

You know that the students wrote a thesis as an answer to (2) because the first part of 書いた *kaita*, that is 書い, gives you this information. For (3) you get an answer from 修士論文 *shūshi-ronbun*, or more precisely from

98

its second part, that is 論文 *ronbun*, and the object marker を tells you that 修士論文 is what the students targeted. The first part of this word then tells you the type of thesis the students wrote (4). (5) asks you about the time of the writing of the thesis. You will say that it was written in the past because the verb 書いた carries the past marker た. Similarly, で functions as an instrumental marker showing that the thesis was written in Japanese. You know that more than one student is involved in this activity from the plural marker たち attached to 学生 *gakusē*. How would you characterize は in (1)? は will be characterized as a discourse particle in Chapter 3 in JLU, which means that it carries a meaning determined by the discourse. (8) demonstrates how (1) is dissected into morphemes.

(8) 学生 たち は 日本 語 で 修士 論文 を 書い た

   The discussion above shows that a Japanese sentence such as (1) consists of morphemes with meanings that may be **lexical** (meanings of lexical items), **grammatical** (meanings of syntactic or morphological units) or **discursive** (meanings derived from discursive functions). The crucial difference between lexical and grammatical meaning is that the latter arises only when the language expresses certain meanings using grammatical forms. Languages encode different grammatical meanings. Malay, for instance, employs different grammatical means to express plural (by repeating the noun *pelajar*), past (by adding a word *telah* meaning 'completion') and means (by combining a preposition *dengan* and a verbal noun *menggunakan*).

(9) Pelajar-pelajar   telah   menulis   tesis   Master   dengan
     student-student   completion   write   thesis   Master   by
     menggunakan   Bahasa   Jepun.
     use   language Japan
     The students wrote a master's thesis in Japanese.

Table 5.1 opposite schematizes the three meanings and also shows that the most salient meaning used is the lexical.

5.2 Ideograms

Before we continue, a word of caution is in order. Unlike English, Japanese (and Chinese) employs characters, or *kanji*, which themselves convey meanings. These characters are called **ideograms**. Ideograms represent a concept, an idea, or a thing without necessarily becoming a word or a morpheme by themselves. Thus, the word 日本語 *nihongo* 'Japanese language' in (1) comprises three ideograms whereby the first two combine to mean 'Japan', and the third carries the meaning of 'language'. It is the combination of these two parts that convey the meaning 'Japanese

99

> 日 stands by itself, but changes from に to び making it a "different" ideogram

Table 5.1

Morpheme	Lexical	Grammatical	Discursive
学生	○		
たち		○	
は			○
日本	○		
語	○		
で		○	
修士	○		
論文	○		
を		○	
書い	○		
た		○	

language'. However, the first two ideograms (日 for 'sun, day' and 本 'source, origin, book') by themselves are, strictly speaking, not 'meaning-ful' with regard to the meaning of 'Japan'; they become meaningful only when combined with each other. This leads one to suggest that the ideograms 日 and 本 by themselves do not form morphemes but that 日本 is a morpheme.

語 is an ideogram bearing the meaning of 'language' but serves, by contrast, as a morpheme (in section 5.6.2.2 it is shown that 語 is an affix and a bound morpheme). It is meaningful in terms of the entire word, which means 'Japanese language'. It is not an independent morpheme (e.g., ×私は語に興味があります, whose intended meaning is 'I am inter-ested in **language**') but is attached meaningfully to the name of the coun-try, creating the name of the language spoken there.

In a similar vein, 修士 *shūshi* 'master' and 論文 *ronbun* 'thesis' are meaningful units for the construction of 修士論文 'master's thesis'; the meaning of these two units corresponds to the meaning of the entire word. However, neither ideogram (i.e., 修 and 士 versus 論 and 文) is considered a morpheme because the combination of 修 'learn' and 士 'qualification' or 論 'discuss' and 文 'writing' can only suggest a clue to the meaning of each component part; they can hardly be regarded as meaningful units for the entire word. The point is that the meaning of ideograms does not always correspond to the meaning of the morpheme.

5.3 Free and bound morphemes

Japanese possesses two major ways of forming words; one is compounding (sections 5.5 and 5.7) and the other is affixation (section 5.6). Compound-ing combines two independent characters (e.g., 親子 *oyako* 'parent and

100

child') or two (or more) independent words (e.g., 親子電話 *oyako-denwa*). They can be either ideograms or morphemes. When parts of compounds can stand on their own, they are generally called **free morphemes**. In Japanese, independent units are not restricted to free morphemes; they can also be ideograms. As you will see in section 5.5, many compounds in Japanese consist of ideograms that may not qualify as morphemes. Examples in (10) to (12) give an idea of how compounds are formed in Japanese. 親, 子, and 親子 are meaningful units of each sentence; (12) demonstrates a case in which a compound 親子 consists of two free morphemes 親 and 子.

> (10) 私の**親**は田舎で農業をしている 。
> *Watashi no oya wa inaka de nōgyō o shite iru*
> My **parents** live by farming in my home town.

> (11) あの**子**はだれですか 。
> *Ano ko wa dare desuka*
> Who is that **child**?

> (12) **親子**の絆はたやすく絶つことはできない。
> *Oyako no kizuna wa tayasuku tatsu koto wa dekinai.*
> You cannot easily sever the bonds between **parent and child**.

Affixation is a process in which an independent word is expanded by using an affix (e.g., 日本語 *nihongo*). Affixes are dependent units of words known as **bound morphemes**. You have so far seen how a character 語 functions as an affix, and other types of affixes will be provided in section 5.6. A character 手, for example, which originally means 'hand', carries a meaning of profession when it is attached to certain words (e.g., 歌手 *kashu* 'singer', 交換手 *kōkanshu* 'telephone operator', 運転手 *untenshu* 'driver').

5.4 Inside the compound

When two parts are combined, a new word is formed that has an 'additive' meaning. The term 'additive' indicates that the meaning of the new word is derived from the addition of the meaning of the original characters or morphemes. For example, 親子 *oyako* corresponds to 親 and 子, and 青空 *aozora* 'blue sky' to 青 *ao* 'blue' and 空 *sora* 'sky'. What is noteworthy is that the meanings of two parts are not always added in the same way. The 'relationship' between the two parts needs to be considered. For example, the compound 親子電話 *oyako-denwa* 'telephone with extensions' consists of two independent morphemes (i.e., 親子 *oyako* 'parent and child' and 電話 *denwa* 'telephone'), but does not mean a telephone used or possessed by a parent and a child. The point is that 親子 is not used in its literal sense but refers to the way the telephone functions. In other words, 親子

101

'modifies' 電話 in that it tells us what type of telephone the second element is. The whole expression points to a phone system in which the main (= 親) telephone is connected to subordinate (= 子) telephone(s) within the same building. In another compound, 携帯電話 *kētai-denwa* 'mobile telephone', the first element also tells us what type of telephone the second element is, but it associates a verbal element – a phone that one carries with oneself. Thus, 携帯電話 can be paraphrased as 電話を携帯する *denwa o kētai suru* 'to carry a phone'. This verbal element is absent from 親子電話, as the ungrammaticality shows: ×電話を親子する. Thus the meaning of compounds depends on the relationships between their component parts.

When a new word is created, it has a core part that represents its entire meaning. Core and supplementary parts are identified by the relationship between the two. What do you think is the core part of 電話 'telephone'? In this compound, the character 話, which means 'speaking', must be the core part because it is modified by 電, which specifies how speaking is conveyed, that is, electrically. There are similar words such as 対話 *taiwa* 'dialogue', in which speaking is modified by 対 referring to two or more people, and 手話 *shuwa* 'talk with the hands', in which speaking is modified by 手 referring to hand movements. As these examples exemplify, it is often the case that the rightmost part of a composite is the core, and the left part serves to add additional information to it.

Activity 1

Text 5.1 is a passage taken from the novel *Calling You*. Words consisting of more than two words are represented in bold. Try to decide which part is the core and explain the relationship between the two parts.

Text 5.1

彼女はそう言うと、この見えない**電話回線**について、いくつかのことを教えてくれた。例えば、実際に口でしゃべったり、まわりで発生した空気の振動による音は、どんなに大きな音でも頭の電話の向こう側には伝わらない。頭の電話に向かって心の中で話しかけたことだけが、相手に伝わるそうだ。また、多くの場合、電話の持ち主は**自分自身**の**電話番号**を知らない。**電話帳**や**番号案内**は存在せず、知らない相手に電話をかけるには、偶然に頼るしかないそうだ。わたしも、自分の電話番号を知らなかった。

© 2003 Otsu, Ichi / *Calling You* (pp. 18–19), Kadokawa

Commentary

Table 5.2

Examples	Core part
電話回線	回線
自分自身	?
電話番号	番号
電話帳	帳
番号案内	案内

All compounds except 自分自身 *jibun-jishin* have the same relationship between the composite parts. The first element modifies, or tells more about, the second element. Three compounds contain 電話 'telephone' as the first element, which serves to give more information about the nature of the second element. In 電話回線 *denwa-kaisen* 'telephone circuit', 電話 tells us which kind of 回線 'circuit' the second element is. Likewise, in 電話番号 *denwa-bangō*, 電話 specifies what kind of 番号 'number' the second element is. 電話帳 'telephone directory' differs from the other two in that it contains an affix 帳 *chō* 'book' that cannot stand alone (×私は帳を買った 'I bought a book'). There are examples such as 日記帳 *nikki-chō* 'diary' or らくがき帳 *rakugaki-chō* 'scribbling book' in which 帳 is used as a bound morpheme. 番号案内 *bangō-an-nai* 'telephone number service' also has the second element as its core; 案内 'information' is modified by 番号 'number' to show that the information is about telephone numbers. One problem in this activity is how to deal with 自分自身 'self'. This compound contains two free morphemes whose meanings are very similar. In other words, we cannot determine which part is the core. There is more information about the different types of compounds, nominal (section 5.5) and verbal (section 5.7), in the following sections, and the answer to this puzzle will be provided accordingly.

5.5 Nominal compounds

Let us look at **nominal compounds** more closely. Nominal compounds refer to compounds that are classified as nouns. They stand in contrast to verbal compounds or, more generally, compound verbs (section 5.7). While compound verbs consist of two independent verbs, many noun compounds in this section are not composed of independent nouns but rather two ideograms or *kanji*. The discussion in 5.4 indicates there are specific relationships between the two composite parts of a compound. The following seven classifications are preliminary suggestions for these

103

relationships. E stands for element. E1 is the first element and E2 is the second element. Most of the compounds in this section are formed by two ideograms that may not qualify as morphemes. The purpose of this section is to explicate meaningful relationships that exist between two parts of a compounded noun.

5.5.1   E1 opposes E2

Compounds consist of two *kanji* whose meanings stand in contrast. Some compounds such as 上下 *jōge* or 明暗 *mēan* have an extended meaning: 上下 can mean 'a suit' (clothes) or 'two volumes' (books), while 明暗 can be associated with aspects of life meaning 'happiness and hardship' or 'various aspects'. This type of compound has no core part; instead the two parts are treated equally to achieve the entire meaning of the compound.

Work on the rest of the compounds in the box below. Discuss with your fellow students whether the compounds exhibit an extended meaning or whether they simply express the opposition of two parts.

親子 *oyako* 'parent and child', 兄弟 kyōdai 'elder brother and younger brother, sibling(s)', 姉妹 *shimai* 'elder sister and younger sister', 男女 *danjo* 'man and woman', 明暗 *mēan* 'lightness and darkness', 朝晩 *asaban* 'morning and evening', 天地 *tenchi* 'heaven and earth', 上下 *jōge* 'up and down', 大小 *daishō* 'large and small size', 高低 *kōtē* 'height and lowness'

5.5.2   E1 parallels E2

This type of compound is created by joining two *kanji* with similar meanings. 照 in 照明 *shōmē* indicates lighting up something and 明 means that something is bright. 泳 in 水泳 *suiē* means 'swimming', which is already associated with water, but the addition of 水 'water' emphasizes that the movement is carried out in water. 水泳 is in fact categorized as a sport that is typically carried out by humans. This connotation is absent in 泳ぐ *oyogu* 'to swim', its native equivalent. As such, it is possible to say 魚が川で泳いでいる *sakana ga kawa de oyoide iru* 'Fish are swimming in the river', while it is unacceptable to say 魚が水泳をしている. Both *kanji* in 思考 *shikō* refer to having opinions in a particular way, implying that one thinks with logic, although independent *kanji*, 思う *omou* 'think' and 考える *kangaeru* 'think', do not denote logical thinking. Like the compounds with two opposites (section 5.5.1), this type of compound does not have a core part. For the remaining compounds in the box below, discuss with your fellow students how the two *kanji* are related.

照明 *shōmē* 'illumination', 水泳 *suiē* 'swimming', 思考 *shikō* 'thinking', 検査 *kensa* 'examination', 選別 *senbetsu* 'selection', 故障 *koshō* 'trouble, breakdown', 優秀 *yūshū* 'outstanding', 時期 *jiki* 'time', 掃除 *sōji* 'clean', 製造 *sēzō* 'manufacture', 創作 *sōsaku* 'create', 散歩 *sanpo* 'walk, stroll', 停止 *tēshi* 'suspend, stop', 河川 *kasen* 'river'

5.5.3 E1 is repeated

When compounds are formed by repeating the same *kanji*, they normally impart a plural meaning such as 人々 *hitobito* and 山々 *yamayama*. E1 of 物々交換 *butsubutsu-kōkan* also indicates plurality. Note, however, that not all *kanji* can be repeated. For example, 丘々 'hills' and 川々 'rivers' are not acceptable. 物々交換 is only acceptable when 物々 'things' is followed by 交換 'exchange'. Like the previous two groups of compounds, this type of compound does not exhibit a core part (except 物々交換, which has E2 as its core; in this regard it also belongs to 5.5.7).

人々 *hitobito* 'people', 山々 *yamayama* 'mountains', 物々交換 *butsubutsu-kōkan* 'barter', 少々 *shōshō* 'a little', 度々 *tabitabi* 'repeatedly'

5.5.4 E1 modifies E2

Three types of compounds fall under this category. Let us look at the first type, in which E1 and E2 both refer to nominal entities. E1 in the compound modifies E2 in various ways. By 'modify' we mean that E1 of a compound provides supplementary information about E2 so that the referent of E2 is specified. 腕 *ude* 'wrist' in 腕時計 *ude-dokē* makes clear what kind of clock it is. E1 in 墓石 *hakaishi* and 名案 *mēan* details the characteristics of E2; in 墓石, E1 indicates that the stone is used for the grave, and in 名案, E1 qualifies E2. Likewise, in 花畑 *hanabatake*, 花 as E1 tells what kind of field 畑 is. In 私邸 *shitē*, 私 as E1 indicates that the residence is a private one.

腕時計 *udedokē* 'watch', 墓石 *hakaishi* 'gravestone', 名案 *mēan* 'a good idea', 花畑 *hanabatake* 'flower field', 私邸 *shitē* 'private residence'

The second type is where compounds contain an adjective or an adjectival element as E1 that serves to supplement the meaning of E2. For example, 青空 *aozora* consists of 青 *ao* 'blue' and 空 *sora* 'sky', meaning

105

'blue sky'. Note that the meaning of 青空 is the same as that of its adjectival expression 青い空 *aoi sora*, though this paraphrase is not always possible with all compounds. Some compounds refer to a specific referent. For example, an adjectival expression 軽い石 *karui ishi* refers to any stones that are light in weight, but a compound 軽石 *karuishi* is a volcanic stone used for softening the skin or removing stains by rubbing it over the skin. グリーン車 *gurīnsha* is not a car painted in green but refers to a special reserved-seat coach in trains in Japan. 親友 *shinyū* is slightly different from 親しい友達 *shitashī tomodachi* in that it refers to one's best friend, while the latter can indicate any close friend. These compounds (except 青空) undergo semantic narrowing (see Chapter 3, section 3.3.2.4).

> 青空 *aozora* 'blue sky', 軽石 *karuishi* 'pumice stone', グリーン車 *gurīnsha* 'green car', 親友 *shinyū* 'best friend'

The third type is where E1 is an adverbial element modifying E2 when E2 refers to a verbal element denoting an action. 明記 *mēki* means that one writes clearly, while 独占 *dokusen* refers to a situation in which someone possesses or dominates something alone. Similarly, 自治 *jichi* means that the people residing in an area govern that area independently of the government of a country, while 速読 *sokudoku* means reading rapidly. These compounds may be divided into two groups depending on the category of the resulting compound. One group can appear with する *suru* (e.g., 明記する, 独占する, 速読する), while the other cannot occur with する (x自治する).

> 明記 *mēki* 'writing clearly', 独占 *dokusen* 'monopolization', 速読 *sokudoku* 'reading rapidly', 自治 *jichi* 'self-governing'

5.5.5   E2 is part of E1

Compounds also exhibit both the part and the whole relationship (see Chapter 6, section 6.1.6). In the examples below, E2 refers to a part of what is indicated by E1. In 山頂 *sanchō*, the summit (= 頂) is a part of a mountain (= 山); likewise, in 川上 *kawakami*, the upper stream (= 上) is a part of a river (= 川). Similarly, 川下 *kawashimo* refers to the lower course (= 下), which is also part of the river (= 川).

> 山頂 *sanchō* 'the summit of a mountain', 川上 *kawakami* 'the upper part of a river', 川下 *kawashimo* 'the lower part of a river'

5.5.6 E1 acts on E2

This compound contains a verb or a verbal element as E1 that modifies E2. That is, E1 expresses the action and E2 is the entity the action targets. For example, 読書 *dokusho* refers to the activity of reading (読 = E1) books (書 = E2). 殺人 *satsujin* consists of killing (殺 = E1) and a person (人 = E2). Both 結婚 *kekkon* and 離婚 *rikon* contain 婚 'marriage' as E2, while E1 characterizes the marriage; in the first, the marriage comes into existence by joining (結 = E1), while in the second, the marriage breaks apart by separation (離 = E2). 映 means 'filming' and, hence, 映画 *ēga* refers to the filming of pictures (画 = E2). Both 着陸 *chakuriku* and 離陸 *ririku* refer to 'arriving' (着 = E1) and 'leaving' (離 = E1) the ground (陸 = E2). 発音 expresses uttering (発 = E1) sounds (音 = E2), while 延期 *enki* means delaying (延 = E1) time (期 = E2). Both 転職 *tenshoku* and 転居 *tenkyo* contain 転 as E1, which means 'change' or 'move'. While the first refers to one's changing (転 = E1) a job (職 = E2), the second refers to one's moving from an old residence (居 = E2) into a new.

Because of the verbal nature of E1, these compounds as a whole often function as verbs, and they are combined either with verbs such as 犯す *okasu* or 観る *miru*. Most compounds take the verb する 'do' (see the remaining verbs).

殺人 *satsujin* 'manslaughter', (を犯す *okasu*), 映画 *ēga* 'movie', (を観る *miru*), 離陸 *ririku* 'taking off', 着陸 *chakuriku* 'landing', 読書 *dokusho* 'reading', 結婚 *kekkon* 'marriage', 離婚 *rikon* 'divorce', 発音 *hatsuon* 'pronunciation', 延期 *enki* 'postponing', 転職 *tenshoku* 'changing a job', 転居 *tenkyo* 'changing one's address'

5.5.7 E2 acts on E1

This compound has E2 as a verbal element that acts on or specifies the referent of E1. In 稲作 *inasaku* and 詩作 *shisaku*, E1 is the object produced by the activity of E2. In 日没, E1 is the object whose movement is specified by E2, while E1 in 日照 *nisshō* refers to the object whose state is described by E2. 自殺 has E1 that is not an object but a person to whom E2, the action (i.e. killing), is directed.

稲作 *inasaku* 'rice production', 詩作 *shisaku* 'creation of poem', 日没 *nichibotsu* 'sunset', 日照 *nisshō* 'sunshine', 自殺 *jisatsu* 'suicide'

Activity 2

Japanese texts contain quite a few compound words. The following extract is part of a daily column 天声人語 *tensē-jingo* 'Heaven's Voice, Men's Words'. The writer describes the tragic accidents that occur repeatedly every year in Mecca, Saudi Arabia. List noun compounds (ignore 繰り返される *kuri-kaesareru* in line 1 as it is a compound verb) and explain how they are structured according to the seven classifications proposed in section 5.5.

Text 5.2

1 今年も２０００人以上が死亡した。毎年のように繰り返されるイスラ

ム教の聖地メッカでの事故である。９０年には１４２６人の死者が出

た。世界中から２００万人もの巡礼者が集まるだけに混乱がつきまと

う。メッカ巡礼とあわせて催される犠牲祭はイスラム世界 最も重要な

5 祭りの一つだ。アフガニスタン・バーミヤンの大仏を破壊したタリバ

ーンもこの期間は爆破作業を中断した。今年は犠牲祭に集まった人々

をねらったテロが発生、イラクのクルド人自治区で多数の犠牲者が出

た。生活の隅々まで宗教が支配している。

© 2004 *Asahi Newspaper* 5 February

Translation:
More than 2000 people died this year – an accident that occurs repeatedly almost every year in the Islamic holy place of Mecca. 1990 was marked by 1426 deaths. More than 2 million pilgrims gather, and this certainly triggers chaos. A ceremony of sacrifice held together with the Mecca pilgrimage is the most important ritual in the Islamic world. Even the Taliban who destroyed the Buddha of Bamiyan, Afghanistan, stopped their routines of destruction during this period. However, the terror occurred this year, which targeted people who gathered for this ceremony. Consequently, the number of victims was large in self-governed Kurdistan in Iraq. Religion is ruling every nook and corner of life.

Commentary

Below is the same text as Text 5.2 with notations of words. Some words include E1 in *katakana*.

---

¹今年も２０００人 ²以上が ³死亡した。⁴毎年のように繰り返される ⁵イスラム教の ⁶聖地メッカでの ⁷事故である。９０年には１４２６人の ⁸死者が出た。⁹世界中から２００万人もの ¹⁰巡礼者が集まるだけに ¹¹混乱がつきまとう。メッカ ¹²巡礼とあわせて催される ¹³犠牲祭は ¹⁴イスラム世界で最も ¹⁵重要な祭りの一つだ。アフガニスタン・バーミヤンの ¹⁶大仏を ¹⁷破壊したタリバーンもこの ¹⁸期間は ¹⁹爆破作業を ²⁰中断した。¹今年は ¹³犠牲祭に集まった ²¹人々をねらったテロが ²²発生、イラクの ²³クルド人 ²⁴自治区で ²⁵多数の ²⁶犠牲者が出た。²⁷生活の ²⁸隅々まで ²⁹宗教が ³⁰支配している。

There are 30 noun compounds in total. Table 5.3 summarizes the distribution of compounds found in the passage above. The first and fifth classifications are not present in Text 5.2.

Table 5.3

	Classifications	Examples
C2	E1 parallels E2	³死亡, ¹¹混乱, ¹²巡礼, ¹³犠牲, ¹⁵重要, ¹⁷破壊, ¹⁸期間, ¹⁹爆破, ²²発生, ²⁷生活, ³⁰支配
C3	E1 is repeated	²¹人々, ²⁸隅々
C4	E1 modifies E2	¹⁴イスラム世界, ¹⁶大仏, ¹⁹爆破作業 (N=N) ⁶聖地, ²⁵多数 (A=N)
C6	E1 acts on E2	²⁰中断 (ADV=V), ²⁴自治 (ADV=V)
C7	E2 acts on E1	²⁹宗教 (N=V)

The structure of two words, that is, ²以上 *ijō* and ⁷事故 *jiko*, may not fall under the classifications proposed in Table 5.3. 以 refers to the reference point from which something starts or is measured. When combined with 上, it refers to something that is above the reference point R. ２０００人以上 *nisen-nin ijō* 'more than two thousand' means that the number of people goes beyond two thousand. There are 以下 *ika* 'below R, under R', 以外 *igai* 'apart from R, except R', 以後 *igo* 'after R', 以来 *irai* 'since R', all of which behave similarly to 以上. 事故 is an example in which E2 modifies E1: 故 means anything evil (e.g., disaster, misfortune, harm), and it specifies 事, which refers to a situation or event. As you may agree, 事故 'accident' is an evil event. Since E2 in 事故 merely

109

modifies E1 but does not act on it, it would be coercive to subsume it under C7.

Not all words found in the text are regarded as compounds, however. Words such as [5]イスラム教 *isuramukyō*, [8]死者 *shisha*, [9]世界中 *sekaijū*, [10]巡礼者 *junrēsha*, [13]犠牲祭 *gisēsai*, [23]クルド人 *kurudojin*, and [26]犠牲者 *gisēsha* contain a suffix as E2, while words such as [1]今年 *kotoshi* and [4]毎年 *maitoshi* have a prefix as E1. These affixes can be attached to many different words that possess an independent lexical meaning. For example, 者 occurs with different elements in the passage (i.e., [8]死者 *shisha*, [10]巡礼者 *junrēsha*, [26]犠牲者 *gisēsha*) and carries the same meaning (者 = person). Although 今 or 毎 occur only once in the text, they can be attached to 週 'week', 月 'month', or 日 'day' (see section 5.6.1.1). When we compare [5]イスラム教 and [29]宗教 *shūkyō*, however, we encounter a problem: while イスラム 'Islam' can be an independent word (私は**イスラム**の芸術に関心がある 'I am interested in **Islamic** art (literally, the art of Islam)'), 宗, which means 'doctrine' by itself, cannot stand alone (×私は**宗**に関心がある 'I am interested in **religion**'). This fact suggests that 教 may not be a suffix in this particular case but rather that 宗教 *shūkyō* is a compound consisting of two idiograms, each of which has its own meaning (see discussion in section 5.2).

5.6 Affixation

Let us now look more closely at **affixation**. Having discussed compounds, the morphological difference between the following words may be noticed.

> ど真ん中 *domannaka* 'right in the centre'
> 楽しみ *tanoshimi* 'pleasure, joy'
> 親子 *oyako* 'parent and child'
> 親子電話 *oyako-denwa* 'telephone with extensions'

It should be noted that the first two words contain ど in front and み at the end. These little words are **affixes**, which have two characteristics: (i) they are **bound morphemes**, and (ii) they are **productive**, meaning they are attached to many words. ど serves to emphasize the meaning of the noun that follows it. ど真ん中 means 'right in the centre', while 東京のど真ん中 means 'right in the centre of Tokyo'. ど can also be attached to adjectives: どぎつい色 refers to colours that are intense (such as 'shocking pink'). Note that the first sound /k/ of きつい becomes voiced /g/ because of the presence of the voiced sound /do/ in ど. This is reminiscent of sequential voicing (Chapter 2, section 2.2.4). It should be noted, however, that this voicing process does not pertain to the principle of sequential voicing since ど is an affix. This appears to be an exception in which an affixed word behaves like part of a compound. By contrast, the addition of み

in 楽しみ turns the adjective 楽しい 'pleasant, joyful' into a noun (nominalization). Although affixes are generally considered to be productive, their distribution remains limited. Some illustrations are in order (words marked by × mean unacceptability):

(13) ど根性 *dokonjō* 'strong willpower', どえらい 'very famous', ど田舎 *doinaka* 'very rural area', ×ど勇気 *doyūki* 'a lot of courage', ×ど若い *dowakai* 'very young'

(14) 痛み *itami* 'painfulness, pain', 悲しみ *kanashimi* 'sadness', ×嬉しみ *ureshimi* 'happiness', ×寒み *samumi* 'coldness'

These examples illustrate that when the affix is attached to certain groups of words, its function as 'emphasis' or 'nominalization' takes effect. Similar phenomena can be observed in English, too. The affix *un* in *unkind* cannot stand alone: its meaning of negation is available when it is attached to a lexical base such as *kind*, but not *patient* (× *un*-patient), *honest* (× *un*-honest), or *pretty* (× *un*-pretty).

Affixation subsumes **prefixation** (e.g., ど) and **suffixation** (e.g., み) depending on which part of the word the affix is attached to. Generally speaking, suffixation seems to be used more than prefixation in Japanese.

As briefly observed in Activity 2 above, it is not always easy to clearly differentiate affixation from compounding in Japanese. The problem lies in the fact that words written in *kanji* integrate a meaning in themselves (because of their being ideograms), but not all *kanji* words are morphologically independent. Activity 1 contained the example 電話帳 *denwachō*, where 帳 is classified as a suffix because it can be attached to independent words such as 日記 *nikki* 'diary' and らくがき *rakugaki* 'scribble', maintaining its meaning as a book. When we look at a compound word such as 通帳 *tsūchō* 'account book', the second element maintains the same meaning of 'book', though it is hard to say that 通 is morphologically independent in the sense of 日記 or らくがき. This suggests that 通帳 may be an example of a compound consisting of two ideograms. These examples readily show that 帳 is an ambiguous case that can be considered an affix with some words and part of a compound with other words. As mentioned already in Text 5.2, 教 in 宗教 and イスラム教 demonstrate the same ambiguity.

The classification of affixes in the next sections follows the classification proposed by major previous studies in Japanese linguistics. To reiterate, the main criteria for the selection of affixes is that they are bound morphemes attached to morphologically independent words and they are used productively.

5.6.1 Prefixation

Prefixes are placed in front of a word.

5.6.1.1 Size, degree, time

By specifying the **size** (e.g., 大, 小), **degree** (e.g., 超) or **frequency** (e.g., 毎, 今, 来, 先) of the base, new words are created. 超 'very' is more frequently used among young people (see JLU: Chapter 4, section 4.5). Prefixes such as 今, 来 or 先 are used in relation to the time of speaking. If the speaker is located in the first week of May, the second week of May is for him the 'next week'. When the second week comes, the first week of May is then considered the 'last week'. Thus, the allocation of these prefixes depends on the week in which the speaker is located.

> 大 (大雨 *ōame* 'heavy rain', 大雪 *ōyuki* 'heavy snow', 大風 *ōkaze* 'heavy wind', 大火事 *ōkaji* 'big fire', 大喧嘩 *ōgenka* 'big quarrel')
> 大 (大渋滞 *dai-jūtai* 'heavy traffic jam', 大事故 *dai-jiko* 'serious traffic accident', 大失敗 *dai-shippai* 'a big mistake')
> 小 (小雪 *koyuki*, 小雨 *kosame*)
> 超(超おもしろい *chō-omoshiroi* 'very interesting')
> 毎 (毎日 *mainichi* 'every day', 毎週 *maishū* 'every week', 毎月 *maigetsu* 'every month', 毎年 *maitoshi* 'every year', 毎秒 *maibyō* 'every second', 毎時間 *mai-jikan* 'every hour')
> 今 (今週 *konshū* 'this week', 今月 *kongetsu* 'this month', 今年 *kotoshi* 'this year')
> 来 (来週 *raishū* 'next week', 来月 *raigetsu* 'next month', 来年 *rainen* 'next year')
> 先 (先日 *senjitsu* 'the other day', 先週 *senshū* 'last week', 先月 *sengetsu* 'last month')

5.6.1.2 Emphasis

Prefixes serve to **emphasize** or **accentuate** the meaning of the base. These two prefixes are exclusive to each other. That is, ど in ど根性 cannot be replaced by 真. 真 triggers gemination when a voiceless consonant comes afterwards.

> ど (ど根性 *dokonjō* 'strong spirit, mind', ど真ん中 *domannaka* 'right at the centre' どぎつい *dogitsui* 'gaudy, loud', どえらい *doerai* 'immense, great, astounding', どしろうと *doshirōto* 'non-professional, layman', ど百姓 *dobyakushō* 'real farmer')
> 真 (真っ白 *masshiro* 'pure white', 真っ赤 *makka* 'deep-red, very red', 真っ黒 *makkuro* 'deep-black', 真緑 *mamidori* 'pure green', 真水 *mamizu* 'fresh water')

5.6.1.3 Negation

Several prefixes express **negation**. These prefixes are not interchangeable, that is, none of the prefixes 不, 非 or 未 can replace 無, and vice versa.

無 (無意味 *mu-imi* 'no meaning', 無関心 *mu-kanshin* 'no interest', 無頓着 *mu-tonchaku* 'indifference')
不 (不必要 *fu-hitsuyō* 'no necessity', 不可能 *fu-kanō* 'impossibility', 不法 *fuhō* 'against law')
非 (非道徳 *hi-dōtoku* 'amoral', 非運 *hiun* 'misfortune', 非凡 *hibon* 'unique, extraordinary')
未 (未完結 *mi-kanketsu* 'incompletion', 未成年 *mi-sēnen* 'minor')

5.6.2 Suffixation

Suffixes are placed at the end of a word.

5.6.2.1 Profession

Depending on the type of **profession**, different suffixes are chosen to derive the names of these professions. It seems that all suffixes are complementary to each other. It is impossible to say ×花者 to mean someone who sells flowers as a profession, or ×運転家 to mean someone who drives a lorry as a profession. Although it is not easy to identify the exact relationship between a suffix and the derived word, 屋 is related to a profession involving a shop, and 家 is used for a profession having something to do with schools or groups where particular opinions are shared. 手 seems to refer to professions in which one utilizes skills such as singing or driving. 人 and 者 not only refer to professions but also to people in general; hence, we have 愛人 'mistress' or 美人 'a good-looking woman', and 患者 'patient' or 識者 'expert', none of which can occur with other suffixes.

人 (歌人 *kajin* 'poet, poetess', 軍人 *gunjin* 'soldier')
者 (司会者 *shikaisha* 'moderator, master of ceremonies', 指揮者 *shikisha* 'conductor', 医者 *isha* 'doctor', 記者 *kisha* 'journalist')
手 (歌手 *kashu* 'singer', 助手 *joshu* 'assistant', 交換手 *kōkanshu* 'operator', 運転手 *untenshu* 'driver')
屋 (花屋 *hanaya* 'flower shop, florist', 電気屋 *denkiya* 'electric appliance store, electrician', 薬屋 *kusuriya* 'pharmacy, pharmacist')
家 (政治家 *sējika* 'politician', 作家 *sakka* 'author, novelist, writer', 翻訳家 *honyakuka* 'translator')

5.6.2.2 Nationality or language

By adding 人 *jin* or 語 *go*, **nationalities** or names of **languages** are derived.

人 (外国人 *gaikoku-jin* 'foreigner', アメリカ人 'American', フランス人 'Frenchman', ベトナム人 'Vietnamese', ベルギー人 'Belgian')
語 (外国語 *gaikoku-go* 'foreign language', フランス語 'French language', ベトナム語 'Vietnamese', マレー語 'Malay language')

5.6.2.3 Period

A specific **period** can be expressed by 期 *ki*, 中 *chū* or 後 *go*.

期 (倦怠期 *kentai-ki* 'a period of lassitude', 思春期 *shishun-ki* 'the age of puberty', 更年期 *kōnen-ki* 'menopause')

中 (恋愛中 *ren-ai-chū* 'being in love', 試験中 *shiken-chū* 'during the exam, during the exam weeks')

後 (試合後 *shiai-go* 'after the match', 試験後 *shiken-go* 'after the exam')

5.6.2.4 Feeling or point of view

The sense of **feeling** or **point of view** can be expressed by adding 感 *kan* and 観 *kan*, respectively. 使命 *shimē* means mission or appointed task. When 感 is attached, it means a self-awareness of completing the task appointed. 世界 *sekai* means 'the world', and when 観 is attached, it means 'world view'.

感 (使命感 *shimē-kan* 'awareness of fulfilling one's mission', 疎外感 *sogai-kan* 'a sense of alienation', 優越感 *yūetsu-kan* 'feeling of superiority')

観 (世界観 *sekai-kan* 'world view', 人生観 *jinsē-kan* 'one's view of life', 厭世観 *ensē-kan* 'pessimistic view of life')

5.6.2.5 Turning a noun into an adjective (adjectivization)

When nouns are attached by the suffix 的 *teki*, they are **adjectivized**. This suffix has the meaning that something or someone has a particular quality. 西洋的な女の人 *sēyōtekina on-na no hito* refers to a woman who has a Western manner. Likewise, 魅力的な女性 *miryokutekina josē* refers to a woman who has a charm in her character or physical appearance. All resulting adjectives with 的 form a *na*-adjective (e.g., 静かな 'quiet'), ending with な or だ depending on what it modifies or qualifies.

的 (魅力的 *miryoku-teki* 'attractive', 女性的 *josē-teki* 'feminine', 伝統的 *dentō-teki* 'traditional', 日本的 *nihon-teki* 'in a Japanese manner', 歴史的 *rekishi-teki* 'historical', 科学的 *kagaku-teki* 'scientific')

5.6.2.6 Turning an adjective into a noun (nominalization)

There are three representative affixes that turn adjectives into nouns, a process called **nominalization**. 悲しい 'sad' can take all three affixes, さ, み and げ, that is, 悲しさ, 悲しみ and 悲しげ, but the meanings of the derived nominals are not always identical. In addition, おもしろい is nominalized by the addition of さ or み only. While it is possible to say 重さ and 重み, it is impossible to say ×重げ. 寂しげ and 恐ろしげ can also be said as 寂しさ and 恐ろしさ but not as ×寂しみ and ×恐ろしみ.

Making a clear distinction between the uses of these suffixes is not easy. However, one can say that while さ serves merely to change the category of the word, み and げ add extra nuances to the resulting nominal. み implies that the referent the nominal modifies is judged or evaluated by the speaker, while げ describes how the referent is perceived by the speaker. For example, if you want to know about the weight of a box, you will say 箱の重さはいくらですか 'How much does the box weigh?' Here the use of 重み is awkward. When you say これは重みのある箱だ 'This is a heavy box', you may evaluate the weight of the box not by weighing it but basing it on your past experience (e.g., you compare this box with another box). 重みのある人間 refers to someone who behaves with dignity. In both cases, the speaker evaluates the referent that 重み modifies based on his experience or knowledge. ×重さのある人間 therefore does not make sense unless we simply mean that he or she weighs a lot. 悲しげな顔 'sad face' lays emphasis on the sad expression on someone's face as judged by the speaker (see also Sakairi et al. 1991: 228–231). In this regard, it can be paraphrased as 悲しそうな顔 'the face that looks sad' (see JLU: Chapter 1, section 1.2.6). Because the speaker's judgement or impression of the other person is the issue, it is impossible to say 私は悲しげな顔をしている 'I have a sad face' (intended meaning) when the speaker is talking about himself.

These resulting nominals (i.e., 重み and 悲しげ) are in fact used as adjectives: 重み is attached to の, serving as an adjective (= 重みのある箱); likewise 悲しげ is combined with な and serves as an adjective (= 悲しげなまなざし 'sad-looking eyes'). Here, the nominalization seems to be a process of creating an extra adjectival meaning that cannot be achieved by the original adjective (e.g., 重い 'heavy' and 悲しい 'sad').

> さ (悲しさ *kanashisa* 'sadness', おもしろさ *omoshirosa* 'interest, fun', 短かさ *mijikasa* 'shortness', 重さ *omosa* 'weight')
> み (悲しみ *kanashimi* 'sadness', おもしろみ *omoshiromi* 'interest, fun', 重み *omomi* 'weight')
> げ (悲しげ *kanashige* 'sadness, sorrowfulness', 寂しげ *sabishige* 'loneliness', 恐ろしげ *osoroshige* 'fright')

5.6.2.7 Turning a noun into another type of noun

It is worth mentioning that some nouns create other types of nouns when they are attached to suffixes such as 化 *ka* or 性 *sē*, whereby an extra meaning is added to the resulting noun.

> 化 (西洋化 *sēyō-ka* 'westernization', 活性化 *kassē-ka* 'activation')
> 性 (独自性 *dokuji-sē* 'originality', 二面性 *nimen-sē* 'two-facedness')

西洋 *sēyō* refers to the West. When it is attached to 化, it denotes a change from one state to another. After the Meiji Restoration (1868), Japan was claimed to be westernized, or 日本は西洋化した 'Japan was westernized'.

This means that Japan underwent changes to assimilate Western ways of life. For example, the government encouraged the people to cut off their topknots or stop wearing swords (see also 英文で読む日本史 *Eibun de yomu nihonshi* 'Reading Japanese History in English' 1996: 118–119). As a result of this westernization, Japanese society blended with different cultures, or 日本社会が活性化した 'Japanese society became active'. Resulting nouns with 化 often appear with a light verb する 'do'. In contrast, 性 adds the meaning of disposition. For example, 独自性のある作品 *dokujisē no aru sakuhin* 'original work', refers to the originality possessed by the work. 独自性のある人 refers to the person who behaves in an original way. 独自 alone refers to an individual. For example, when a teacher says to his students, 独自の意見を持ちなさい *dokuji no iken o mochinasai* 'Do have your own opinions', it does not mean that the ideas are original but that they are the students' own. 二面 means two sides, but when it appears with 性, it refers to a person's two-facedness. Unlike 西洋化 and 活性化, it is impossible to say ×独自性する and ×二面性する, but all the derived words with 性 take が/のある.

5.6.2.8 Plural markers

Different **plural markers** are attached to nouns. The first three markers are used frequently, although inanimate entities do not express plurality (e.g., ×二冊の本たち, ×二冊の本ども, ×二冊の本ら 'two books'). など and なんか (the latter is a spoken form of the former) are used when the speaker does not state explicitly the number of objects but only implies that there is more than one object. Text 5.3, an extract from *Calling You*, contains 電化製品なんか *denka-sēhin nanka* (line 4) to refer to unused items littering an unoccupied land (= 空き地 *akichi*). From the context it is clear that the phrase refers to the plurality of items.

たち	(子どもたち 'children', 学生たち 'students')
ども	(私ども 'we')
ら	(子供ら 'children')
など	(ノートなど 'notebook and other')
なんか	(電化製品 なんか 'electric appliances')

Text 5.3

1 「そんなの、誰だってやるよ。当然の隠蔽工作だね。きみは『時間
稼ぎ』の場所、どこにしてる？」「『時間稼ぎ』？ああ、わかった。
私は図書館。あなたは？」「僕はごみ捨て場を使ってる。と言って
も、近所の空き地に**電化製品なんか**が放置されているだけなんだけ

116

> **5**　どね。だれもこないところだから、すごく落ち着くんだ。錆のうい
> た冷蔵庫の真似をして、膝をかかえて座っていると、楽しい気持ち
> になれる。時々、まだ使えるものまで捨てられていて、このまえ、
> まだ映るワイドテレビを拾ったよ」

© 2003 Otsu, ichi / *Calling You* (p. 24), Kadokawa

Vocabulary:
隠蔽工作 *inpē-kōsaku* (line 1) 'concealment maneuvering'

Brief explanation:
In this novel, two high school students are having a conversation. A female student who has no friends and feels isolated tells a male student that she told her mother a lie that she has many friends at school. He responds in line 1 that such concealment is what everyone normally does with their parents. The differentiation between 'male' and 'female' speakers can be identified by the use of きみ *kimi* (line 1), あなた *anata* (line 3) and 僕 *boku* (line 3), or the use of sentence final particles such as よ *yo* (lines 1 and 8) and だね *dane* (line 1) (see JLU: Chapter 4, section 4.1.3).

Activity 3

This activity comprises ten sentences extracted from the novel *Calling You* (pp. 1–27). Each sentence contains morphologically complex words. Identify whether **words in bold** are compounds or affixed words.

Text 5.4

> **1.** **教室**が**楽しげ**に騒がしくなればなるほど、わたしのまわりの空間だけ
> 切り離され、**孤独感**が**増大**する。
>
> **2.** **昼休み**になると、よく**図書館**を訪れた。
>
> **3.** 我が家の前に**到着**すると、玄関の鍵をポケットから取り出す。
>
> **4.** 原田さんの**説明**を聞きながら、さきほどの彼が番号を**非通知**にして
> いたことを思い出す。
>
> **5.** つまり、お互いにエース**最新号**の内容を知らないわけだ。
>
> **6.** 心の中でつぶやいた言葉が、六十分という時間の隔たりと、日本列島
> の半分という**空間的**距離を越えて彼に届いているという。

---

7. ぼくは**内向的**な性格なんだ。

8. 原田さんともしばしば連絡をとり、彼女に尋ねてみたが、まだ一度も**請求書**が届いたことはないらしい。

9. 彼が英語のテストを受ける時、わたしは電話越しに、**英和辞典**を用意してアドバイスした。

10. 大学での生活や、一人暮らしをする上で経験した**悲喜**こもごもを話してくれた。

© 2003 Otsu, ichi / *Calling You*, Kadokawa

Commentary

The following table presents suggested answers to the task in Activity 3. 'Com' indicates compound and 'A' indicates affix. 'P' or 'S' in parentheses refers to prefix and suffix, respectively. Complete the table by giving the reading and meaning of each word.

Table 5.4

Words	Reading	Compound or affix	Meaning
教室		Com	classroom
楽しげ	たのしげ	A(S)	
孤独感		Com+A(S)	
増大		Com	
昼休み		Com	lunch break
図書館		Com+A(S)	
到着		Com	
説明		Com	
非通知		A(P)+Com	
最新号		A(P)+A(S)	
空間的		Com+A(S)	
内向的	ないこうてき	Com+A(S)	
請求書		Com+A(S)	
英和辞典		Com	
悲喜		Com	

As shown above, words such as 孤独感 *kodokukan* 'loneliness' (1), 図書館 *toshokan* 'library' (2), 非通知 *hitsūchi* 'not notifying' (4), 空間的 *kūkanteki* 'spacious' (6), 内向的 *naikōteki* 'introversion' (7) and 請求書 *sēkyūsho* 'bill' (8) contain both processes of compounding and affixation. 最新号 *saishingō* should be an example of double affixation. 最 is a prefix to mean the degree (see McClure 2000: 83), and 号 indicates a number or

issue for magazines or newspapers. 楽しげ(1) is not interchangeable with
楽しさ or 楽しみ. 悲喜 *hiki* (10) emphasizes the manner in which sorrow
and joy alternate; the person did not explain a single experience but
instead alternated sad or pleasant incidents in her telling. こもごも often
appears with 悲喜, but not with other compounds such as 明暗 *mēan* or
高低 *kōtei*.[1]

Exercise

Visit the websites of newspapers and collect examples of affixed words,
which you have learned in 5.5. Discuss with your fellow students why these
words contain a particular affix but not others.

5.7   Verbal compounds

In sections 5.1 to 5.6, the main concern has been noun morphology. In
this final section the focus is on verb morphology. This section deals
with **compound verbs** (or 複合動詞 *fukugō-dōshi*), which are composed of
two verbs. As with noun compounds (see section 5.5), it is important
to recognize that compound verbs are not merely a composite of two
elements but that there are semantic relationships between the elements.
Consider, first, the four examples in (15) to (18).

(15)   Xは扉を開けた。 *Tobira o aketa.*
X opened the door.

(16)   Xは扉を押し開けた。 *Tobira o oshi-aketa.*
X pushed the door open.

(17)   Xは車を押し始めた。 *Kuruma o oshi-hajimeta.*
X began to push the car.

(18)   Xは新聞をポケットに押し込んだ。
Shinbun o poketto ni oshi-konda.
X stuffed a newspaper into his pocket.

All the examples except (15) contain a compound verb. While (15) demonstrates basic information about the opening of the door, (16) supplements
(15) by providing information as to how the door is opened. In other
words, the first verb (V1 henceforth) specifies the manner in which the
activity encoded in the second verb (V2 henceforth) is carried out.
Example (17) indicates not only that X pushes the car but that the pushing
is also in its initial stage. V1 and V2 in (16) and (17) maintain their original
lexical meaning in the compound, while V2 in (18) expresses the direction
of the action, which is not part of its original meaning (e.g., バスが込んだ
basu ga konda 'A bus was crowded'). Most compound verbs semantically
have a core part. The core part represents the entire meaning of a com-

119

pound. If V1 is semantically the core part, V2 modifies its meaning. If V2 is semantically the core part, V1 modifies the meaning of V2. The examples above can be paraphrased according to this criterion. In (17), V2 modifies V1 by indicating at which temporal stage the action is carried out. Likewise, V2 modifies V1 in (18) by specifying the direction of the action. In (16), V2 is the main part, and V1 modifies V2 by indicating that the opening of the door is performed by pushing it.

It is important to mention here the **transitivity** of V1 and V2 in a compound. V1 or V2 is syntactically either a transitive verb or an intransitive verb. As shown in Table 5.5, there are in principle four patterns.

Table 5.5

	Syntactic patterns	Example
①	intransitive + intransitive	しゃがみ + 込む (see (22))
②	intransitive + transitive	走り + 始める (see (24))
③	transitive + transitive	振り + 回す (see (44))
④	transitive + intransitive	はずし + 終わる (see (27))

What is noteworthy here is that an intransitive verb can be combined with a transitive verb or vice versa, as in ② and ④. The transitive verb 始める *hajimeru* has 始まる *hajimaru* as its intransitive counterpart, but 始まる cannot occur with 走る *hashiru*; that is, 走り始まる does not exist in Japanese. Similarly, the intransitive verb 終わる *owaru* has 終える *oeru* as its transitive counterpart, but it is awkward to say はずし終える. As a rule, the transitivity status of V2 is not relevant in the formation of the compound. More precisely, 始める in ② is transitive, but the compound in which it appears functions as an intransitive verb because V1 is intransitive. Likewise, 終わる in ④ is an intransitive, but the compound in which it appears functions as a transitive verb because V1 はずす *hazusu* is transitive. The discussion above indicates clearly that the main function of a compound is not syntactic but semantic.

The following sections from 5.7.1 to 5.7.12 elaborate on the patterns of compound verbs. The resources of the discussion are from a children's story 車のいろは空のいろ *Kuruma no iro wa sora no iro* 'The Colour of the Car is the Colour of the Sky' (Aman 1977). In this story (173 pages long), compound verbs number 163 total. Of these, 130 compounds derive their meaning from their component parts. These 163 compounds are formed according to the following four principles:

1. V1 is a core element and V2 is a modifying element. Modification is realized by providing either the aspectuality of V1 (Table 5.6), direction of V1 (Table 5.7), reciprocality of V1 (Table 5.8)

or manner in which V1 takes place (Table 5.9). Most V1 words express action or motion, while only a few express change of state (e.g., 走り出す *hashiri-dasu* 'start running', 流れ込む *nagare-komu* 'flow into', 泳ぎ回る *oyogi-mawaru* 'swim round').

2. V2 is a core element and V1 is a modifying element. Modification is realized by specifying the manner or the method by which the given event is carried out. V2 in all compounds except one (Table 5.11) expresses change of state (Table 5.10) (e.g., 立ち上がる *tachi-agaru* 'stand up', 見送る *mi-okuru* 'see off').

3. V1 and V2 express semantically equal events; thus there is no distinction between core and modifying elements (Table 5.12) (e.g., 折れ曲がる *ore-magaru* 'broken and bent').

4. V1 and V2 are fused, that is, the entire meaning of the compound does not depend on the meaning of its component parts; instead the compound generates its own meaning by itself (e.g., すれちがう *sure-chigau* 'pass each other').

Aspect (the expression of the internal stages of an event) is the most frequently used modifying element in the formation of compounds in the story. Among all the aspectual functions, the inceptive use of 出す *dasu* is the most frequent, as shown in Table 5.6 (see also Chapter 7, section 7.4. for the concept of 'aspect').[2]

Table 5.6   Aspect (75 total)

V2	Total	Examples	Function of V2
- 出す	43	走りだす	inceptive
- 始める	12	走りはじめる	initiation
- なおす	4	すわりなおす	repetitive
- 付ける	3	しめつける	intensive
- 込む	3	すわりこむ	intensive
- 返す	2	ききかえす	repetitive
- 掛ける	2	いきかける	prospective/intentive
- 続ける	1	話しつづける	continuative
- 着く	1	たどりつく	terminative
- 終わる	1	はずし終わる	terminative
- 付く	1	こおりつく	intensive
- そこなう	1	きりそこなう	incompletive
- 干す	1	のみほす	terminative/intensive

Table 5.7   Direction (16 total)

V2	Total	Example
- 上げる	7	つみあげる
- 込む	6	ながれこむ
- 掛ける	2	はなしかける
- 出す	1	とりだす

Table 5.8   Reciprocal (5 total)

V2	Total	Example
- 合わせる	4	見あわせる
- 合う	1	おしあう

Table 5.9   Manner (10 total)

V2	Total	Example
- まわる	3	およぎまわる
- まわす	7	ふりまわす

Table 5.10   Manner + change of state (20 total)

V2	Total	Example	Meaning of V2
- 上がる	12	まいあがる	rise
- 止まる	2	立ちどまる	stop
- 降りる	2	とびおりる	descend
- 乗る	1	とびのる	get on
- 出る	1	ふきでる	come out
- 消す	1	もみけす	eliminate
- 去る	1	かけさる	disappear

Table 5.11   Manner + action (1 total)

V2	Total	Example	Meaning of V2
- 送る	1	見おくる	send

Table 5.12   *Equal events (3 total)*

V1	V2	Total
おれ	まがる	1
すき	とおる	1
とおり	すぎる	1

5.7.1   だす as V2

The most frequently used meaning of だす (出す) *dasu* as V2 is as an **inceptive** aspect, that is, the initial point at which an event begins to transpire, as shown in (19) to (21). The first two examples describe the way in which the taxi begins to start (19) and starts to return (20). Example (21) focuses on the inceptive moment of Mr Matsui's getting out of his taxi.[3] 飛ぶ *tobu* originally means 'fly', but in this compound it emphasizes that someone exits an object vigorously. In the context of (21), Mr Matsui runs out of the taxi to chase down an old female passenger who gave him a ¥1000 note – an amount much more than she had to pay. Note that Japanese has an intransitive verb 出る *deru* 'come out, go outside'. It might be thought that this verb could be combined with 飛ぶ to mean that Mr Matsui exits his taxi (see (21)). However, Japanese already has 飛び出る *tobi-deru*, meaning that something (e.g., eyes or bones) protrudes or projects. 出る, meaning that something comes out from something else, is the main part of the compound here.

(19) 空いろの車は、また、すべるように**走りだします**。 (p. 45)
The blue car **begins to start** again as it slides away.

(20) 車は、五本松のところでユーターンして、**もどりだし**ました。
(p. 13)
The car **begins** to return at the five pine trees.

(21) (松井さんは) 車のそとに**とびだし**ました。 (p. 50)
Mr Matsui **went outside** of the car.

5.7.2   こむ as V2

こむ (込む) *komu* as V2 expresses not only aspect but also direction. Example (22) expresses the **completeness** or **exhaustiveness** of sitting. It is possible to say しゃがんで without having V2. However, this would simply express the fact of sitting. What is at issue in this scene is that Mr Matsui has been sitting behind the car for a long time repairing the flat tyre. The exhaustiveness of an action runs parallel to his eagerness to complete the work (a repair in this case). Example (22) contains an adverb

123

(さっきから 'for some time'), which points to the lengthy work and Mr Matsui's eagerness associated with it. Example (23) refers to the direction of the water that enters the taxi. The usage of こむ in (23) is the same as that of (18).

> (22) 空いろのぴかぴかのタクシーが、一台、とまっていました。その
>   うしろに**しゃがみこんで**、さっきから、ねっしんにタイヤをしら
>   べているのは、この車のうんてんしゅー、松井五郎さんです。
>   (p. 6)
>
> The blue-coloured taxi was being parked. Mr Matsui, the driver of this car, was **sitting** to the back of it and seriously examining the tyre for some time.
>
> (23) 水が、ひんやりと、風のように**ながれこん**できました。(p. 25)
>   The cold water **came inside** the car like a wind.

5.7.3   はじめる as V2

はじめる (始める) *hajimeru* 'begin' indicates the **initial** temporal stage of an action. Although はじめる and 出す are synonymous (see Chapter 6, section 6.1.2 for the term 'synonym'), はじめる encompasses a longer period of time in which the initial stages of an action take place. Notice that (24) has はじめる instead of だす (see (19)). It would not be appropriate to use だす here. Why not? Upon looking closer, we recognize that (24) does not merely express the inceptive moment of driving. This is implied by the presence of いまきた道 – the road on which Mr Matsui has driven his taxi – denoting that the taxi will now drive back along the same road. The process indicated here covers more than an inceptive moment of driving. Look at (25), which contains うとうと, an adverb that expresses the manner in which the guest sleeps in the taxi. The presence of this adverb implies that the sleeping occupies more than its starting point, that is, the process of sleeping that follows its inception. It is not possible to replace ねむりはじめた with ねむりだした. だす puts an emphasis on the initiation of an action rather than the continuation that follows it. Similarly, it would not be adequate to use 走りはじめ instead of 走りだし in (19) because of the presence of an adverb すべるように 'like sliding', which denotes the force used for starting the car off powerfully.

> (24) 車は、いまきた道をもうーど**走りはじめ**ました。(p. 80)
>   The car **began to go back** along the road that Mr Matusi had just used.
>
> (25) お客が、うとうと**ねむりはじめ**たのです。(p. 20)
>   The guest **began to fall** into a doze.

124

The replaceability of はじめる with だす is not an absolute criterion but instead depends on the meaning of the verb. As in (26), when もえる 'burn, be in flames' is used as V1, もえだす fits the given context. This can be explained by the fact that burning does not have a clear-cut initiation point (unlike the driving of a car) but is immediately followed by the process of burning. This fact makes もえだす compatible with the context here.

(26) 松井さんの目のまえに、すずかけ通りが見え、ずらっとならんで
いた木の大きな葉が、ほのおをふいて、**もえはじめ**ました。赤や
みどりのやねが、オレンジ色のすさまじいほのおにつつまれてい
ます。 (pp. 47–48)

Mr Matsui sees Suzukake Street in front of him, and the big leaves of the trees ordered in lines **began burning**. Red or green roofs are in orange-coloured, powerful flames.

5.7.4   おわる or ほす as V2

おわる (終わる) *owaru* 'finish' expresses a **terminative** aspect. That is, it conveys an event that ceases happening. In (27), the protagonist has finished taking out the onions being hung at the window frames. Another terminative aspect is conveyed by ほす (干す) *hosu* 'desiccate'. It is possible to say のみ終わって in (28). The use of ほす as V2 adds a nuance that a bear gentleman (a bear dressed as a gentleman) not only finishes drinking the whisky but drinks it up, so that nothing is left in the glass.

(27) 私は、自分が勝手口から外にでて、窓のわくにぶらさがっている
玉ねぎを、一個ずつはずしました。 [...] 二つめのたまねぎを、
ひもから**はずし終わ**った時、私は、はっとしました。 (pp. 125–126)

I went out the exit and took out the onions hung at the window frames one by one. As soon as I **finished taking** the second onion, I was startled.

(28) くましんしは、グラスのなかみをぐいっと**のみほして**、はなしを
つづけました。 (p. 86)

A bear gentleman **drank up** the content of the glass and continued talking.

5.7.5 つける or つく as V2

つける (付ける) *tsukeru* (transitive) 'attach', 'to append' or つく (付く) *tsuku* (intransitive) 'be stuck to' is used to describe an event performed with a degree of **intensity**. Compound verbs with these verbs as V2 all have a figurative meaning in the story (see JLU: Chapter 2, section 2.5 for the concept of 'figure of speech'). しめつける is normally used when we tie something tightly, but in (29) it is used figuratively. It describes the protagonist's inner emotions: her heart is greatly wrung by the question of where her hometown is. Because her hometown no longer exists, the bitter word moves her greatly. Intensity in (30) refers to the complete coldness that can almost freeze the stars. こおりつく basically means that something (e.g., water, lake) freezes hard, but it is used figuratively to emphasize the very low temperature outside.

(29) ふるさと . . . 。私の胸はじいんと**しめつけ**られました。つらいこと

ばを、ここで聞くとは思いませんでした 。 (p. 141)

My hometown . . . It **wrung** my heart. I didn't expect to hear the bitter word here.

(30) ずいぶんさむそうだな。まるで、星まで**こおりついて**いるよう

な夜 。 (p. 76)

It looks very cold outside – as if even stars can become **completely frozen** tonight.

Example (31) also uses intensity to emphasize the brightness of the colour of a mandarin. It is possible to say そめたような without an intensifier, but this fails to accentuate the strong impression the mandarin imparts in a given context.

(31) うんてんせきからとりだしたのは、あの夏みかんです。まるで、

あたたかい日の光をそのまま**そめつけ**たような、みごとないろで

した 。 (p. 32)

It is the mandarin that Mr Matsui took out from his driver's seat. It has a beautifully bright colour as if the warm sunlight **is painted** naturally on it.

5.7.6 かける as V2

かける (掛ける) *kakeru* originally means 'hang' (壁に絵をかけた *kabe ni e o kaketa* 'I hung a drawing on the wall'). When it is attached to V1, one meaning is **prospective** aspect, the point of time just prior to the beginning of an event. It is also called an 'intentive' in the sense that the event is expected to occur but does not transpire (see Frawley 1992: 322). In (32), the gentleman was about to go to the other side but failed to do so because Mr Matsui stopped him. Another meaning of かける is a direction, as in (33). When it is attached to V1, which denotes communication between two (or more) people (e.g., 話す *hanasu* 'speak', 言う *yū* 'say', 説明する *setsumei suru* 'explain'), it emphasizes that someone attends to someone else by speaking.

> (32) 松井さんはポケットから白いハンカチをだして、ひたいのあせを
>
> ふきました。むこうに**いきかけ**たしんしのうでを、いそいで、で
>
> もしっかりとつかみました。(pp. 106–107)
>
> Mr Matsui took out a white handkerchief from his pocket and wiped the sweat on his forehead. He grasped the arm of the gentleman who **was about to go** to the other side – hurriedly but tightly.

> (33) ほりばたでのせたお客のしんしが、**はなしかけ**ました。(p. 29)
>
> The guest, a gentleman whom Mr Matsui picked up from the moat, **spoke to** him.

そこなう 'fail to do' resembles the first meaning of かける in that it denotes that an event does not succeed in transpiring. Contrary to かける, however, そこなう does not imply that the event is expected to transpire; it merely expresses that an event fails to take place. There are also other expressions such as いいそこなう 'fail to say', 食べそこなう 'fail to eat' and 見そこなう 'fail to see'. ハンドルをきりそこなう in (34) means that someone fails to steer the car correctly. きる (切る) here means 'to turn the wheel properly', and when そこなう is added to it, it means literally 'to fail to turn the wheel correctly'. Because the sentence in the text contains ところでした 'was in the point of', it actually means that Mr Matsui was about to steer the wheel in the wrong direction (because of his surprise), but fortunately this did not happen. The emphasis is on the non-occurrence of the failure.

> (34) びっくりした松井さんは、もうすこしでハンドルを**きりそこなう**
>
> ところでした。そのひょうしに、車はガタンと大きくゆれました。
>
> (p. 79)
>
> Mr Matsui, startled, **almost steered** the car in the wrong direction. At this moment, the car jolted heavily.

5.7.7 かえす as V2

かえす (返す) *kaesu* originally means 'return' (e.g., 不良品だったのでCDを返した *furyōhin datta node sīdī o kaeshita* 'I returned the CD because it was defective'). When it appears as V2, it denotes a **repetitive** aspect; that is, something is done once again or repeatedly. Mr Matsui asks the female guest a question by repeating what the woman said because the name of the street is unfamiliar to him. It is possible to say ききました without V2, but this refers to the act of asking only and does not make explicit what Mr Matsui actually did, that is, ask her back.

(35) 「すずかけ通り三丁目までいってください。」そのお客は、車に

のると、しずかな声でいいました。四十ぐらいの、色のたいへん

白い、ふっくらした女の人でした。「すずかけ通り？」と、松井

さんは**ききかえし**ました。そんな通りは、まだきいたことがなか

ったからです。(p. 39)

'Can you go to Suzukake Street?'
The guest got in the car and spoke quietly. A woman was in her forties, her skin being very white and a little shabby.
'Suzukake Street?'
Mr Matsui **asked** her **back** because he had not heard of that street.

5.7.8 あわせる or あう as V2

あわせる (合わせる) *awaseru* 'put together' and あう (合う) *au* 'agree with' both express **reciprocality** when combined with V1. As shown in (36) and (37), two people or two things take part in an action. In (36), Mr Matsui rubs his hands, and in (37), three passengers push their bodies together. Where あわせる and あう differ lies in how the reciprocal action is carried out. When あわせる is used, something (e.g., hands) is put together, and this reciprocal action can last for some time. In (36), Mr Matsui rubs his two hands while they are placed together. When あう is used, as in (37), it connotes that something comes into contact with something else, and that this reciprocal action may not last long. For example, there are similar examples such as 殴り合う *naguri-au* 'hit each other', 打ち合う and *uchi-au* 'knock each other'; both actions express the repetition of a series of small actions. あわせる and あう are not interchangeable.

(36) そこで、りょうてを二ど三ど**こすりあわせ**てから、松井さんは、

おもいきって、ハンドルをまわしました。(p. 152)

And then, Mr Matsui **rubbed** both his hands **together** two or three times and manipulated the wheel boldly.

(37) それから、三にんは、きゃくせきにのりこむと、ほくほくしたよ

うに、おたがい、からだを**おしあっ**たり、くっくっとわらったり

しています。(p. 155)

After that three people got into the passenger seat. They were very pleased to be in there and were **pushing** themselves **together** or giggling at each other.

5.7.9 Manner + V2 (change verb)

When **manner** is expressed by V1, V2 normally denotes **change of state**. Table 5.10 contains twenty verbs that occur in the story. あがる (上がる) *agaru* 'rise' is used most frequently. It describes an entity going in a higher direction. When change of state is expressed by V2, V1 represents how the change takes place. In (38), the taxi goes up by way of floating. In (39), Mr Matsui goes up the steps in the station by running. In (40), Mr Matsui gets in the car as if he jumped into it, that is, in a hurried manner. In (41), foxes come to a stop in an upright posture. たつ (立つ) *tatsu* 'stand' modifies V2 in that it implies that the foxes (who wear clothes and can stand like humans in the story) stop their actions while remaining standing.

(38) ブレーキを、力いっぱいふみました。車は、ゆらっと**うきあがっ**

てとまりました。(p. 22)

(Mr Matsui) pressed the brakes with all his power. The car **came up** and stopped.

(39) 千円さつをしっかりにぎったまま、松井さんは、駅の長い長いか

いだんを、**かけあがっ**ていきました。(p. 51)

Mr Matsui grasped the ¥1000 note and **went up** the very long steps in the station.

(40) 松井さんは、口をあけて見とれている女の子のよこから、足音を

しのばせてはなれました。車に、あわてて**とびのり**ました。

(p. 74)

Mr Matsui walked away on tiptoe from the side of a girl who was gaping. He hurriedly **jumped into** the car.

(41) そのとき、どこからか、かくせい機がビービーガーなるような、

高い音がしました。すると、その音がなにかの合図のように、

きつねたちは**たちどまり**ました。(p. 100)

At that moment, one could hear a high tone sound as if a loudspeaker beeped. At this moment, the foxes **stopped their movement** as if the sound meant some signal.

5.7.10 V1 (action verb) + manner

When V1 is the core element, V2 expresses how the event denoted by V1 is carried out. Most V1 words are action verbs – verbs that express action. Action verbs are differentiated clearly from change verbs (see section 5.7.9) in that they express processes that someone carries out relatively deliberately. Swimming, flying or running are processes that either humans or animals conduct deliberately. The story exhibits only two manner verbs as V2: まわす (回す) *mawasu* 'turn' (transitive) and まわる (回る) *mawaru* 'turn' (intransitive). Both express an action (denoted by V1) in which something goes or moves around. In (42) and (43), V1 and V2 are intransitive verbs (およぐ (泳ぐ) *oyogu* 'swim', とぶ (飛ぶ) *tobu* 'fly' and にげる (逃げる) *nigeru* 'flee away'). In (44), V1 and V2 are both transitive verbs (ふる (振る) *furu* 'swing' + まわす (回す) *mawasu* 'swing').

(42) 大きいの、小さいの、長いの、みじかいの、赤、青、黄、みどり

のさかなが、すこし水色にそまって、ついつい、すいすいと、

かさなるように**およぎまわっている**のです。(p. 24)

Fish, whether they are big, small, long, short, red, blue, yellow, or green, are coloured in a little marine blue and **swimming around** lightly and smoothly in layers.

(43) 昭和二十年の春から、"空襲"がはじまりました。七月の"大空

襲"のとき、三十機のB29が、町の空を**とびまわり**、しょうい

弾をつぎつぎにおとしました。あちらもこちらも火事になり、

町は、もうもう火の海でした。三さいだったふたりのむすこを、

わたしは、ひとりをせおい、ひとりはだいて.......ええ、

ふた子だったんですよ...**にげまわり**ました。(p. 46)

An air attack started in the twentieth year of the Showa Period. In the big July air attack, B29s were **flying around** in the sky of the town and bombed incendiaries one after another. There were fires everywhere and the town was entirely a sea of fire. Two sons being three, I carried one on my back and held another. Yes, they were twins. I was **running around** from one place to another.

(44) そしてぼうしをつまみあげたとたん、ふわっとなにかがとびだし

ました。

「あれっ！？」

モンシロチョウです。

あわててぼうしを**ふりまわし**ました 。(p. 31)

And as soon as (Mr Matsui) picked up the hat, something flew out.
'What was it!?'
It was a white cabbage butterfly.
He hurriedly **waved** it **around**.

5.7.11   Two similar events

A certain group of compound verbs coordinate two similar events. Similar events are those events with equal semantic status. In (45), 通る *tōru* 'pass' and すぎる (過ぎる) *sugiru* 'pass' encode almost the same meaning. In (46), おれる (折れる) *oreru* 'be broken' and まがる (曲がる) *magaru* 'be bent' are also semantically quite similar. The repetition of two similar words describes the situation more emphatically and effectively.

> (45)   小さなぼうしをつかんで、ためいきをついている松井さんのよこ
>
>   を、ふとったおまわりさんが、じろじろ見ながら通**りすぎ**ました 。
>
>   (p. 32)
>
>   Looking him up and down, a fat policeman **walked past** a place where Mr Matsui was holding a small hat and sighing.

> (46)   ピエロは、とがったはなに、赤いいろをつけ、目には大きなまつ
>
>   げをかき、**おれまが**ったぼうしをかぶり、だぶだぶのふくをきて
>
>   います。 (p. 154)
>
>   A pierrot has a red colour on a sharp nose, draws big eyelashes at the eyes, wears a **bent** cap, and puts on baggy clothes.

This type of compound does not occur frequently in the story. Tagashira and Hoff (1986: 7) provide three other examples: 泣き叫ぶ *naki-sakebu* 'cry and shout', 喜び勇む *yorokobi-isamu* 'rejoice and get excited', 飛び跳ねる *tobi-haneru* 'jump and leap'.

5.7.12   Fused compounds

The story contains 33 fused compounds. Fused compounds have a meaning not directly derived from the combined meanings of the component parts. Fused compounds can be sub-classified into two groups, 'weak fusion' and 'strong fusion'. Weak fusion refers to compounds whose meaning is related in some way to the meaning of one part. Strong fusion refers to compounds whose meaning has no bearing on the meaning of any part (see also Tagashira and Hoff 1986: 8–9). Strongly fused compounds therefore behave as if they were individual units with their own

131

meaning. For example, (47) contains だす 'take out, to put out' as V2 whose meaning is still related to the action of Mr Matsui who sticks out his face. In contrast, つく (突く) *tsuku* 'push strongly' does not contribute to the overall meaning of the compound. Example (48) contains both weak and strong compounds. ちかづく *chikazuku* 'to come closer to' is an example of weak fusion, since its first part, that is, ちか 'close' is meaningful for the compound, while its second part, 付く *tsuku* 'be stuck to' appears to be irrelevant. すれちがう *surechigau* 'to pass by someone' is an example of strong fusion since its meaning does not derive from the constituents of the compound (擦れる *sureru* 'to be rubbed' and 違う *chigau* 'to be different').

(47) 松井さんは顔を**つきだす**ようにしました。目を大きくして、ヘッド

ライトがてらしている道を、いっしょけんめいにみつめました。
(p. 21)
Mr Matsui **sticks out** his face. He opened his eyes and stared at the road that the headlight was lighting up.

(48) ハンドルをまわしながら、松井さんはおもいました。とおくに

オレンジ色のひかりがあらわれて、みるみるうちに**ちかづき**、

ビュン、と風のうなりをのこして、**すれちが**っていきます。

(p. 76)

An idea came to Mr Matsui's mind while turning the wheel. An orange light turned up in the distance and **came close** to him in an instant. It leaves a sound of wind and **passes by**.

Notes

1 McClure (2000: 81–104) has an extensive list of prefixes and suffices. Interested readers are advised to consult it.
2 McClure (2000: 65–76) demonstrates a list of compound verbs with representative examples. Interested readers are advised to consult it.
3 Mr Matsui is a taxi driver who owns a blue car, the same colour as the sky. In the story, he encounters many people as his customers. Each chapter of the book contains an episode.

6 Word meaning

When constructing sentences, the **meaning of words** plays an important role because this element controls, or determines, the acceptability of a sentence. Meaning is studied in the domain of **semantics**, and the sub-area of semantics that deals with word meaning is called **lexical semantics**. Consider the difference in meaning between words such as 熱い *atsui* and 暑い *atsui*. We can say スープが熱い 'The soup is hot' but we cannot say ×今年の夏は熱い *Kotoshi no natsu wa atsui* 'This summer is hot', both of which contain the adjective 熱い. The second sentence becomes grammatical when 熱い is replaced by 暑い, that is, 今年の夏は暑い *Kotoshi no natsu wa atsui* 'It's hot this summer'. 熱い and 暑い are pronounced the same way (i.e., [atsɯi]), but their meanings are not identical. We call this pair of words **homonyms**, since they share a common pronunciation but differ in meaning. Words are listed as entries in the **lexicon**, or mental dictionary, that a language user has at his or her disposal. These entries build a network because word meanings are not discrete entities but are instead related to each other. Take, for example, another pair, 暑い and 暖かい *atatakai* 'warm'. Again, the meanings of these adjectives are not the same but are still related, though their relationship is different from that which holds between 熱い and 暑い. Not only are they pronounced differently but, more significantly, the difference in meaning lies in the speaker's differing perception of 'high temperature'. As with 'hot' and 'warm' in English, 暑い indicates a temperature higher than that indicated by 暖かい. The important point is that their difference not only concerns the temperature, but 暑い also includes a sense of discomfort caused by a high temperature, while 暖かい expresses an agreeable feeling derived from a relatively high temperature. Thus, この部屋は暖かくて気持ちがいい *kono heya wa atatakakute kimochi ga ī* 'This room is warm and it makes me feel good' is a correct sentence, while この部屋は暑くて気持ちがいい 'This room is hot and it makes me feel good' is unacceptable under normal circumstances.

In what follows, we look more closely at the **lexical relations** (6.1) that hold between words, and the **meaning components** (6.2) within words.

6.1 Relations between words

6.1.1 Homonymy

Homonyms, or 同音異義語 *dōon-igigo*, refer to words that are pronounced the same way but differ in meaning, such as 暑い and 熱い above. The nature of homonyms is identified when we look at the linguistic environment or co-text (see JLU: Chapter 2, section 2.2) in which the words appear.

(1) 三郎が泣く。
    Saburō ga naku
    Saburo cries.
    鳥が鳴く。
    Tori ga naku
    Birds sing.

The difference between the homonyms 泣く and 鳴く in (1) depends on the semantics of the entity the verb is related to. If a human (三郎) appears as the subject, 泣く is chosen, while if a non-human such as a bird (鳥) is the subject, 鳴く is chosen. Both humans and birds make sounds, but they do so in different ways, and this difference is reflected in the choice of verb. Interestingly, homonyms are distinguished not only by their meaning but also by their syntactic or phonological properties.

(2) 大きな蛙
    ōkina kaeru
    a big frog
    旅行日程を変える。
    ryokō-nittei o kaeru
    to change one's travel plans

Example (2) contains 蛙 and 変える, which read as [kaeru], but the first is a noun meaning 'frog' and the second is a verb meaning 'to change'. To choose the right word, one must look at its syntactic properties. 蛙 is chosen because it is preceded by an adjective, while 変える is chosen because an object marker を takes a verb that follows it. The semantic environment is not the decisive factor in explaining the choice of homonymous words. For example, when 大きな *ōkina* changes its syntactic category into an adverb, such as 大きく *ōkiku* 'on a large scale', it can occur with 変える but not with 蛙. Thus, the distinction between 蛙 and 変える is made by reference to syntactic categories, in this case noun and verb.

(3) 橋
    箸
    端

The examples in (3) all read as [haʃi] and all are categorized as nouns. They can also take the same adjective. It is possible to have pairs such as 長い橋 *nagai hashi* 'long bridge' and 長い箸 *nagai hashi* 'long chopsticks', or 狭い橋 *semai hashi* 'narrow bridge' and 狭い端 *semai hashi* 'narrow corner'. These pairs can be neither semantically nor syntactically disambiguated. Instead the difference between them is determined phonologically or through the pitch accent (see Chapter 2, section 2.5). To reiterate, in standard Japanese, 橋 is pronounced with the Low–High–Low pitch accent, 箸 with High–Low and 端 with Low–High. Similar examples are 海 *umi* 'sea' and 膿 *umi* 'pus', the former with High–Low and the latter with Low–High–Low.

Activity 1

Japanese has many homonyms that share similar meanings. The following extracts are taken from newspaper articles in Asahi.com. Homonyms are marked by ☐ in the text. Fill in the blanks with an appropriate verb, and explain why you chose a particular word. The first four texts, 6.1, 6.2, 6.3 and 6.4, concern either 聞く *kiku* or 聴く *kiku*, both of which have the basic meaning of 'listening', while the next three texts, 6.5, 6.6 and 6.7, concern either 見る *miru*, 観る *miru* or 診る *miru*, all of which refer to the basic meaning of 'seeing'.

Text 6.1 [聞く・聴く]

> このケースのように退職を考える場合、辞めること、あるいは転職する
>
> ことのメリットとデメリット、会社に残ることのメリットとデメリット
>
> をすべて書き出してみよう。毎月の支出額の２４ヶ月分の手持ち資金が
>
> あると安心だ。その際には、家計を預かる妻の意見を ☐ ① ☐ ことも
>
> 大事だ。

© 2004 Asahi.com 10 April

Text 6.2 [聞く・聴く]

> 昼間に外で銃声を ☐ ② ☐ こともあったが、ほとんどは夜、事務所にい
>
> る時や寝ている時だった。

© 2004 Asahi.com 9 April

135

Text 6.3 (聞く・聴く)

それまでにない価値観を提示したバンドが次々現れました。ウォークマンで ③ ながら街を歩くと、見慣れた東京の街が一変して見えました。

© 2004 Asahi.com 15 March

Text 6.4 (聞く・聴く)

鶏卵は野外に、段ボール箱に詰めた状態で置かれていた。運送会社によると、浅田農産側が1日に運び出す予定だったが引き取られなかった。県はこうした経緯について詳しく ④ 方針だ。

© 2004 Asahi.com 9 April

Text 6.5 (見る・観る・診る)

ここニューヨークでは、NHKをメインとした日本語放送を高い視聴料を払って ⑤ ことができます。今はほとんど天気予報以外 ⑥ ことありません。集金人さんが来る度に最近では「天気予報だけ ⑥ ていますのでその分だけ支払います。料金はいくらですか」と言いますが、料金を提示されたことなくそのままになっています。

© 2004 Asahi.com 6 February

Text 6.6 (見る・観る・診る)

各地の田園風景などにはそう大きな変りはなかったし、戦災を免れ無傷

のままで残されている京都周辺のようなところもあったが、日本の

都市部の被った損害の莫大さが並大抵のものではないことは、車窓の向

こうに ⑦ 光景を通して十分に推察がついた。

© 2004 Asahi.com 10 March

Text 6.7 (見る・観る・診る)

当番日は一夜で平均２０人の患者を ⑧ 。

© 2004 Asahi.com 6 April

Commentary

Answers for Activity 1 are as follows:

① 聞く
② 聞く
③ 聴き
④ 聴く
⑤ 観る
⑥ 見る・見
⑦ 見える
⑧ 診る

聞く is a general word used frequently to express one's perception of sound through the ears. For instance, this word would be used when hearing something spontaneously (that is, without intention) such as the sound of gunfire, as shown in ②. 聞く can also be used when listening to something (that is, intentionally), as shown in ①. When the act of listening is associated with one's interest or eagerness, 聴く is used. As shown in ③, you 'listen to' the music because you are interested, or as shown in ④, you also 'listen to' someone's explanations because you are eager to inquire about specific information.

見る is a general word used when noticing or perceiving an entity with the eyes. When looking at the scenery through a window, one will use 見る, as in ⑦. By contrast, 観る is used when paying special attention to

137

an entity; as a result, one enjoys looking at it and appreciates its good qualities. As exemplified by ⑤, watching a TV programme requires 観る, while watching the weather report requires 見る, as in ⑥. As such, watching a Japanese TV programme brings pleasure, while a weather report normally does not. In fact, it is interesting to learn from the passage (Text 6.5) that the author has not been asked to pay his NHK bills since he watches only weather reports. 観る has a Sino-Japanese counterpart 観賞 *kanshō*, which emphasizes that someone looks at something (e.g., a movie, poem or fish) with enjoyment and appreciation, while 見る does not form such a compound (cf. 見物 *kenbutsu* 'sightseeing', which does not encode enjoyment or appreciation). 診る in ⑧ is differentiated semantically from 見る and 観る in that it is used in a medical domain such as the examination of patients. It also has a Sino-Japanese equivalent 診察 *shinsatsu* 'examination'.

Exercise 1

Some additional groups of homonyms are given below. Using the Internet, find passages in which they are used. Similar to Activity 1, identify how their meanings differ from each other.[1]

- 意志　意思　遺志
- 触る　障る
- 打つ　撃つ　討つ
- 送る　贈る
- 町　　街

6.1.2 Synonymy

Synonyms, or 類義語 *ruigigo*, refer to two words whose meaning is very similar but not exactly the same. In Japanese, synonyms are characterized in various ways. Some synonyms refer to different lexical items (4) (see Activity 2). The contrast shown in (5) refers to the distinction between different vocabulary strata (see Chapter 3). Synonyms are also found with respect to cultural factors (6) and social structures (7) (see JLU: Chapter 4, Tables 4.1, 4.4 and 4.8).[2]

(4) Lexical differences:
愛 *ai* 'love' － 愛情 *aijō* 'love'

(5) Differences between vocabulary types:
(漢語 *kango* versus 外来語 *gairaigo*)
座席 *zaseki* － シート *shīto* 'seat'
運転手 *untenshu* － ドライバー *doraibā* 'driver'
食堂 *shokudō* － レストラン *resutoran* 'restaurant'

季節 *kisetsu* －シーズン *sīzun* 'season'
機会 *kikai* －チャンス *chansu* 'chance'
昼食 *chūshoku* －ランチ *ranchi* 'lunch'
旅館 *ryokan* －ホテル *hoteru* 'hotel'
運動 *undō* －スポーツ *supōtsu* 'sports'
(和語 *wago* versus 外来語 *gairaigo*)
手紙 *tegami*－レター *retā* 'letter'
考え *kangae* －アイディア *aidia* 'idea'
(外来語 *gairaigo* versus 外来語)
カップ *kappu* －コップ *koppu*
(漢語 *kango* versus 和語 *wago*)
家屋 *kaoku* 'house, building' －家 *ie* 'house'
接触する *sesshokusuru* －触る *sawaru* 'come into contact with'
旅行する *ryokōsuru* －旅する *tabisuru* 'make a journey/trip'
許可する *kyokasuru* －許す *yurusu* 'permit'
祝福する *shukufukusuru* －祝う *iwau* 'celebrate'
読書する *dokushosuru* －読む *yomu* 'read'

(6) Differences reflecting cultural factors:
俺 *ore*－私 *watashi* 'I'
便所 *benjo* －お手洗い *otearai* トイレ 'toilet'
水 *mizu* －お冷 *ohiya* 'water'
うまい *umai* －おいしい *oishī* 'tasty'
食う *kū* －食べる *taberu* 'eat'
来る *kuru* －いらっしゃる *irassharu* 'come'

(7) Differences reflecting social structures:
父 *chichi* －お父さん *otōsan* 'father'
母 *haha* －お母さん *okāsan* 'mother'
姉 *ane* －お姉さん *onēsan* 'elder sister'

Activity 2

Fill in the blanks with either 家 *ie* or 家屋 *kaoku*. This activity will test your ability to infer the meaning of new words from a given context. After choosing the appropriate words, try to explain their different meanings.

Text 6.8

民家　全焼し１人死亡、２人けが　東京・八王子市

東京都八王子市諏訪町、自営業Ｘさん（５８）方から９日午後９時１０

分ごろ出火、木造モルタル２階建て住宅約１４０平方メートルが全焼し

た。Ｘさんの娘で、この　①　に住むＹさん（２４）と見られる焼死体

が、１階から見つかった。Ｘさんがのどをやけどし、救助しようとした

隣家に住む男性がガラスで脚を切るけがをした。

© 2004 Asahi.com 10 April

Text 6.9

ブッシュ大統領が現地視察へ　カリフォルニア州 山火事

米カリフォルニア州南部山火事はさらに広がり、３１日午後（日本時間

１日朝）までに焼失面積は約３０００平方キロに達し、焼けた　②

も計２８７４軒になった。ホワイトハウスは同日、ブッシュ大統領が４

日に被災地を視察すると発表した。３１日、同州南部では雲が広がり、

冷たく湿った風が太平洋側から吹き付けた。

© 2003 Asahi.com 1 November

140

Text 6.10

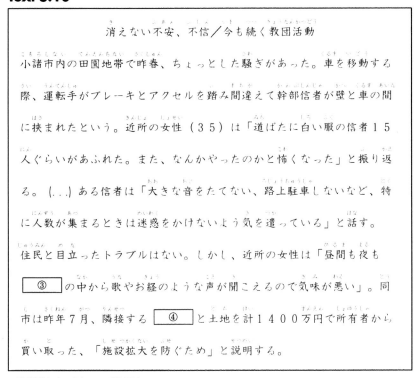

消えない不安、不信／今も続く教団活動

小諸市内の田園地帯で昨春、ちょっとした騒ぎがあった。車を移動する

際、運転手がブレーキとアクセルを踏み間違えて幹部信者が壁と車の間

に挟まれたという。近所の女性（３５）は「道ばたに白い服の信者１５

人ぐらいがあふれた。また、なんかやったのかと怖くなった」と振り返

る。［…］ある信者は「大きな音をたてない、路上駐車しないなど、特

に人数が集まるときは迷惑をかけないよう気を遣っている」と話す。

住民と目立ったトラブルはない。しかし、近所の女性は「昼間も夜も

③ の中から歌やお経のような声が聞こえるので気味が悪い」。同

市は昨年７月、隣接する ④ と土地を計１４００万円で所有者から

買い取った、「施設拡大を防ぐため」と説明する。

Commentary

The appropriate words for each blank are as follows:

① 家
② 家屋
③ 家
④ 家屋

Both 家 and 家屋 refer to the English word 'house'. When 家 is used, it implies that people live in the house – the place where people tend the hearth. When 家屋 is used, however, it refers to the house as a building and is not connected to a place for living. When you look at the linguistic environment in which each word appears, you readily find that the use of ① and ③ has something to do with our daily activities: ① appears with 住む *sumu* 'live' and ③ refers to the place where people sing and chant sutras. Look at the environments in which 家屋 is used. In both cases, 家屋

does not refer to the place used for living. What ② expresses is the number of houses destroyed by a mountain fire in the state of California. Similarly, ④ refers to houses sold to the municipal government.

Activity 3

Activity 3 is part of a passage from 天声人語 *tensē-jingo* 'Heaven's Voice, Men's Words'. What makes this column interesting is the alternative use of 'seat' as 座席 *zaseki* and シート *sīto*. Discuss why the writer alternates these two synonymous words. Note that ⑥ベンチシート *benchi-sīto* cannot be replaced by ベンチ座席, and that 7人掛けの座席 *shichiningake no zaseki* as a paraphrase of ① 7人掛けのシート sounds awkward.

Text 6.11

東京から大阪へ転勤した同僚が「通勤の電車内に違和感がある」という。結構こんでいるのに、7人掛けの①シートを6人、ときには5人で占領している光景によくぶつかる。「関西の人は体が触れ合うのを嫌うのかなあ」などと思っていたが、しばらくして、はたと気づいたそうだ。東京の路線は、くぼみがついている②座席が少なくない。7人なら7人が座るように仕向けられている。「秩序か自由か」は大げさにしても、③座席に関東と関西で違いがあるようなのだ。JR東日本は92年から、くぼみつきの④座席を導入し始めた。新車両には⑤シートの間に、お年寄りなどのための「握り棒」もつけたから、座る場所は、くぼみと棒で二重に決められれる。JR西日本の車両は今も平らなベンチ⑥シートだ。

© 2002 *Asahi Newspaper* 9 June

Translation:
A colleague who was transferred from Tokyo to Osaka told me that he feels uneasy in the commuter train. He often encounters a situation in which six people or even five people occupy the entire seven passenger seat (シート). He first wondered if people in Kansai do not like to come into contact with other people's bodies, but then suddenly realized that trains in Tokyo have seats (座席) with divisions and this urges passengers to sit correctly if the seat is for seven people. It may be an exaggeration if we ask whether this is an issue of 'an order or freedom', but there is definitely a difference between Kanto and Kansai in the manner of seating

(座席). JR (Japan Rail) in the East started to introduce seats (座席) with divisions in 1992. New trains even have a 'handle' for elderly people between the seats (シート), and this means that the place we sit on is decided doubly by the division and the handle. JR trains in the West still have a flat bench seat (シート).

Commentary

When foreign loanwords (most coming from English) enter the Japanese lexicon, they often become responsible for one or two senses of their original Japanese counterparts. From the context of the passage above, it can be inferred that 座席 is a more general word for 'seat' than シート to express furniture that is sat on. For example, ③座席 refers to the seat or the way passengers take a seat in a commuter train. Because of this general meaning of 座席, it cannot be replaced by シート. By contrast, ④座席 can be replaced by シート since it refers to a specific seat, that is, the long seat in a commuter train. The meaning of シート is more restricted because of its foreign origin, and it is certainly narrower than the meanings encoded in the English word *seat*. For example, 座席を指定する *zaseki o shitēsuru* is said to reserve a seat on a train or a plane. The seat in this usage can refer to any type of furniture that can be sat on. It is also appropriate to use this expression when booking a seat for a play, a show or a concert. It is impossible to use シート in this context. This means that シート has a more specific or narrower meaning and is used only to refer to a long seat in a train. シート is an example of semantic narrowing (see Chapter 3, section 3.3.2.4).

Imagine now a situation in which you find an independent chair (with four legs) vacant in a train. This would hardly be referred to as シート but instead as 座席 because it is a chair for one person. Thus, 座席が空いています *zaseki ga aiteimasu* 'There is a vacant seat' is grammatical when referring to this situation, while ×シートが空いています may not be acceptable. By contrast, シート evokes the idea that there are other seats attached to it. ベンチシート (literally 'bench seat') therefore cannot be paraphrased as ベンチ座席, the reason being that 'bench' implies a long seat that can be shared by several people. The fact that the expression 7人掛けの座席 *shichiningake no zaseki* (see ①) sounds awkward can also be explained along the same lines; 7人掛け 'for seven people' contradicts the implication of 座席.

6.1.3 Polysemy

Polysemy, or 多義語 *tagigo*, resembles homonyms in that it refers to words that share the same pronunciation. The difference is that polysemous words share the same orthography (熱い₁熱い₂) and have several meanings closely related to each other. Homonyms are normally written differently and expressed in different *kanji* (e.g., 蛙 versus 変える). The meaning of homonymous words is either unrelated (i.e., 'frog' versus 'to change') or shares a similar meaning (e.g., 見る 'see' versus 観る 'see'). Consider the two related meanings of 熱い once again. One meaning is a high temperature perceived by means of physical contact (熱いコーヒー — *atsui kōhī* 'hot coffee'), while the other refers to a degree of intensity that is emotionally determined (熱いカップル *atsui kappuru* 'a couple deeply in love'). The relationship between the two senses lies where they both refer to the higher point of a situation, that is, the temperature of coffee and the degree of love.

Activity 4

When you look at body part expressions such as 足 *ashi* 'leg', 顔 *kao* 'face', or 目 *me* 'eye' in a dictionary, you will find several meanings under each entry since these are polysemous words. This activity gives you passages containing 足. Identify its various meanings, and then explain why 足 is polysemous on the basis of the given examples.

After you have finished this task, compare the behaviour of 足 with that of 'leg' or 'foot' in your mother tongue. Are the explanations you arrived at in terms of Japanese 足 also valid for your mother tongue? Or would you suggest that polysemy is a language-specific phenomenon?

Text 6.12

福岡の１７歳の体型は足が長いことが特徴で、男女とも全国１５位だっ

たことが県の学校保健統計調査でわかった。身長に占める足の長さの

割合を０３年度までの５年間の平均値として算出した。

© 2004 Asahi.com 6 April

Text 6.13

夏隊が昭和基地を去る日が２日後に迫り、１３日は送別会が開かれました。食堂の**テーブルの足**を短くし、イスを片づけて、お座敷に模様替え。寄せ鍋をつつきながら、短い夏の思い出を語り合いました。

© 2004 Asahi.com 14 February

Text 6.14

日本の大手ビールメーカーが、中国市場の本格攻略にこぞって取り組み始めた。９０年代半ばから取り組んだ生産・販売の**足場**固めを終え、利幅の厚い日本と同等の高級ビールの売り込みに挑む。

© 2004 Asahi.com 12 January

Text 6.15

そういう中で訴訟を起こすわけなんですけど、本来、民事訴訟というのは、自分の損害を補てんするための訴訟でなきゃいけないんですけども、必ず**足が出る**んですね。

© 2004 Asahi.com 23 September

Text 6.16

春は卒業と入学の季節だ。Ｊリーグにも引退する選手がいる一方で、増鳩やカレンのようなプロの世界で戦おうという選手が現れる。そんな新人たちを新しいシーズンの見どころと考えながら、スタジアムへ**足を運ぶ**のはサッカー観戦の大きな楽しみだ。

© 2004 Asahi.com 1 April

Commentary

In Text 6.12, 足 *ashi* refers to those parts of our body on which we stand. This example exemplifies the basic sense of the word 'leg'. The other meanings, as Texts 6.13 to 6.16 show, arise by extending this basic meaning, that is, by using it figuratively (see JLU: Chapter 2, section 2.5).

In Text 6.13, 足 is used metaphorically for inanimate entities such as tables. The legs of a table are the parts of the furniture that rest on the floor and support the table's weight.

足場 *ashiba* 'foothold, footing' in Text 6.14 has a related meaning in that 足 is used to support the place (場) on which you can safely put your feet. When 足場 'scaffold' occurs with a verb such as 固める *katameru* 'to harden', it has the extended meaning of a strong or firm position from which further advance can be made. 足場固め *ashiba-gatame*, as used in this passage, refers to the establishment of a fertile ground for the production and sale of beer.

足が出る *ashi ga deru* in Text 6.15 is not used to support an entity; instead it refers to something that projects or sticks out beyond a surface or an edge. When someone's legs stick out from a *futon*, we can say 足が布団から出る *ashi ga futon kara deru* 'Legs stick out from the *futon*'. If used figuratively, 足が出る alludes to a situation where something goes beyond the limit, resulting in a deficit or loss of money. The issue in Text 6.15 is that a civil action should help a client compensate for his previous deficits, but instead it often ends with a new financial loss.

In Text 6.16, 足 in 足を運ぶ *ashi o hakobu* literally means the movement of one's legs; its metaphorical sense is that someone goes to, comes to, or visits some place. スタジアムへ足を運ぶ 'to carry one's legs to the sports stadium' in the passage is the same as スタジアムへ行く 'go to the sports stadium'.

Exercise 2

Try working on 顔 *kao* and 目 *me* by yourself. Consult a dictionary (e.g., 基礎日本語辞典 *Kiso Nihongo Jiten* 'A Dictionary of Basic Japanese' by Morita (1989)) and pick up some examples. Your task is to figure out why these words have several (related) meanings.

6.1.4 Antonymy

Antonyms, or 対義語 *taigigo*, refer to a pair of words whose meaning is opposite or near opposite. This opposite relationship can be identified in three ways. The first is the so-called **complementary pair**, that is, an antonymous pair A and B stands in relation such as 'B is not A'. One example is the relationship between 勝つ *katsu* 'win' versus 負ける *makeru* 'lose': if someone wins a match, it means that he or she did not lose the match. The positive of 'win' is related to the negative of 'lose'. A similar example might be 試験に受かる *shiken ni ukaru* 'to pass the exam' versus 試験に落ちる *shiken ni ochiru* 'to fail the exam', in the sense that someone not passing the exam means that he fails it.

The second type of antonym is a pair standing in a **gradable relationship** that holds between words such as 暑い *atsui* 'hot' versus 寒い *samui* 'cold'. That is, not being hot does not necessarily mean being cold, as the grammaticality of the sentence indicates: 暑くもないが、寒くもない 'It is not hot but it is not cold, either'. The fact that 暑い and 寒い do not stand in complementary opposition, as in 勝つ and 負ける, lies in the nature of adjectives in that their meanings are in essence gradable. As shown below, between 暑い and 寒い there are 暖かい 'warm' and 涼しい 'cool'. Because of the gradable nature of adjectives, we can thus say 暑くはないが、暖かい 'It's not hot but warm'.

(8) 暑い *atsui*, 暖かい *atatakai*, 涼しい *suzushii*, 寒い *samui*

The gradability of adjectives can be demonstrated by the ability to describe coldness in different ways, as shown in (9). Likewise, 'being hot' can further be refined, as shown in (10).

(9) 薄ら寒い *usurasamui* 'lightly cold', 肌寒い *hadazamui* 'chilly'

(10) 暑苦しい *atsugurushii* 'sultry, oppressively hot', むし暑い *mushiatsui* 'hot and stuffy, sticky'

The third type of antonym is a **paraphrasable pair**, as exemplified in the relationship between 前 *mae* 'front' and 後ろ *ushiro* 'back'. Like the pair 勝つ and 負ける, 'being in the front' can mean 'not being at the back'. However, these concepts do not imply positive or negative sides to the meaning. Instead they are used to 'paraphrase' the same situation. As shown in (11), a and b refer to the same scenario.

(11) a. よう子が三郎の**前**にいる。
       Yōko ga Saburō no mae ni iru
       Yoko is in front of Saburo.
     b. 三郎がよう子の**うしろ**にいる。
       Saburō ga Yōko no ushiro ni iru
       Saburo is behind Yoko.

前 and 後ろ count as alternative views of the same situation from two different perspectives; the spatial positions of よう子 and 三郎 remain the same in both expressions. This paraphrase-relation does not hold with other types of antonyms.

147

6.1.5 Hypernyms and hyponyms

Hypernyms, or 上位語 *jōigo*, refer to superordinate, or more general, words whose meaning stands at the top of a group of related words. For example, *flower* is a hypernym for *rose* or *tulip* because *rose* and *tulip* are two instances of *flower*, thus, being specific to *flower*. To put it differently, *rose* and *tulip* always 'include' their hypernym, *flower*, as their more general meaning. Words that rank lower in the hierarchy are called **hyponyms**, or 下位語 *kaigo*. We say that *rose* is a hyponym of *flower* and *tulip* is also a hyponym of *flower*, whereby *rose* and *tulip* have a horizontal sisterhood. This inclusion of *flower* is sustained regardless of how many subordinates the hypernym possesses. Consider that *rose* can also function as a hypernym for different sub-types of roses (e.g., 'Christmas rose', 'rose of Sharon'), and these hyponyms continue to include *flower* as a hypernym. In this manner, words are 'related' with respect to their superordinate and subordinate structures.

Our knowledge of this lexical relationship sometimes helps us understand the connection between two sentences. In the first sentence of (12), for example, 花 *hana* requires a demonstrative この *kono* to emphasize its anaphoric relation to the previous バラ *bara* (see JLU: Chapter 2, section 2.1.3, for the term 'anaphoric'). The speaker does not choose 花 arbitrarily but is also conscious of the lexical relationship between 花 and バラ. This lexical relation reinforces the connection between the two. As the ungrammaticality of (12b) indicates, when 花 is replaced by its hyponym チューリップ *chūrippu*, the anaphoric relationship is not realized despite the existence of the demonstrative この. Example (12c) exemplifies an alternative to (12a), which still maintains an anaphoric relationship, though it does not sound as elegant as (12a) because of the repetition of the same word バラ 'rose'. This type of sentence is often written by students of Japanese who lack sufficient knowledge of the relationship between hypernyms and hyponyms.

(12)　a. バラは美しい。この(×∅)花はみんなに愛されている。
　　　　Bara wa utsukushī. Kono hana wa minna ni aisarete iru
　　　　Roses are beautiful. This flower is loved by everyone.

　　　b. ×バラは美しい。このチューリップはみんなに愛されている。
　　　　Bara wa utsukushī. Kono chūrippu wa minna ni aisarete iru
　　　　Roses are beautiful. This tulip is loved by everyone.

　　　c. バラは美しい。このバラはみんなに愛されている。
　　　　Bara wa utsukushī. Kono bara wa minna ni aisarete iru
　　　　Roses are beautiful. This rose is loved by everyone.

Text 6.17 ハゴロモ

> 1　私のふるさとである**その町**は、川の隙間に存在するようなところだ
>
> 　った。夏はわりと涼しいが、冬はとても寒く、山のほうではたくさ
>
> 　ん雪が降る。どこを歩いていても川の音が、闇の中をついてくるよ
>
> 　うだった。(...) 町中に大小さまざまな橋があり、橋はある種のリズ
>
> 5　ムを作り、**その川ばかりの景色の中で** まるで句読点のように人々を
>
> 　ふと水辺に向かって立ち止まら;せていた。

© 2003 Yoshimoto, Banana / Hagoromo (p. 3), Shinchosha

Translation:

The town where I was born is located in a place like an opening in a river. It is relatively cool in summer, but it is very cold in winter. It snows a lot in the mountains. Wherever you walk, you may have the impression that the sound of the river is chasing you in the dark. (. . .)
There are many bridges of various sizes, and these bridges create a certain rhythm. **In this rivered scenery**, bridges suddenly get you to pause and look at the surface of the water – as if we were disrupted by punctuation marks.

This passage is the beginning of the novel ハゴロモ *Hagoromo*. The first-person narrator describes her birthplace, which is symbolized by the big river that runs through the town. Her memories are tied to this river. In this novel, there are two places (marked in bold) that have an anaphoric relationship to the previous part. A nominal expression that follows a demonstrative その *sono* serves as a hypernym that reinforces the ana-phoric relationship. The first instance is in line 1. The author says that 私のふるさと *watashi no furusato* 'my hometown' is presented as a specific example of 町 *machi* 'town', thereby the former (私のふるさと *watashi no furusato*) being a hyponym of the latter (その町 *sono machi*). The second and third sentences describe the town, underlining the importance of the river. In lines 4 and 5, the author refers to the bridges of various sizes and the rhythm they create, concluding that all her surveillance is subsumed under 景色 *keshiki* 'scenery, landscape'. Here we suggest that all her observations and emotional sensations are subordinates, or hyponyms, of the scenery, the hypernym. In this novel, the lexical strategy of inclusion contributes to the creation of an effective literary text that succeeds in meticulously expressing the narrator's sentiments.

6.1.6 Meronymy

There is another hierarchical relationship that holds between lexical words. **Meronymy** denotes the part–whole relationship. It is important to note that the relationship between 木 *ki* and 枝 *eda*, 幹 *miki*, 根 *ne* and 葉 *ha* is different from the inclusive relationship held between *flower* and *rose*. In other words, the more general word (e.g., 木 'tree') does not represent more specific words (e.g., 幹 'trunk' or 葉 'leaf'), but specific words are considered parts of a general word. As a rule of thumb, meronymy can be paraphrased as 'X has Y'; thus, we can say, 'trees have branches' or 'trees have roots', but it is impossible to say 'flowers have roses', showing that the part–whole relationship is distinct from the relation of inclusion. In (13) the words 幹, 葉, 根 and 枝 are all related to the tree by the part–whole relationship. In (14) the tree is perceived differently because there is no part–whole relationship between *tree* and *garden*, *house*, *swimming pool* and *car*.

(13) 巨大な**木**がある。**幹**は太くて、**葉**も厚い。**根**は長くのびてい

るし、**枝**も頑丈だ。

Kyodai na ki ga aru. Miki wa futokute, ha mo atsui. Ne wa nagaku nobite irushi, eda mo ganjō da

There is a huge tree. Its trunk is big, its leaves being thick. The roots stretch widely and the branches are stable, too.

(14) 巨大な**木**がある。庭は広くて、家も大きい。プールは二つ

あるし、車も外車だ。

Kyodai na ki ga aru. Niwa wa hirokute, ie mo ōkii. Pūru wa futatsu arushi, kuruma mo gaisha da

There is a huge tree. The garden is wide, the house being big. There are two swimming pools and the car is foreign-made.

Activity 5

When reading newspaper articles, we may start with a dictionary to look up unknown words or phrases. It is of course important to know the lexical meaning of the words. However, we can also approach the text in a different way. We can start by recognizing the lexical relations of the words on the basis of their use of が *ga* and は *wa*. You may have learned in the classroom that が is used when something is introduced for the first time, and は is used when it is repeated a second time (see JLU: Chapter 3, section 3. 5). When dealing with a text such as 6.18, the use of が and は does not always follow this general principle. At this point, the concept of meronymy comes into play, and you should be able to explain why 一台の車 *ichidai no kuruma* is marked by が, while ボンネット *bon-netto* and 窓に *madoni* contain は. ヘッドライト *heddoraito* is marked by も 'too' (it suffices to say that も resembles は in that both of them have a discursive function).

Text 6.18

JR横浜駅から数分のコインパーキング。昨年夏、**1台の車が**1ヵ月近く

止めっぱなしになっていた。**ボンネットは**へこみ、**ヘッドライトも**割れ

ている。**窓には**べたべたと張り紙。

© 2004 *Asahi Newspaper* 29 January

Translation:
There is coin-parking a few minutes from the JR-Yokohama Station. Last summer one car remained parked for nearly a month. The bonnet was dented, and the headlights were also broken. There were patches of paper on the window.

Now, look at Text 6.19 in which 屋台 *yatai* is marked by は, although it appears in the text for the first time. Do you think this example is explained by the same strategy at work in Text 6.18, or would you suggest another lexical relation at work?

Text 6.19

春風に誘われて、「とげぬき地蔵」として知られる東京・巣鴨の高岩寺

に出かけた。境内に小さな露店を出している耳かき職人(53)のエッセー

を日経新聞で読んだからだ。**屋台は**すぐみつかった。さっそく注文して

1本作ってもらうことにした。

© 2003 *Asahi Newspaper* 31 March

Translation:
Invited by the spring-like breeze, I went out to the Takaiwa temple, the temple known for its statue for splinter-removal in Sugamo, Tokyo, since I read an essay in Nikkei newspaper on a producer of ear-cleaning utensils (53) who keeps an open kiosk in the precinct. The stall was easily found. I immediately asked him to make one for me.

Commentary

The reason は is used for the nouns introduced for the first time in Text 6.18 is that they are meronymies to the car 一台の車 *ichidai no kuruma* mentioned in the second sentence. They refer to parts of the car. も *mo* in ヘッドライトも emphasizes the fact that not only the bonnet but also the headlights are damaged. も has the same discursive function as は *wa* in that both of them topicalize the noun to which they are attached because of their part–whole relation to the noun 'car', the difference being that the use of も makes it clear that the mention of headlights is in addition to information about the bonnet.

The use of は in Text 6.19 is influenced by the presence of 露天 *roten* 'open kiosk' in the second sentence because they are synonymous, referring to the same shop where a craftsman is selling utensils. There is, however, no meronymic relationship between 露天 and 屋台 *yatai* 'stall' since neither of these is part of the other.

6.2 Meaning components

In 6.1.1, 熱い *atsui* and 暑い *atsui* were categorized as homonyms. The question now being raised is how to explain why they are homonyms. The best way to tackle this question is to examine their linguistic or co-textual environments (see JLU: Chapter 2, section 2.2, for the notion 'co-text') and discover fine-grained meanings – what we call **meaning components**, or 意味要素 *imi-yōso*.

It is clear that both adjectives 熱い and 暑い are related to the central meaning that the temperature is high. The ungrammaticality of ×今年の夏は熱い shows that the use of these adjectives is sensitive to the nature of the entity they qualify; for example, the difference between 'soup' and 'summer'. When we say that the soup is hot, it implies that we have already tasted it or touched the plate that contains it. That is, 熱い refers to the hot temperature that we can judge based on our inspection of tangible evidence. By contrast, 暑い refers to the high temperature we experience with regard to the weather or the environment (e.g., in a room). Hence, the sentence 暑い日に、熱い砂の上を歩いた 'I walked on the *hot* sand on a *hot* day' is grammatical, because the hot temperature refers to two different scenarios (one that the day is hot, and the other that the sand is hot).

What differentiates the behaviour of the expressions mentioned above are the meaning components that elaborate the meaning of the hot temperature. Table 6.1 summarizes the meaning components of three adjectives. Because they do not contain the exact same meaning components, they do not behave in the same manner.

Table 6.1 *Meaning components with high temperature*

Adjectives	Meaning	Meaning Components		
	Temperature	Weather	Contact	Comfort
暑い 'hot'	high	○	×	×
熱い 'hot'	high	×	○	×
暖かい 'warm'	high	○	×	○

Activity 6

Pick out the meaning components of the synonymous adjectives 寒い *samui*, 冷たい *tsumetai* and 涼しい *suzushī* based on the following passages from Asahi.com.

Text 6.20

①オーロラを撮るときは零下１５度くらいでとても**寒い**ので、カメラに羽毛カバーをし、バッテリーも服の中に入れ、おなかで暖めながら撮ります。(28 March 2004)

When I take a picture of an aurora, I cover the camera with a feather, put the battery into my jacket and warm it up with my stomach, since the temperature goes down to minus 15 centigrade and it is freezing.

②お金はいらない。その代わり、**冷たい**ビールを１杯、ごちそうしてください。(1 April 2003)

I wouldn't need money. Instead I would like to be treated to a glass of cold beer.

③太陽が傾き始めると、海からの**冷たい**風をほほに感じます。

(26 March 2004)

When the sun begins to go down, I feel the cold wind from the sea on my cheek.

④晴れた日は山頂から淡路島を見晴らせる。平野部より気温は５度ほど**涼しい**。(14 October 2003)

On a sunny day, we can look over Awaji Island from the summit of the mountain. It is cooler here than in the plain area by about five centigrade.

⑤**涼しい**夏のせいかもうイチョウの落ち葉が散っていた。
(29 August 2003)

Perhaps because of the cool summer, ginkgo leaves have already fallen.

Commentary

Table 6.2 *Meaning components with low temperature*

Adjectives		Meaning Components		
	Temperature	Weather	Contact	Comfort
寒い	low	○	×	×
冷たい	low	○	○	×
涼しい	low	○	×	○

Table 6.3 *Replaceability and meaning components*

Adjectives	No./ Referent in text				
	① 天気 *tenki*	② ビール	③ 風 *kaze*	④ 気温 *kion*	⑤ 夏 *natsu*
寒い	◎ w	×	○	×	□
冷たい	×	◎ con	◎ w/con	×	×
涼しい	×	×	○	◎ w/com	◎ w

Table 6.2 shows that all the adjectives refer to the low temperature, but similar to the contrast between 熱い 'hot', 暑い 'hot' and 暖かい 'warm' (Table 6.1), Weather, Contact and Comfort are important meaning components for the distinction between the adjectives. Table 6.3 summarizes the use and availability of adjectives according to the referent they modify. Adjectives are marked by ◎ when they are actually used in Text 6.20, while ○ refers to an alternative adjective that can replace the original one. For example, 寒い and 涼しい can modify 風 in the context of ③, as shown in (15).

(15) 太陽が傾き始めると、海からの**寒い・涼しい**風をほほに感じます。

*Taiyō ga katamuki-hajimeru to umi kara no **samui/suzushī** kaze o hoho ni kanjimasu*

While × means that the designated adjective cannot replace the original one, □ indicates the awkwardness of replacement by another adjective unless the linguistic setting is modified. For example, 寒い will be accepted in ⑤ if the sentence is reformulated the following way:

(16) **寒い**夏のせいかセーターが必要だ。

***Samui** natsu no sēka sētā ga hitsuyō da*

We need a sweater because of the cold summer.

Look first at Weather. All three adjectives are compatible with expressions that include weather. As indicated in Table 6.3, all examples except ② are in use because of their weather component.

Next consider Contact. This meaning component is found with examples in ② and ③, which contain 冷たい *tsumetai*. The coldness of beer can be recognized by tangible evidence such as touching, drinking or observing the beer bottle in a refrigerator. The fact that ③ can also accept 寒い *samui* (e.g., 海からの寒い風 'The cold wind from the sea') means that 風 *kaze* 'wind' can have two types of coldness. First, the coldness of the wind can be detected when the person is exposed to it; that is, he or she comes into contact with it (冷たい風). Second, the coldness of the wind can be detected by the low temperature in the atmosphere; that is, the person perceives the coldness of the wind without coming into contact with it (寒い風). The first option is more natural because of the predicate (ほほに感じます) indicating the contact. The unacceptability ×寒いビールを一杯 'a glass of cold beer' shows that the coldness of the beer can only be detected through contact.

Finally, consider Comfort. This meaning component can be used to explain the behaviour of 涼しい *suzushī*. The coldness expressed by 冷たい in ③ does not refer to comfort, while the coolness expressed by 涼しい in ④ may. When 冷たい in ③ is replaced by 涼しい, the sentence will then express a sense of comfort in the wind (e.g., you may enjoy being exposed to it). Comfort comes into play when the temperature stays low in moderation, and this coolness is expressed by 涼しい and in certain contexts by 冷たい. The reason ① does not accept 涼しい is that the temperature is indeed very low (minus 15°C) and it is hardly possible to feel comfort. But the use of 涼しい is not always linked to comfort; it can simply express the relatively low temperature, as shown in ⑤.

Our exposition of six adjectives in this section proposes that these adjectives can form three antonymous pairs (i.e., 暑い versus 寒い; 熱い versus 冷たい; 暖かい versus 涼しい), sharing similar meaning components. It has also been shown that meaning components are identified when examining the given linguistic environment in which they are used. Because adjectives are gradable elements, these pairings are not complementary antonyms. To illustrate, 風 'wind' takes 暖かい 'warm' (暖かい風) but not 暑い 'hot' (×暑い風) or 熱い 'hot' (×熱い風). But this asymmetry does not apply to their counterparts of 涼しい 'cool' (涼しい風), 冷たい 'cold' (冷たい風) and 寒い 'cold' (寒い風) in that 風 accepts all three adjectives.[3]

It can be concluded that what underlines the lexical relations of words demonstrated in section 6.1 might well be the existence of meaning components. It goes without saying that more meaning components could be suggested to explain more cases and more words. Nevertheless, this section has demonstrated that the nature of lexical relations such as homonyms, synonyms and antonyms can be clarified in the light of this analysis.

Exercise 3

Tackle antonyms and try to discover their meaning components or behaviours. Does the same method work with antonyms? Suggested antonyms you may start with are as follows:

死ぬ *sinu* versus 生きる *ikiru*
借りる *kariru* versus 貸す *kasu*

Notes

1   Detailed explanations of the synonymous pairs are illustrated in Yamaguchi (2005).
2   Detailed explanations of the word pairs presented here are found in Yamaguchi (2005).
3   It is important to note that 風 can take 熱い only when it forms a Sino-Japanese word, that is, 熱風 *neppū* 'hot wind'.

7 Sentence structure

This chapter examines how Japanese sentences are constructed to become meaningful units. Six topics are selected for this purpose: (i) the distinction between は and が as the markers of subject and topic, (ii) particular types of verbs, (iii) expressions of states and actions with て, (iv) case particles, (v) basic sentence patterns versus patterns of spoken language, and (vi) noun modifications. These selected topics illustrate structural and semantic properties at the level of the sentence. Pragmatic (i.e., use of language) properties relevant to Japanese sentences are dealt with in JLU, Chapters 1 and 2. Properties specific to the level above the sentence are dealt with in JLU, Chapters 3 and 4.

7.1 Subject and predicate

As discussed previously, language does not exist in a vacuum but functions on the basis of 'units'. With sound structure (Chapter 2), language takes as its basic unit phonemes, which distinguish the meanings of words. With word structure (Chapter 5), language takes as its basic unit morphemes, which are considered meaningful parts of a word. When native speakers of Japanese write or speak, a sentence serves as a unit of grammar in such a way that it conveys meaningful, that is, self-contained, information. When an expression such as 犬が *inu ga* 'dog-ga' stands alone outside of context and is uttered at the beginning of a conversation, it is hard for the Japanese hearer to understand what it means, and he or she would rather expect something else to follow it. 犬が is unintelligible because it lacks the information that represents what is said of 犬. It becomes intelligible, however, when we say 犬がほえた *inu ga hoeta* 'The dog barked', since the second part of the sentence conveys the information about the activity of the dog. This example shows that the basic sentence in Japanese, as in many other languages, requires a **subject** (主語 *shugo*) and **predicate** (述語 *jutsugo*). The subject is the first part of a sentence that refers to someone or something, of which something is said or predicated, and it is normally marked by が (note that not all nouns marked by が are subjects (see section 7.6)). The predicate is the second part of a sentence that says something about the subject. Thus, the sentence 犬がほえた consists of a subject (犬が) and a predicate (ほえた); the latter describes what the dog did. The presence of the two parts makes the sentence grammatically intelligible and self-contained, because they provide the basic information.

A short note is in order for the label 'subject'. For some scholars, the use of this label might be controversial because, unlike Western languages, Japanese does not exhibit the subject–verb agreement. However, the 'first noun phrase' in a sentence is an important indicator for honorification (i.e., respect honorifics in JLU: Chapter 4, section 4.4), since this grammatical process is dependent on the presence of this noun phrase. 'Subject' is therefore used here to signal the presence of this first noun phrase in a sentence (see also Iwasaki 2002: 101–102).

The subject and predicate structure also holds for adjectives. In Example (1), サクラ is the subject and 満開だ and 美しい are predicates. Both predicates tell us about the state of cherry blossoms. Example (1) differs from the example above (犬がほえた 'The dog barked'), since the subject is not the entity that acts or moves.

(1)　a.　サクラ**が**満開だ。
　　　　 Sakura ga mankai da
　　　　 Cherry blossoms are at their best.
　　 b.　サクラ**が**美しい。
　　　　 Sakura ga utsukushii
　　　　 Cherry blossoms are beautiful.

7.2　Topic and comment

Although Japanese has the structure of subject and predicate, it is important to remember that it also has what is called the **topic** (主題 *shudai*) and **comment** (叙述 *jojutsu*) structure. The difference between the subject and predicate structure (SP henceforth) and the topic and comment structure (TC henceforth) is that in the latter, the speaker takes an element from the sentence, categorizes it as a topic, and comments on it in the rest of the sentence. The topic is marked by the particle は *wa*. Compare the two sentences in (2), which categorize a phrase 決勝戦 *kesshōsen* 'final game' as the subject (marked by が *ga*) and the topic (marked by は). Both describe the same proposition (i.e., state of affairs) such that the final game will be held on the 21st. While in (2a) the fact is described, in (2b) 決勝戦 is taken as the topic on which the speaker comments in the rest of the sentence. A significant difference between TC and SP is that TC views a fact through the speaker's eyes. We can paraphrase topic X as 'Speaking of X' or 'Talking about X', emphasizing that X attains special attention in a given discourse. Compare the English glosses for (2a) and (2b). The presence of TC becomes clearer when we observe (3a), where the topic is the World Cup, which cannot appear as a subject marked by が (3b). What (2) and (3) show is that when the referent of the topic is not the same as that of the subject, as in (3), there is a semantic cue as to why one element becomes a topic and the other is a subject; in (3a), we find the part–whole relationship between ワールドカップ *wārudo-kappu* 'World Cup' and 決勝戦 'final game' (see Chapter 6, section 6.1.6); the final game is one event (part) of the World Cup (= whole). This explains why (3b) is unacceptable. In (4) there are further examples: the Merlion and the Twin Towers are parts of Singapore and Kuala Lumpur, being eligible to co-occur with their topic.

(2) a. 決勝戦**が**２１日に行われる。
　　　 Kesshōsen ga nijūichi-nichi ni okonawareru
　　　 The final game will be held on the 21st.
　　 b. 決勝戦**は**２１日に行われる。
　　　 Kesshōsen wa nijūichi-nichi ni okonawareru
　　　 Speaking of the final game, it will be held on the 21st.

(3) a. ワールドカップ**は**決勝戦**が**２１日に行われる。
　　　 Wārudo-kappu wa kesshōsen ga nijūichi-nichi ni okonawareru
　　　 Speaking of the World Cup, the final game will be held on the 21st.
　　 b. ×ワールドカップ**が**決勝戦**が**２１日に行われる。

(4) a. シンガポール**は**マーライオン**が**観光名所だ。
　　　 Singapōru wa māraion ga kankō-meisho da
　　　 Speaking of Singapore, the Merlion is a tourist attraction.
　　 b. クアラルンプール**は**ツインタワー**が**観光名所だ。
　　　 Kuara-runpūru wa tsuin-tawā ga kankō-meisho da
　　　 Speaking of Kuala Lumpur, the Twin Towers are a tourist attraction.

We can also alter (1b) to TC by topicalizing サクラ.

(5) サクラ**は**美しい。
　　 Sakura wa utsukushii
　　 Speaking of cherry blossoms, they are beautiful.

We can add 八重桜 *yaezakura* into the comment part to elaborate on what type of cherry blossom is being talked about. The relation between cherry blossoms and 八重桜 is not a part–whole relation, but 八重桜 is one type of cherry blossom and is seen to be subordinate to it. We have here another semantic relationship between topic and subject (see Chapter 6, section 6.1.5).

(6) サクラ**は**八重桜**が**美しい。
　　 Sakura wa yaezakura ga utsukushī
　　 Speaking of cherry blossoms, yaezakura (= double cherry blossoms) are beautiful.

The locational phrase can also be topicalized, as shown in (7b), whereby the preposition で is retained. Let us expand (2a) as in (7b). Example (7a) is SP with the addition of the location as factual information.

(7) a. 静岡スタジアム**で**決勝戦が２１日に行われる。
    *Shizuoka-sutajiamu **de** kesshōsen ga 21-nichi ni okonawareru*
    The final game will be held on the 21st in the Shizuoka Stadium.

   b. 静岡スタジアム**では**決勝戦が２１日に行われる。
    *Shizuoka-sutajiamu **dewa** kesshōsen ga 21-nichi ni okonawareru*
    Speaking of the Shizuoka Stadium, the final game of the 21st will be held there.

It is important to note that the overall use of the particle は as topic is related to the structure of the discourse (see JLU: Chapter 3). The reason why the speaker/writer chooses は as the topic is motivated ultimately by the organization of the discourse, since sentences are not isolated entities but become more meaningful when they are interpreted inter-sententially. For the sake of clarity, consider the beginning of a newspaper article (*Mainichi* 22 June 2002) in Text 7.1. The choice of は rather than が in two places (in bold) is motivated by the 'theme' of the article the writer has in mind (see JLU: Chapter 3, section 3.5.4). The **theme** is understood as the main idea on which the article elaborates. In this article, the theme should be the progress of the games in the World Cup. It is possible to remove は from 静岡スタジアムでは, as shown in (8), but the sentence would then describe the fact only, and the link between this sentence and the theme would not be emphasized. By using は, the writer underlines that the events reported are chained to one another, serving as evidence that は functions as a discourse marker. This line of explanation also illustrates the difference between (7a) and (7b) above.

Text 7.1

独、ブラジル４強

サッカーのワールドカップ**は**２１日、日本と韓国で準々決勝試合が行われ、ブラジルがイングランドを降し、ドイツも米国を破って、ベスト４に進出した。静岡スタジアム**では**、ブラジルとイングランドの注目の一戦が行われた。

© 2002 *Mainichi Newspaper* 22 June

Translation:
Germany – Brazil Quarterfinals
In the World Cup (WA) on the 21st, two quarter-final games were played in Japan and Korea. Brazil and Germany entered the best four by defeating England and America, respectively. In the Shizuoka Stadium (WA), the game between Brazil and England, which attracted much public attention, took place.

160

(8) 静岡スタジアムで∅、ブラジルとイングランドの注目の一戦が
行われた。

*Shizuoka stajiamu de burajiru to ingurando no chūmoku no issen
ga okonawareta*

The awaited match between Brazil and England was held in the
Shizuoka Stadium.

You may have been taught the sentence 私はXです *watashi wa X desu* to
introduce yourself. 私 is marked by は but not by が, because you are now
talking about yourself, which is regarded as the theme of your self-
introduction. Because 私 is an important element, it has the status of
topic. By attaching は to 私, you are stressing your own relevance in the
discourse (the self-introduction) and the link between you and what you
are going to tell your audience.

7.2.1 Topics other than は

It is important to note that the topic is not always marked by は. There
are other expressions that can replace は without losing their status as a
topic. When they appear in a sentence, they express an additional speaker
meaning apart from being a topic. For example, when (9) contains は
instead of こそ *koso*, it describes Professor Yoshio, who is a great scholar,
but when こそ is used, it connotes that there may be no one better than
Professor Yoshio, who is regarded as a great scholar. By using こそ, the
speaker attaches exclusiveness of the topic. Likewise, (10) not only says
that higher education is the place where one builds one's personality, but it
also defines the nature of higher education. The use of these short words
enables the speaker to integrate various speech acts (see JLU: Chapter 1,
for the term 'speech act') into the topic.[1] All the examples from (9) to (16)
can be replaced with は.

(9) 吉野先生こそ、立派な学者だ。
*Yoshino-sensē **koso**, rippana gakusha da*
It is Professor Yoshino, who is a great scholar.

(10) 高等教育とは、人格を形成する場である。
*Kōtō-kyōiku **towa**, jinkaku o kēsē suru ba de aru*
Higher education is the place where we build our character.

(11) 仙台といえば、かまぼこがうまい。
*Sendai **toieba**, kamaboko ga umai*
Talking about Sendai, kamaboko (boiled fish paste) is tasty.
(The speaker characterizes the topic.)

(12) うちの主人たら、高い指輪を買ってくれたんですよ。
*Uchi no shujin **tara**, takai yubiwa o katte kuretandesu yo*
My husband has bought me an expensive ring.

161

(The speaker attaches her special emotion (e.g., intimacy) to the topic.)

(13) ボールペン**なら**、ここにありますよ。
*Bōrupen **nara**, koko ni arimasu yo*
If you mean this ballpoint pen, it is right here.
(The speaker spotlights the topic.)

(14) 私**も**参加します。
*Watashi **mo** sanka shimasu*
I will join it, too.
(The speaker denotes the presence of someone else apart from the topic.)

(15) ラクサ**って**何ですか。
*Rakusa **tte** nandesu ka*
What is laksa?
(The speaker is uncertain of the nature of the topic.)

(16) 幽霊**なんて**いないさ。
*Yūrē **nante** inaisa*
There are no such things as ghosts.
(The speaker harbours doubt about the existence of the topic.)

7.3 Types of verbs

The main part of the predicate is often the verb. As in the examples above, the verb ほえる *hoeru* requires one obligatory element that is doing the barking. Verbs such as ほえる, which require only a subject to make a grammatical sentence, are called **intransitive verbs** (自動詞 *jidōshi*). Some verbs need to have one or two obligatory objects to make the sentence grammatical. Verbs that take a direct object are called **transitive verbs** (他動詞 *tadōshi*), while verbs taking two objects, indirect and direct, are called **ditransitive verbs** (二項動詞 *nikōdōshi*). The difference between indirect and direct object is that the former refers to the person (= recipient) who receives the transferred object, while the latter refers to the object that moves from one person (= giver) to the other person (= receiver). In (19) Midori (= recipient) is the indirect object and 'flowers' is the direct object. 送る *okuru* 'send' is another ditransitive verb that requires two objects (e.g., XがYに花を送った *X ga Y ni hana o okutta* 'X sent flowers to Y'). The transferred object is not always a concrete tangible object; instead it can be an abstract concept. With the verb 教える *oshieru* 'teach', what is transferred between the giver (e.g., teacher) and recipient (e.g., student) is knowledge (e.g., XがYに日本語を教える *X ga Y ni nihongo o oshieru* 'X teaches Japanese to Y').

162

(17)   Intransitive
       a. 犬がほえた 。
          Inu ga hoeta
          A dog barked.
       b. かびんが割れた。
          Kabin ga wareta
          The vase broke.

(18)   Transitive
       山田さんがお茶を飲んだ。
       Yamada-san ga ocha o nonda
       Mr Yamada drank a tea.

(19)   Ditransitive
       山田さんがみどりさんに 花をあげた 。
       Yamada-san ga midori-san ni hana o ageta
       Mr Yamada gave flowers to Midori.

The following sections will look more closely at two subtypes of intransitive verb (change of state verbs (7.3.1) and passive verbs (7.3.2 to 7.3.4)) and one subtype of ditransitive verb (donative verbs (7.3.5)). These verbs deserve special attention.

7.3.1   Change of state verbs

Ikegami (1978) and his followers in Japanese linguistics (e.g., Kageyama 1990) have stated that Japanese is a 'become-language', while a language such as English is a 'do-language'. This suggests that Japanese pays special attention to **change-of-state** (become) verbs, one sub-category of intransitive verbs. One good example is an intransitive verb 建つ *tatsu* 'to be built', as shown in (20).

(20)   空き地にアパートが建った。
       Akichi ni apāto ga tatta
       An apartment was built in the vacant plot.

Example (20) will be uttered when the speaker refers to an apartment that has recently been built in a place where no house existed before. This example shows that Japanese speakers perceive the situation in such a way that the absence of an apartment changes into the presence of an apartment. In Japanese linguistics literature, 'change of state', as used here, corresponds to the term 自発 *jihatsu*, which emphasizes, as its *kanji* implies, 'spontaneity'. In other words, the change of state expressed in (20) is perceived to have taken place spontaneously, whereby the fact that there were carpenters who built the apartment is paid no attention. Apart from 建つ *tatsu*, there are representative change-of-state verbs such as 見つかる *mitsukaru* 'to be found', 焼ける *yakeru* 'to be baked' or 出る *deru* 'to come out, to come up'. The difficulty with the use of this type of intransitive

163

verb is that no exact equivalent may exist in other languages. English, for example, uses a passive construction to express the same situation (Miura 2002: 108–9), as the English translation for (20) indicates.

Text 7.2 is an excerpt from ドラえもん *Doraemon*. のび太 *Nobita*, a protagonist, left his house because he could not stand being scolded by his parents. Since he does not wish to be easily discovered, he tries to find an uninhabited island. Although he knows the difficulty of locating such an island, he encounters one unexpectedly. At this moment he says かんたんにみつかった *Kantan-ni mitsukatta* 'I've found the island easily'; thus, みつかった here emphasizes the change from not finding an island to finding one.

Text 7.2 みつかった

© Fujiko Production / *Doraemon: Nobita-Grafity* (p. 112), Shogakukan

Let us look at a change-of-state verb 出る in a newspaper. Part of a daily column, 天声人語 *tensē-jingo* 'Heaven's Voice, Men's Words', describes Mr X, who runs a small Chinese restaurant where Chinese noodles are offered for only ￥ 100. Because of such a surprisingly cheap price, '￥ 100 Ramen' becomes a daily topic among people in the area. The passage goes as follows.

Text 7.3

鉄工所や銀行の朝礼でXさんの話が**出た**。銀行の課長は商売道を学びたい

といって、店を訪ねて**きた**。地下鉄職員、酒屋の店員たちは、頻繁に

「飯店」への道順をたずねられるものだから、教えた道順が間違っていて

はいけないと、店の所在を確かめにきた。

© 1985 *Asahi Newspaper* 12 December

The verb 出た *deta* is an intransitive verb that emphasizes the change of state: X's story 'became' the topic of the morning meeting in workplaces, which it had not been before. What is noteworthy is the presence of きた *kita* attached to 訪ねて. This verb is the same as an intransitive motion verb 来た *kita* 'came', but is used here as an auxiliary verb following the particle て. By adding きた *kita*, the journalist succeeds in embedding the change of state (i.e. a new development in a situation) expressed in the passage (see also Kaiser et al. 2001: 505). The English translation does not have equivalent forms for this shade of meaning, as exemplified in Text 7.4 below (from Asahi Editorial Board 天声人語 *tensē-jingo* 1985; 冬 *fuyu* 1986: 122–123). The usage of V + てきた *tekita* will be dealt with in more detail in section 7.4.2.5.

Text 7.4

> Tanaka's story **was taken up** in the morning meeting of a steelworks and a bank. A bank section chief **visited** the restaurant, saying he wanted to learn how to do business. Because subway station personnel and liquor store clerks are frequently asked the way to the restaurant, they checked on the exact location of the restaurant since it would be wrong for them to give inaccurate directions.

Exercise

Think about how the two verbs in Text 7.3 are expressed in your mother tongue. Does your mother tongue express the meaning of change of state explicitly just like Japanese, or does it behave more like English?

7.3.2 Passive verbs

In using change of state, the speaker places no importance on the agent (who is responsible for the conduct of the action). Instead an alternative means is used to defocus the agent in Japanese. When the speaker admits the existence of the agent but judges the mention of that person as irrelevant, **passive verbs** are used. The following two examples illustrate the difference between change-of-state and passive verbs. The change of state (21a) does not accept the agent who has built the apartment, while the passive (21b) does. The point is that although the agent can be expressed in the passive, the speaker prefers not to express it overtly. This type of passive is called **direct passive** as opposed to indirect passive (see section 7.3.3). Direct passives without an overt agent are also called **agentless passives**.

(21) a. 空き地にアパートが (×大工によって) 建った。
     Akichi ni apāto ga (daiku niyotte) tatta
     The apartment was built in a vacant plot (by the carpenters).
   b. 空き地にアパートが (大工によって) 建てられた。
     Akichi ni apāto ga (daiku niyotte) taterareta
     The apartment was built (by the carpenters).

Text 7.5 demonstrates two cases in which passives appear with ている *teiru* (see section 7.4.2.1 for a more detailed discussion of ている). When passive verbs appear with ている, they normally do not express the agent. In the first passive ①, the writer does not care who sells vodka in airports, and in the second ② the writer does not care who has printed the figures on the bottle. These passives differ **aspectually**: the first expresses the progressive aspect, that is, the selling situation is still continuous at the time the article is written, and the second expresses the resultative aspect, that is, two figures appearing on the bottle (one is Kalashnikov in a military uniform and the other is the gun named Automatic Kalashnikov) are the result of a past act of printing.

Text 7.5

空港の売店でもっとも①売れている商品は「カラシニコフ」という銘柄

のウォッカだ。中身は普通なのだが、ラベルに軍服姿 のカラシニコフと

AK銃が印刷②されている。

© 2004 *Asahi Newspaper* 5 February

7.3.3 Indirect passive

The function of passive verbs is not only to make the agent weak or non-existent but also to express adverse or unfavourable situations from which a person suffers. This affected person is expressed by a topic marker は *wa* (see section 7.2), and the passive is called **indirect** as opposed to direct passive. The reason is that this affected person only 'indirectly participates' in the denoted event, in the sense that he or she is influenced by the ensuing result of the event. Note that the affected person is not always verbalized in authentic texts as it is inferable from the context. Because adversity is not a grammatical but a psychological property of language, the passive verb with this usage is formed by transitive as well as intransitive verbs.

Texts 7.6 and 7.7 demonstrate cases for direct and indirect passives respectively. ころされた? *korosareta* 'Was he killed?' in Text 7.6 is an agentless direct passive, because のび郎 *Nobirō* (のび太's *Nobita*'s uncle) does not know who killed the elephant (his name is ハナ夫 *Hanao*). In Text 7.7, のび太 is reading his son's diary in a future setting. His son (のび介 *Nobisuke*) has written that his father (i.e., のび太 himself) does not buy him a toy set despite his strong wish to have it. With this indirect passive, のび介's unfavourable, dissatisfied feeling is conveyed. It is important to note that のび郎 in Text 7.6 is in fact badly influenced by はな夫's death in the story; he went home crying and cried out the whole night. The question is why ころされた？ is considered direct passive but not indirect. In Text 7.6, it is not perceived linguistically as adversative despite this storyline. The answer seems to be that adversity is evoked when the person who is influenced by the event possesses the thing that directly receives the unfavourable action. The acceptability of (23) (corresponding to Text 7.7) arises from the fact that the request, which is rejected by the father, belongs to the speaker (ぼく *boku*), while はな夫 does not belong to the speaker, and thus the unacceptability of (22) (corresponding to Text 7.6) (see also Iwasaki 2002: 134).

(22)　△ぼくははな夫をころされた。
　　　Boku wa Hanao o korosareta
　　　Hanao was killed and I am sad about it (intended reading).

(23)　ぼくはねがい事をことわられた。
　　　Boku wa negaigoto o kotowarareta
　　　My wish was rejected and I am sad about it.

Text 7.6 Agentless passive ころされた？

© Fujiko Production / *Doraemon*: *Kandō-hen* (p. 19), Shogakukan

Text 7.7 Adversative passive ことわられた

© Fujiko Production / *Doraemon: Nobita-Grafity* (p. 213), Shogakukan

7.3.4 Causative–passive

Passive verbs are combined with the causative form of a verb to express the forcefulness of a situation. When verbs belong to Class I verbs (or U-verbs), shortened causative verbs are available (泣かす *nakas-u* 'to cause someone to cry', 読ます *yamas-u* 'to cause someone to read'). In Text 7.8, a causative form 立たす *tatasu* 'to cause someone to stand' is followed by a passive form れる. Because のび太 *Nobita* has gotten up late, he is afraid of standing in the corridor in the school. Here, the speaker is silent about who the agent is; the important thing is that the causative–passive form of a verb is used to express the speaker's being forced to do something and feeling uncomfortable with the consequence.

Text 7.8 Causative–passive たたされる！

© Fujiko Production / *Doraemon: Nobita-Grafity* (p. 79), Shogakukan

Activity 1

Text 7.9 contains passive verbs. Select FIVE passive verbs and make sense of their functions in the text. Note that two passives contain a phrase that expresses the agent, but whose referent is not a specific person: まわりから *mawarikara* (lines 15–16) and 人に *hitoni* (line 18). Text 7.9, taken from *Calling You*, is a continuation of Text 5.1 in Chapter 5 (p. 102). It describes the refreshing experience of a female student わたし *watashi* 'I', who is greatly surprised to learn that シンヤ *Shinya*, her male friend, enjoys talking with her.

Text 7.9

1 シンヤがごみ捨て場で座り込み、ぼーっとしている場面をよく想像

した。家にも帰らず、そんなところで、いったい何を考えているの

か、私にはよく分かった。おそらく私が図書館で考えていることと、

そんなにかわらないだろう。

5 「今度ごみ捨て場で、ラジカセを探しておいてよ。軽くて、小さな

やつ。前から欲しいと思っていたんだ」

わたしがそう言うと、彼は笑って「オーケー」と答えた。それから、

わたしとの会話がとても楽しいと言ってくれた。

「楽しい？」

10 「うん」

「はじめてそんなこと言われた。かなり今、びっくりしてる。だっ

て、わたしには、会話をかみあわなくさせる欠陥があるものだと信

じていたから」

「欠陥？」

15 わたしは彼に話をした。他人の社交辞令を真に受けてまわりから

苦笑される。物事を信じこみやすいから愚かな女の子の物語である。

「臆病だと思われるかもしれないけど、もうわたしは、失敗をして

人に笑われたくないんだよ」

怖くて、人に話しかけることができない。話しかけられると、緊張

20 してしまう。このことを考えるたびに、わたしはこの先ずっと、み

んなのように決してはなれないのだという沈んだ気持ちになる。

© 2003 Otsu, Ichi / *Calling You* (pp. 25–26), Kadokawa

Commentary

Table 7.1 contains five passives. The passive parts are in **bold.**

Table 7.1

No	Lines	Passives	Meaning
①	11	言**われ**た	X said to me
②	16	苦笑**され**る	be laughed at
③	18	思**われ**る	be thought of
④	19	笑**われ**たくないんだよ	do not want to be laughed at
⑤	20	話しか**られ**ると	be talked to

All passives in this passage do not express the agent explicitly. All passives except ① are direct passives. Consider first ② and ④. Since it is clear from the context that the person who is laughed at is the first-person narrator, わたし *watashi* 'I', she is not mentioned overtly in the passage. The agent is made overt in ② (まわりから *mawari kara* 'from the classmates around わたし' (literally: 'from the surroundings') and ④ (人に *hito ni* 'by people'). わたし is ridiculed and laughed at by her classmates because she utterly believes their diplomatic language. These passives are formed by verbs (苦笑する *kushō suru* 'to give a wry smile' and 笑う *warau* 'to laugh') and can take an object marked by を *o* in active sentences. Numbers ③ and ⑤ are also direct passives, but no agent is expressed; neither is the person who receives the action expressed. In the former, the suppressed agent is the person to whom わたし is talking (i.e., シンヤ *Shinya*). In the latter, 人 *hito* 'person' (i.e., people in general) is suppressed. Because it is expressed overtly in the previous sentence (line 20) (人に話しかけることができない *Hito ni hanashi-kakeru koto ga dekinai* 'I can't speak to people'), it is omitted in the next.

What is noteworthy is the use of the passive in ①. At first glance, it looks as if it serves to express adversity. 言う *yū* 'to say, tell' is an intransitive verb, and, hence, there is no object to be promoted as subject; わたし is the person who experiences the action of saying, but her participation is psychological and indirect. Upon closer inspection, it can be seen that わたし's reaction to シンヤ's comment (lines 8–10) is a positive one; she is pleased to know that シンヤ enjoys talking with her. It is obvious that わたし is influenced psychologically by what シンヤ tells her about herself. Where this passive differs from other indirect passives may be that the influence is a pleasant experience (not adversative) for the affected person. This text points out that the indirect passive is not always an indicator of adversity but also of positivity. Following Alfonso (1966), Martin (2004: 298) draws attention to the fact that some passives of his data express emotional affects that are not adversative. Our example here substantiates his claim in the sense that the main role of the indirect passive is apparently to reveal the affected person's emotional affect, be it positive or negative. In the above story, it refers to the female student's pleasant surprise.

7.3.5 Donative verbs

Donative verbs refer to verbs of giving and receiving. The three most important donative verbs are あげる *ageru*, くれる *kureru* and もらう *morau*. Each verb has its own honorific form, 差し上げる *sashi-ageru*, くださる *kudasaru* and いただく *itadaku*, respectively. Let us focus first on あげる and くれる. Both verbs mean 'to give', but the difference lies in the direction of giving. With あげる, the direction of giving goes from 'I' to the other person, who can be 'I's' in-group members or 'I's' out-group members (24). In-group members include 'I's' family members or relatives. Out-group members are those outside of 'I's' in-group members (e.g., 'I's' classmates, friends, acquaintances, colleagues) (see JLU: Chapter 4, section 4.2). Not only 'I' but other members of 'I's' in-group can appear as a giver (25). 'I's' out-group members can also serve as a giver if the giving is not directed to 'I' (26). The crucial point is that 'I' can never be a receiver (27). When the receiver is socially higher than the giver, 差し上げる *sashi-ageru* is used (28). ☐ signals the giver. ☐ signals the receiver.

(24) わたし が 妹・いとこ・母・佐藤さん にお人形を **あげた**。
   *Watashi ga imōto/itoko/haha/Satō-san ni o-ningyō o **ageta***
   I gave my younger sister/cousin/my mother/Mr Sato a doll.

(25) いとこが 佐藤さん・妹に花びんを**あげた**。
*Itoko ga Satō-san/imōto ni kabin o **ageta***
My cousin gave a vase to Mr Sato/my sister.

(26) 佐々木さんが 佐藤さんに花びんを**あげた**。
*Sasaki-san ga Satō-san ni kabin o **ageta***
Mr Sasaki gave a vase to Mr Sato.

(27) ×いとこ・父・佐々木さんが 私にチョコレートを**あげた**。
*Itoko/Chichi/Sasaki-san ga watashi ni chokorēto o **ageta***
My cousin/father/Mr Sasaki gave me a chocolate.

(28) わたし・父・いとこが 先生に贈り物を**差し上げた**。
*Watashi/Chichi/Itoko ga sensē ni okurimono o **sashiageta***
I/My father/My cousin gave a gift to the teacher.

With くれる, the direction of giving moves from the other person to 'I' (29) or 'I's' in-group member (30). The crucial point here is that 'I' can never be a giver (31) and that the receiver must be either 'I' or 'I's' in-group member. When the receiver is either 'I' or 'I's' in-group member, anyone except 'I' can be a giver regardless of their group membership (29) (30). The ungrammaticality of (32) is caused by the receiver's being neither 'I' nor 'I's' in-group member. The fact that くれる allows 'I' to be a receiver supplements the use of あげる (as it does not allow 'I' to be a receiver). This complementary distribution (two different directions in a giving activity) makes sense with the presence of two verbs of giving (see also discussions in Rubin 1998: 51–54).

(29) 父・友達・佐々木さんが わたしに本を**くれた**。
*Chichi/Tomodachi/Sasaki-san ga watashi ni hon o **kureta***
My father/My friend/Mr Sasaki gave me a book.

(30) 父・友達・佐々木さんが 弟にプラモデルを**くれた**。
*Chichi/Tomodachi/Sasaki-san ga otōto ni puramoderu o **kureta***
My father/My friend/Mr Sasaki gave my younger brother a plastic model.

(31) ×私が 弟に本を**くれた**。
I gave the book to my brother.

(32) ×父・佐々木さんが 佐藤さんに本を**くれた**。
My father/Mr Sasaki gave the book to my brother/Mr Sato.

もらう means 'to receive'. As a matter of fact, 'to give' and 'to receive' are two sides of the same coin. When you give someone a book, that person receives a book from you. What is noteworthy with もらう is that, contrary to verbs of giving, the direction of receiving is uni-directional, that is, the activity of receiving is that 'I' (or 'I's' in-group member) always functions as a receiver. In (33) and (34), 'I' or 'I's' in-group member gets X from someone. In (35), an out-group member gets X from someone else. Anyone, regardless of group membership, can be a receiver. What is not possible is to have 'I' as a giver (36).

(33) わたしが姉から本を**もらった**。
*Watashi ga ane kara hon o **moratta***
I got a book from my elder sister.

(34) 弟が友達からプラモデルを**もらった**。
*Otōto ga tomodachi kara puramoderu o **moratta***
My brother got a plastic model from his/my friend.

(35) 佐藤さんが佐々木さんから本を**もらった**。
*Satō-san ga Sasaki-san kara hon o **moratta***
Mr Sato got a book from Mr Sasaki.

(36) ×佐藤さんが私から本を**もらった**。
Mr Sato got a book from me.

Verbs of giving and receiving are used as **auxiliary verbs** when attached to the preceding verb. When we say (37), it connotes that 'I gave my younger sister my doing of baking a cake'. Rather than saying わたしが妹にケーキを焼いた 'I baked a cake for my younger sister', which merely describes the fact, it is preferable to integrate the meaning of 'action of giving' into the sentence to express the kindness of a giver or the benefit given to a receiver. From (38) to (40), the speaker draws attention to the benefit obtained from the referent of the subject, who has done some act for the sake of the person in the dotted box.

(37) わたしが妹にケーキを焼いて**あげた**。
*Watashi ga imōto ni kēki o yaite **ageta***
I baked a cake for my younger sister.

(38) 友達がかなちゃんに勉強を教えて**あげた**。
*Tomodachi ga Kana-chan ni benkyō o oshiete **ageta***
My friend helped Kana with her study.
(literally: My friend taught Kana the study).

(39) 友達がわたしに本を貸して**くれた**。
*Tomodachi ga watashi ni hon o kashite **kureta***
My friend lent me a book.

(40) 佐藤さんが弟にプラモデルを作って**くれた**。
*Satō-san ga otōto ni puramoderu o tsukutte **kureta***
Mr Sato assembled a plastic model for my younger brother.

くれた (past tense of くれる *kureru*), as used in (39) and (40) are often found in narrative texts (e.g., novels) in which, as Rubin puts it (1998: 86), the writer 'has a handle on the truth'. Text 7.10 is an extract from *Calling*

You. A female student recalls a conversation with one of her classmates, Miss Harada. She feels inferior to other classmates (Miss Harada is one of them) because she thinks she is incapable of conversing with people (see also Text 7.9). Despite her inferiority, she respects Miss Harada, who gets along with people in a sophisticated manner. In Text 7.10, this female student describes her relationship to Miss Harada. By using くれた three times, the female student refers to favourable actions Miss Harada did for her. She is a receiver of all the giving actions Miss Harada has provided. These favourable actions are to listen to わたし's problems (相談に乗る *sōdan ni noru*), to tell わたし her own past experiences (悲喜こもごもを話す *hiki-komogomo o hanasu*), and to let わたし know which washing cream is suitable for treating her pimples (洗顔クリームを教える *sengan-kurīmu o oshieru*). Through Miss Harada's 'giving actions', the female student begins to feel relieved and even has the illusion at the end that she has known her for a long time. It is still grammatical not to use くれた in this passage, but without it the female student's strong emotions towards Miss Harada would not be expressed effectively.

Text 7.10

```
1  原田さんとも時々、話をした。彼女は大人で、どんなことでも相談
   に乗ってくれた。大学での生活や、一人暮らしをする上で経験した
   悲喜こもごもを話してくれた。ニキビによく効く洗顔クリームも教
   えてくれた。彼女の声は、なぜかわたしをおおいに安心させた。
5  不思議とその声音は以前から知っていたような気がする。彼女の声
   は耳慣れた響きで、清らかな水が染み込むように、頭の中へ浸透し
   ていった。
```

© 2003 Otsu, Ichi / *Calling You* (p. 27), Kadokawa

Translation:
I sometimes talked with Miss Harada, too. She is mature and ready to listen to any of my problems. She also talked about her university life and her own bitter and pleasant experiences while she lived alone. She also taught me about a washing cream that works well for pimples. I don't know why but her voice made me happy and relaxed me greatly.

Strangely enough, I felt that I knew her voice from long before. It has a resonance that was quite familiar to me, and it permeated my brain as if pure water soaks in.

7.4 States and actions with て-forms

Now that different types of verbs and their encoded meanings have been covered, it is important to introduce two concepts, **states** and **actions**. These categories are essential when constructing sentences, since verbs or predicates fall under either of these categories. 'Event' or 事象 *jishō* is a general notion that describes how an entity exists (states) or happens (actions). Stative events have, temporally speaking, a uniform structure, while active events are structured according to different temporal components. For example, 'Mary likes hamburgers' is a stative event, and 'Mary is liking hamburgers' is an active event. The former expresses a continuing or unchanging mental condition of Mary; that is, she likes hamburgers regardless of temporal distributions of her liking. Here the entire event is denoted as an undifferentiated, homogeneous phenomenon. By contrast, the latter implies the existence of substates in which Mary makes efforts to ultimately like hamburgers. Here, the event has dynamic components that develop, and hence is sensitive to the temporal distributions (e.g., beginning and end) of her liking (see Frawley 1992: 147–148). Needless to say, there are several ways in which the internal parts of an event develop and are expressed formally in a language. When we study the internal structure of an event, we talk about **aspect**. Classifications of aspect often depend on the **lexical semantics** (see Chapter 6 for the notion) of the verb. Not all sentences in Japanese encode aspect, however. Some sentences contain verbs that are differentiated by **tense**. Tense is a grammatical encoding of time. Japanese has two tenses, present (also called non-past) and past. When the predicate specifies an aspect, it also specifies tense, but the reverse is not always the case. Text 7.10, for instance, consists of six sentences, all of which are marked by either present or past. Aspect is encoded in the last two sentences (知っていた in line 5 and 浸透していった in line 7). This section deals with expressions with て *te*, which differentiate various meanings of states and actions. A section on states is provided in 7.4.1, followed by sections on actions that are classified according to aspect in 7.4.2 to 7.4.5.

7.4.1 States

The most frequent occurrence of the て-form is ている *teiru*, which contains an existential verb いる 'to be'. When this form is attached to intransitive verbs that encode change of state, it denotes a **state**. Resultant states (or resultative aspect) will be covered in 7.4.2.1. States denoted in

175

examples (41) to (43) are distinguishable from resultant states in that they come into existence independently of a past action. The fact that the road bends does not necessarily mean that someone exerted an effort to change the direction of the road. The road now has a bend in it because of a natural disaster (e.g., an earthquake). Likewise, a badly made shirt can be torn easily when the person who wears it moves her arms widely. Seven Eleven is open for 24 hours, but it does not depend on the actual event of opening the store (e.g., unlocking the entrance door).

Transitive verbs such as 知る *shiru* 'to know' and 覚える *oboeru* 'to remember' may well belong to this class. Knowing the sculpture *Manneken Pis* in Brussels pertains to one's general knowledge, while remembering someone's face relies on one's capacity of memory, both being unrelated to the actual occurrence of a past event. In brief, since the stative events described here do not originate in an actual event in the past, they are referred to as 'pure states' (Jacobsen 1992: 179).

(41) 道が**曲**がっています。
Michi ga magatte imasu
The road bends.

(42) シャツが**破れ**ています。
Shatsu ga yaburete imasu
The shirt is torn.

(43) セブンイレブンは２４時間**開**いています。
Sebun-irebun wa 24-jikan aite imasu
Seven Eleven is open for 24 hours.

(44) 私はブルッセルにある小便小僧を**知**っています。
Watashi wa burusseru ni aru shōben-kozō o shitte imasu
I know Manneken Pis in Brussels.

(45) 私はＳさんの顔を**覚え**ています。
Watashi wa S-san no kao o oboete imasu
I remember Mr S's face.

7.4.2 Actions

As mentioned earlier, actions are distinguished from states by the presence of an internal temporal contour known as an aspect. This section examines different て-forms from this perspective. Forms we consider are ている (7.4.2.1), てある (7.4.2.2), ておく (7.4.2.3), てしまう (7.4.2.4) and ていく/てくる (7.4.2.5).

7.4.2.1 ている

ている has five aspectual meanings: (i) progressive, (ii) durative, (iii) resultative, (iv) habitual and (v) iterative.

176

Progressive   The progressive aspect expresses an event that is in progress or ongoing. As shown in (46) and (47), the progressive aspect is created by combining ている *teiru* with action verbs (encoding an action that demands a certain length of time for it to take place). Both writing a letter and watching a movie occupy time for conducting an activity. In order to show that these activities have duration, durative adverbials such as 一時間 *ichijikan* 'one hour' can be added.

> (46) a. 冬子さんは手紙を書いています。
>   *Fuyuko-san wa tegami o kaite imasu*
>   Fuyuko is writing a letter.
>   b. 冬子さんは手紙を一時間書いています。
>   *Fuyuko-san wa tegami o ichijikan kaite imasu*
>   Fuyuko writes a letter for an hour.
>
> (47) a. 高志君は映画を見ています。
>   *Takashi-kun wa eiga o mite imasu*
>   Takashi is watching a movie.
>   b. 高志君は映画を一時間見ています。
>   *Takashi-kun wa eiga o ichijikan mite imasu*
>   Takashi watches a movie for an hour.

Durative   The durative aspect expresses an event that maintains over time. To the extent that the durative aspect occupies time and continues to exist, it resembles the progressive aspect. It differs in that it does not improve or develop over time. When writing a letter, there is a blank paper at the beginning that becomes filled with sentences by the end. As shown in (48) to (50), sitting on a chair, knowing someone or being married do not have internal composites that can progress. The beginning and the end of these three events are virtually the same. Because durative events are extendable, they can co-occur with adverbials that encode temporal duration (e.g., 一時間 *ichijikan* 'one hour'; 三年間 *san-nenkan* 'three years'). A word of caution is in order. The meaning of 知る in (49) slightly differs from that of 知る in (44) in that the knowledge encoded in (49) originates in a previous action (e.g., Michiko met Mr M at one point in the past).

> (48) a. 友子さんは椅子に座っています。
>   *Tomoko-san wa isu ni suwatte imasu*
>   Tomoko is sitting on a chair.
>   b. 友子さんは一時間椅子に座っています。
>   *Tomoko-san wa ichijikan isu ni suwatte imasu*
>   Tomoko has been sitting on a chair for an hour.
>
> (49) a. 道子さんはMさんを知っています。
>   *Michiko-san wa M-san o shitte imasu*
>   Michiko knows Mr M.

   b. 道子さんはMさんを三年間知っています。
     *Michiko-san wa M-san o **san-nenkan shitte imasu***
     Michiko has known Mr M for three years.

(50) a. 梓さんは**結婚しています**。
     *Azusa-san wa **kekkonshite imasu**.*
     Azusa is married.
    b. 梓さんはもう三年間結婚しています。
     *Azusa-san wa mō **san-nenkan kekkonshite imasu***
     Azusa has already been married for three years.

Resultative   The resultative aspect expresses an event that ends in a result and has neither development nor continuation. As exemplified by (51) and (52), when someone dies, this represents the endpoint of the entire event. The event is exhausted by the result of dying, and what remains at the time of speech is the resultant state. When someone wakes up, this event is likewise exhausted by the result of waking up. Because of its exhaustiveness, the resultative aspect accepts point-like adverbials (e.g., 六時に *rokujini* 'at six o'clock') but, unlike the progressive or durative aspects, it is at odds with adverbials that encode duration (e.g., 一時間 *ichijikan* 'one hour').

(51) a. 犬が**死んでいます**。
     *Inu ga **shinde imasu***
     The dog is dead.
    b. 犬が (×一時間/○六時に) **死んでいます**。

(52) a. 子供が**起きています**。
     *Kodomo ga **okite imasu***
     The child has got up (and is awake now).
    b. 子供が (×一時間/○六時に) **起きています**。

The resultative is formed by punctual verbs that express an instantaneous event. Aside from 'die' or 'wake up', other verbs such as 'arrive' or 'receive' fall under this category. All these verbs are instantaneous because they express an event whose accomplishment does not require temporary duration; that is, it happens momentarily.

(53) a. 秋子さんは家に**着いています**。
     *Akiko-san wa ie ni **tsuite imasu***
     Akiko has arrived home.
    b. 秋子さんは (×一時間/○六時に) 家に**着いています**。

(54) a. まり子さんは手紙を**受け取っています**。
     *Mariko-san wa tegami o **uketotte imasu***
     Marko has received a letter.
    b. まり子さんは (×一時間/○六時に)手紙を**受け取っています**。

Habitual   The habitual aspect expresses an event that occurs habitually. Unlike progressive or durative events, habitual events extend irrespective of time (see Frawley 1992: 316). This means that the habitual is not associated with any specific moment but rather expresses repetition of an event on different occasions. As shown in (55), (56) and (57), the main issue in these events is that the event is distributed over a number of times. Since a series of events extends over a period of time, these examples permit a durative adverbial. The habitual also permits adverbials that express frequency such as 'every week'.

(55)   a. 夏子さんは中国語を**習っています**。
       *Natsuko-san wa chūgoku-go o **naratte imasu***
       Natsuko is learning Chinese.
   b. 夏子さんは**二年間/毎週**中国語を**習っています**。
       *Natsuko-san wa **ninenkan/maishū** chūgoku-go o **naratte imasu***
       Natsuko has been learning Chinese for two years.
       Natsuko learns Chinese every week.

(56)   a. 春子さんは大学に**通っています**。
       *Haruko-san wa daigaku ni **kayotte imasu***
       Haruko goes to the university.
   b. 春子さんは大学に**二年間/毎日通っています**。
       *Haruko-san wa daigaku ni **ninenkan/mainichi kayotte imasu***
       Haruko has been going to the university for two years.
       Haruko goes to the university every day.

(57)   a. 春子さんのお兄さんは大学で**教えています**。
       *Haruko-san no onīsan wa daigaku de **oshiete imasu***
       Haruko's elder brother is teaching at university.
   b. 春子さんのお兄さんは**五年間/週に三回**大学で**教えています**。
       *Haruko-san no onīsan wa **gonenkan/shūni sankai** daigaku de **oshiete imasu***
       Haruko's elder brother has been teaching at university for five years.
       Haruko's elder brother teaches at university three times a week.

Iterative   The iterative aspect expresses an event that has multiple sub-events. An event can also consist of a single event. When we raise our hand, it is a single event, called **semelfactive**. When we wave our hand, the action must normally occur more than once. In other words, waving a hand refers to multiple moments of the hand movement. Likewise, knocking on a door consists of multiple sub-events.

(58)   学生がドアを**叩いています**。
       *Gakusē ga doa o **tataite imasu***
       The student is knocking at the door.

179

(59) 人々が手を振っています。
*Hitobito ga te o **futte imasu***
People are waving a hand.

7.4.2.2 てある

てある *tearu* is another aspectual marker that contains て and another existential verb ある 'to be'. Distinct from ている, which exhibits various meanings (see section 7.4.2.1), てある has one aspectual meaning, that is, the durative. As a result of a past event, a new situation arises that persists for a certain time. Both (60) and (61) express a situation in which the window remains open. However, the meaning of the durative is not exactly the same between ている and てある.

(60) 窓が**開いています**。
*Mado ga **aite imasu***
The window is open.

(61) 窓が**開けてあります**。
*Mado ga **akete arimasu***
The window is open.

The difference is grammatical and semantic. Example (60) contains an intransitive verb (開く *aku* 'to open'), while (61) contains a transitive (開ける *akeru* 'to open'). In (60), there is no indication as to who opened the window; the emphasis is merely on the window being open. In (61), the addressee perceives that the window is open as a result of someone's act of opening it in the near past. てある is used when the speaker is aware of someone having caused the new situation that is currently important. Because てある implies the presence of someone's actual performance, only transitive verbs are used, and the subject in the てある construction is always inanimate. Recall that when ある is used as a proper existential verb, it takes, as a rule, an inanimate object (e.g., 'desk', 'flower') as a subject. To the extent that てある considers the speaker's attitude towards the status of the event, it is obvious that it is not merely an aspectual marker.

7.4.2.3 ておく

ておく *teoku* is another aspectual marker in which て is combined with the verb おく 'to put, to locate, to place'. Unlike いる and ある, おく is a transitive verb that always takes an object. ておく emphasizes the completion of a denoted event. The important thing is that ておく does not merely express the completion but that this completion is seen as a preparation for the near future. The connotation is that it would be convenient or recommendable to have this done so that something else in the future could happen smoothly. A teacher in a classroom may say (62) at the end of the class. This implies that it would be convenient for students to review the vocabulary they had learned today for the preparation of the next lesson. Similar to てある, the exact meaning of the 'completion of the event' is realized with the speaker's attitude towards the given situation.

(62) このレッスンの単語を**復習しておいて**ください。
*Kono ressun no tango o **fukushū shite oite** kudasai*
Please review the vocabularies in this lesson.

7.4.2.4 てしまう

てしまう *teshimau* contains the transitive verb しまう, which literally means 'to put something away', 'to keep' or 'to store'. The form encodes an aspect of completion. Similarly to ておく, the completion expressed does not simply refer to 'the end of an event' but also to the 'finality' or 'irreversibility' of the completion. The speaker gives the impression that the happening of an event cannot be undone or altered; that is, the completion is an irresistible end of the event. Example (63) can be thus interpreted in such a way that there is no other meaning but that the child is crying. Because of the irreversibility encoded in てしまう, it is also used to express the speaker's regret (see JLU: Chapter 1, section 1.2.4); thus, with (63) the speaker can express regret about the child's crying. Like てある and ておく, the speaker's attitude towards the completion of an event influences the interpretation of the aspect.

(63) 子供が**泣いてしまった**。
*Kodomo ga **naite shimatta***
The child cried.

7.4.2.5 ていく and てくる

When て *te* is combined with verbs such as いく *iku* 'to go' or くる *kuru* 'to come', it expresses a direction, that is, a movement between two points. As shown in (64) and (65), the addition of いく gives further information about the direction of the person's movement. Since いく expresses an action away from the speaker, the action of walking (64) and running (65) goes away from the speaker.

(64) 秋子さんが学校へ**歩いていきました**。
*Akiko-san ga gakkō e **aruite ikimashita***
Akiko walked to school.

(65) 子供が公園へ**走っていきました**。
*Kodomo ga kōen e **hashitte ikimashita***
The child ran into the park.

てくる expresses an action that comes closer to the speaker. When examples (66) and (67) are uttered, the addressee knows that the speaker is in the school and in the park, respectively, while in (64) and (65) the

181

speaker could be in his home. Note that the location of the speaker can be mental; that is, he can be somewhere else but his mind is focused on the place to or from which the movement is directed.

(66) 秋子さんが学校へ**歩いてきました**。
Akiko-san ga gakkō e aruite kimashita
Akiko walked and came to school.

(67) こどもが公園へ**走ってきました**。
Kodomo ga kōen e hashitte kimashita
The child ran to the park.

These directional meanings of ていく and てくる can be extended to express different aspects of events. Table 7.2 gives an idea of how each form exhibits the aspectual meanings (see also Kamiya 2001: 170–171; Maynard 1990: 182–183). There are essentially four features important for the interpretation of ていく and てくる: (i) appearance or disappearance of an event, (ii) beginning or end of an event, (iii) stretch of event over past, present and future, and (iv) change of state. When something appears or begins, てくる is used. When something disappears or comes to an end, ていく is used. When an event stretches from the past up to the present, てくる is used, whereas when the event stretches from the present into the future, ていく is used. Bodily change (e.g., a change in one's complexion) is also differentiated by the two uses. When a change is in its initial stage, てくる is used, whereas ていく is used when the focus is on the development of a change. It can thus be said that Japanese people categorize the occurrence of certain kinds of events into two opposing dimensions: one is close to the speaker, while the other is away from the speaker.

Table 7.2 *Aspectual meanings of* ていく *and* てくる

No.	Aspectual meanings	ていく away from speaker	てくる closer to speaker
68	Appearance		○
69	Disappearance	○	
70	Initiation		○
71	Termination	○	
72	Stretching from past to now		○
73	Stretching from now to future	○	
74	Bodily change	○	○

(68) 富士山が見え**てきた**。(×見えていった)
      *Fujisan ga mie **tekita***
      Fuji Mountain comes to appear in my sight.

(69) 雲がだんだん消え**ていった**。(×消えてきた)
      *Kumo ga dandan kie **teitta***
      Clouds disappeared.

(70) 空が晴れ**てきた**。(×晴れていった)
      *Sora ga hare **tekita**.*
      The sky became bright.

(71) 清王朝は力を失い滅亡し**ていった**。(×滅亡してきた)
      *Shin-Ōchō wa chikara o ushinai metsubō shi **teitta***
      The Ching dynasty lost their power and fell.

(72) 関谷君はこれまで絶え間ない努力を重ね**てきた**。
      (×重ねていった)
      *Sekiya-kun wa koremade taemanai doryoku o kasane **tekita***
      Mr Sekiya has so far been making endless efforts.

(73) 関谷くんはこれからも絶え間ない努力を重ね**ていく**つもりだ。
      (×重ねてくるつもりだ)
      *Sekiya-kun wa korekaramo taemanai doryoku o kasane **teiku** tsumori da*
      Mr Sekiya is going to make endless efforts from now on.

(74) 高根さんの顔が赤くなっ**ていった** (development)。/ **てきた**
      (initiation)。
      *Takane-san no kao ga akaku nat **teitta** / **tekita***
      Mr Takane's face was turning red.

Activity 2

Let us look at the children's story 車のいろは空のいろ *Kuruma no iro wa sora no iro* 'The Colour of the Car is the Colour of the Sky', which regularly employs て-forms and expresses the aspect of events the taxi driver 松井五郎 *Matsui Gorō* encounters. Your task is to identify the functions of each form (highlighted in the text) in terms of its aspectual meaning. In the case of ていく *teiku* and てくる *tekuru*, bear in mind that they often occur as a directional marker (but not an aspectual) in the story.

Text 7.11

> **1** 空いろのぴかぴかのタクシーが、一台、①とまっていました。そのう
> しろにしゃがみこんで、さっきから、ねっしんにタイヤを②しらべて
> いるのは、この車のうんてんしゅー、松井五郎さんです。まるいはな
> の上に、つぶつぶのあせが③ひかっています。とおくのひこうじょう
> **5** までお客を④のせていき、からでもどるとちゅうでした。ちっ――
> と松井さんは、らんぼうなしたうちをしながら立ちあがりました。
> おもったとおり、うしろのタイヤが⑤パンクしていたからです。
> むしまんじゅうのようにふくれた顔で、松井さんは、荷台から、銀
> いろのジャッキを⑥とりだしてきました。ふとい車じくにジャッキを
> **10** かけ、この車をもちあげねばなりません。そこで、
> 「ん！」
> と、ジャッキについているねじをまわそうとしました。ところが、う
> ごきません。いつもなら、このくらい力をいれるとうごくはずなのに、
> なかなかうごきません。松井さんの顔は、だんだんだんだん赤みをま
> **15** して、⑦カニのようになってきました。
> 〔...〕
> 「これじゃ、のれないわ。わたしは、あたらしい黒のスーツを
> ⑧きているんですからね。車のシートは、いつも⑨きれいにしておく
> ことよ。」
> こういったのは、つぎのお客です。その人は、ちょうどむこうからき
> **20** た黒いタクシーに、手をあげながらつんつん⑩走っていきました。
> 「？......」
> 車をおり、客せきのドアをあけたとたん、松井さんは、
> 「なんだ？こりゃ.......」
> と、つぶやきました。
> **25** ほそいみじかい金色の毛が、みどりのシートに⑪ちらばっています。

Text 7.12

1 アクセルをふもうとしたとき、松井さんは、はっとしました。

（おや、車道のあんなすぐそばに、小さなぼうしが①**おちている**ぞ。

風がもうひとふきすれば、車が②**ひいてしまう**わい。

みどりが③**ゆれている**ヤナギの下に、かわいい白いぼうしが、ちょこ

5 んと④**おいてあります**。松井さんは車からでました。そして、ぼうし

をつまみあげたとたん、ふわっとなにかがとびだしました。

「あれっ！？」

モンシロチョウです。

あわててぼうしをふりまわしました。そんな松井さんの目のまえを、

10 チョウはひらひら高くまいあがると、並木のみどりのむこうに

⑤**みえなくなってしまいました。**

（ははあ、わざわざここにおいたんだな。）

ぼうしのうらに、赤いししゅう糸で、小さくぬいとりが⑥**してありま**

す。

15 |たけ山ようちえん　たけのたけお|

小さなぼうしをつかんで、ためいきを⑦**ついている**松井さんのよこを、

ふとったおまわりさんが、じろじろ見ながらとおりすぎました。

（せっかくのえものが⑧**いなくなっていた**ら、この子は、

どんなにがっかりするだろう。）

20 ちょっとのあいだ、かたをすぼめて⑨**立っていた**松井さんは、なにを

おもいついたのか、いそいで車にもどりました。

（...）

車にもどると、おかっぱにかわいい女の子が、ちょこんとうしろのシ

ートに⑩**すわっています。**

「みちにまよったの、いってもいっても、四かくいたてものばかりだ

25 もん。」

つかれたような声でした。

「ええと、どちらまで？」

「え？......ええ、あの、あのね、なの花よこ町ってあるかしら？」

「なの花橋のことですね。」

30 エンジンをかけたとき、とおくから、げんきそうな男の子の声が

⑪**ちかづいてきました。**[...]

客せきの女の子が、うしろからのりだして、せかせかといいました。

「はやく、おじちゃん。はやく行ってちょうだい。」

松井さんは、あわててアクセルをふみました。ヤナギの並木が、みる

35 みるうしろに⑫**ながれていきます。**[...]

すると、ぽかっと口を〇の字に⑬**あけている**男の子の顔が、⑭**見えて**

きます。

（おどろいただろうな。まほうのみかんとおもうかな。なにしろ、

チョウがばけたんだから——）

40 「ふふふっ。」

ひとりでにわらいが⑮**こみあげてきました。**でも、つぎに

「おや。」

松井さんはあわてました。バックミラーにはだれも⑯**うつっていませ**

ん。ふりかえっても、だれもいません。

45 「おかしいな。」

松井さんは車をとめて、かんがえ、まどのそとを見ました。

そこは、小さな団地のまえの小さな野原でした。しろいチョウが、

二十も三十も、いえ、もっとたくさん⑰**とんでいました。**クローバー

が青あおとひろがり、わた毛ときいろの花のまざったタンポポが、

50 てんてんのもようになって⑱**さいています。**その上を⑲**とんでいる**チ

ョウをぼんやり見ているうち、松井さんには、こんな声が⑳**きこえて**

きました。

© 1977 Aman, Kimiko / *Kuruma no Iro wa Sora no Iro* (pp. 30–32, 33–34, 36–37), Poplar

Commentary

The following table demonstrates suggested answers to Activity 2.

Table 7.3   *Answers to Text 7.11*

No.	Examples	Meaning
①	タクシーがとまっていました	Durative
②	しらべている	Progressive
③	あせがひかっている	State
④	のせていき	Direction away from the vantage point
⑤	パンクしていた	Resultative
⑥	とりだしてきました	Direction closer to the vantage point
⑦	カニのようになってきました	Initiation of bodily change in Mr Matusi
⑧	スーツをきている	Durative
⑨	きれいにしておく	Completion and suggestion
⑩	走っていきました	Direction away from Mr Matsui
⑪	ちらばっています	State

Table 7.4   *Answers to Text 7.12*

No.	Examples	Meanings
①	おちている	Resultative
②	ひいてしまう	Completion with finality
③	ゆれている	Progressive
④	おいてあります	Completion by someone
⑤	みえなくなってしまいました	Completion with regret/finality
⑥	してあります	Completion by someone
⑦	ためいきをついている	Iterative / semelfactive
⑧	いなくなっていた	Resultative
⑨	立っていた	Durative
⑩	すわっています	Durative
⑪	ちかづいてきました	Direction towards Mr Matsui
⑫	ながれていきます	Disappearance
⑬	口をあけている	Durative
⑭	見えてきます	Appearance
⑮	わらいがこみあげてきました	Initiation
⑯	だれもうつっていません	State
⑰	とんでいました	Progressive
⑱	さいています	State
⑲	とんでいる	Progressive
⑳	きこえてきました	Initiation

7.5 Case particles

Japanese has **case particles**, or 格助詞 *kakujoshi*, which are attached to nouns in a sentence. They comprise が *ga*, を *o*, に *ni*, で *de*, と *to*, へ *e* and の *no*, and their role is to specify the noun's grammatical and semantic relation to other units of the sentence. Some scholars (see Tsujimura 1996: 134–136) regard case particles as representing four cases prominent in many European languages (i.e., nominative, genitive, dative, accusative), and they distinguish them from postpositions. These four cases correspond to が, の, に and を; other particles, that is, で, と, へ, に (に has two functions) are regarded as postpositions, since they encode spatial and temporal relations. In this section, the term 格助詞 is used (its translation is 'case particles' in this book), which encompasses all seven particles mentioned above. In other words, no distinction is made between case particles and postpositions. Case particles stand in contrast to three other types of particles in Japanese grammar, that is, 副助詞 *fukujoshi* (e.g., は, も, こそ), 終助詞 *shūjoshi* (e.g., ね, よ, か), and 接続助詞 *setsuzokujoshi* (e.g., が, て, ので).

When 山田さんØ お茶Ø 飲んだ appears without particles, the presence of the three units does not make sense unless provided with a context. Only when a particle is placed in an appropriate position do the three units become structurally and semantically meaningful (see (18)). By attaching the particle が to 山田さん, 山田さん is identified as the person who acts on お茶. When お茶 is marked by を, it is made clear that what 山田さん does is to drink a tea. Case particles function like pillars that support the parts of a house. Without particles to hold together the units of a sentence, the sentence will not be well-formed. In what follows, we look more closely at the semantic relations of particles (i.e., を (7.5.1), に (7.5.2, 7.5.3 and 7.5.5), へ (7.5.2), で (7.5.3 and 7.5.4), と (7.5.6), が (7.5.7)). The different functions of the particle の are dealt with in Table 7.6, p. 196.

7.5.1 Receiving an action

The use of を points to several semantic relations that exist between subject and object. The most common relation attached to を is to indicate that the object that it marks **receives an action** conducted by the subject. The nature of the relation between subject and object can be further explicated by identifying the way in which the referent of the object receives an action (75) to (79).

> (75) Object is in contact with subject when the action takes place
> (着る *kiru*, 履く *haku*)
> 山田さんが服を着る。

> *Yamada-san ga fuku **o** kiru*
> Mr Yamada wears a cloth.

(76) Object undergoes a change by the action
(食べる *taberu*, 飲む *nomu*, 切る *kiru*)
山田さんが焼き鳥**を**食べる。
*Yamada-san ga yakitori **o** taberu*
Mr Yamada eats a barbecued chicken.

(77) Object is the integral part of an action (読む *yomu*, 書く *kaku*)
山田さんが本**を**読む。
*Yamada-san ga hon **o** yomu*
Mr Yamada reads a book.

(78) Object is created by an action (作る *tsukuru*, 焼く *yaku*)
山田さんがケーキ**を**作る。
*Yamada-san ga kēki **o** tsukuru*
Mr Yamada bakes a cake.

(79) Object is the space where an action takes place
(走る *hashiru*, 歩く *aruku*)[2]
山田さんが公園**を**走る。
*Yamada-san ga kōen **o** hashiru*
Mr Yamada runs in the park.

7.5.2 Direction

Some verbs select に to mark the object to which the subject is **directed**. Mr Yamada, be it his whole body or part, is directed at a particular person such as Midori, as in (80) and (82), or a non-human such as a caterpillar, as in (81). Verbs taking に are 会う *au*, 触る *sawaru*, and 近づく *chikazuku*. The exact meaning of the direction differs depending on the meaning of the verb. When 会う is used, as in (80), it implies that the meeting happens accidentally, whilst the unexpectedness is not present in (81) or (82).

(80) 山田さんがみどりさん**に**会った。
*Yamada-san ga Midori-san **ni** atta*
Mr Yamada met/bumped into Midori.

(81) 山田さんが毛虫**に**触った。
*Yamada-san ga kemushi **ni** sawatta*
Mr Yamada touched a caterpillar.

(82) 山田さんがみどりさん**に**近づいた。
*Yamada-san ga Midori-san **ni** chikazuita*
Mr Yamada approached Midori.

189

に is also used when some motion is directed towards a particular object. In (83) Mr Yamada is directed towards the bus by getting into it, and in (84) the car is directed towards the house by stopping in front of it.

(83) 山田さんがバス**に**乗った。
*Yamada-san ga basu **ni** notta*
Mr Yamada got on the bus.

(84) 車が家の前**に**止まった。
*Kuruma ga ie no mae **ni** tomatta*
The car stopped in front of the house.

Direction is also expressed by using the particle へ, as in (85) and (86). What differentiates へ from に is that the action expressed by に emphasizes a state resulting from the completion of the motion (when X gets on the bus, X remains in the bus), whilst the motion expressed by へ simply expresses a direction, being mute about its resulting state (we do not know whether X stays in school as a result of her going there). Note that へ can be replaced by に in (85) and (86), while (83) and (84) cannot be rephrased by へ.

(85) みどりさんが学校**へ・に**行った。
*Midori-san ga gakkō **e / ni** itta*
Midori went to school.

(86) みどりさんが駅**へ・に**向かった。
*Midori-san ga eki **e / ni** mukatta*
Midori went towards the station.

7.5.3 Location

Apart from expressing direction, に is used when the subject ends an action in a **location**. The implication is that the resultant state remains in place as a result of the previous action. The usage of に in (83) and (84) is, in essence, cognate with this function. Example (87) connotes that Mr Yamada will be working in a company (location) as a result of his starting employment. Likewise, (88) indicates that Mr Yamada will be studying at university (location) as a result of his acceptance as a student. Example (89) implies that the beer will be kept in the refrigerator (location) as a result of being placed in it. As far as に is used, these verbs encode a sense of direction (see (83) and (84)), but the direction here is merely a prerequisite for the resulting activity/situation.

(87) 山田さんが日系の会社**に**勤めた。
*Yamada-san ga nikkei no kaisha **ni** tsutometa*
Mr Yamada became employed at a Japanese company.

(88)　山田さんが大学**に**入学した。
　　　*Yamada-san ga daigaku **ni** nyūgaku shita*
　　　Mr Yamada entered a university.

(89)　山田さんがビールを冷蔵庫**に**入れた。
　　　*Yamada-san ga bīru o rēzōko **ni** ireta*
　　　Mr Yamada put the beer into the refrigerator.

で resembles に in the sense that both express a location. However, で differs from に, as it neither encodes the direction nor the result. As exemplified in (90) to (92), で denotes a location in which an activity is carried out. に is not compatible with verbs here, although the meanings of pairs of verbs are synonymous (e.g., 勤める versus 働く; 入学する versus 勉強する).

(90)　山田さんが日系の会社**で**働いた。
　　　*Yamada-san ga nikkei no kaisha **de** hataraita*
　　　Mr Yamada worked in a Japanese company.

(91)　山田さんが大学**で**勉強した。
　　　*Yamada-san ga daigaku **de** benkyō shita*
　　　Mr Yamada studied in a university.

(92)　山田さんが秋田**で**生まれた。
　　　*Yamada-san ga Akita **de** umareta*
　　　Mr Yamada was born in Akita.

The difference between に and で can be shown by the ways in which adverbial phrases behave. As in (93), に is compatible with adverbials such as 4 月 1 日 から *shigatsu tsuitachi kara* 'from the first of April', expressing the point of time in which an action arises. As in (94), で allows adverbials such as 7年間 *shichinenkan* 'for seven years', expressing the duration of an activity. The crucial point is that the location encoded in に denotes the source from which the action originates. Example (95) exemplifies that に is interchangeable with から 'from', showing clearly that the meaning of に overlaps with that of から.

(93)　山田さんが日系の会社**に** 4 月 1 日から(×7 年間) 勤めた。

(94)　山田さんが日系の会社**で** 7 年間 (×4 月 1 日**から**) 働いた。

(95)　山田さんが奥さん**に・から**ネクタイをもらった。

7.5.4 Instrument

で functions as an **instrument** referring to an entity by means of which an action is carried out. In (96) Mr Yamada uses a crayon as an instrument to draw a picture, while in (97) Japanese people use chopsticks as an instrument to eat meals.

(96)　山田さんがクレヨン**で**絵を描いた。
　　　*Yamada-san ga kureyon **de** e o kaita*
　　　Mr Yamada drew a picture with a crayon.

(97)　日本人は箸**で**ご飯を食べる。
　　　*Nihonjin wa hashi **de** gohan o taberu*
　　　Japanese people eat meals using chopsticks.

7.5.5　Participation

The particle に can be used when the subject **participates** in an activity. In (98), the meeting is an activity in which Mr Yamada takes part. In (99), Mr Yamada takes part in answering a question. Apart from these two examples, verbs such as 反対する *hantai suru* 'to oppose', がまんする 'to endure, stand' and 賛成する *sansei suru* 'to agree' pertain to this group (see Obana 2000: 92). It is reasonable to isolate this group of verbs, as the meaning of に is neither cognate with direction nor location.

(98)　山田さんが会議**に**参加した。
　　　*Yamada-san ga kaigi **ni** sanka shita*
　　　Mr Yamada participated in the meeting.

(99)　山田さんが質問**に**答えた。
　　　*Yamada-san ga shitsumon **ni** kotaeta*
　　　Mr Yamada answered the question.

7.5.6　Reciprocity

When a **reciprocal** relation between the two participants exists, the object is marked by と. Verbs such as 結婚する *kekkon suru* 'to marry', 離婚する *rikon suru* 'to get divorced', 衝突する *shōtotsu suru* 'to collide with', ぶつかる 'to collide with, dash against, clash with', 喧嘩する *kenka suru* 'to have a row with', 争う *arasou* 'to fight with', and 戦争する *sensō suru* 'to be at war with' are representative in that the actions denoted do not exist without the involvement of two parties. Marriage and divorce need two people who participate. Similarly, having a fight needs two parties. Directional verbs such as 会う (see (80)) can accept と, as shown in (102), when reciprocity is stressed. 触る *sawaru* (81) and 近づく *chikazuku* (82) do not allow と; the reason is precisely that the action encoded is germane to the involvement of a single person. Reciprocity thus emphasizes the simultaneous participation of two people. This special emphasis on reciprocity apparently assigns an extra meaning to (102) in such a way that Mr Yamada and Midori 'arranged' to meet each other (see also Obana 2000: 93).

(100) 山田さんがみどりさん**と**結婚・離婚した。
*Yamada-san ga Midori-san **to** kekkon/rikon shita*
Mr Yamada married/divorced Midori.

(101) 山田さんがみどりさん**と**よく喧嘩する。
*Yamada-san ga Midori-san **to** yoku kenka suru*
Mr Yamada often has a row with Midori.

(102) 山田さんがみどりさん**と**会った。
*Yamada-san ga Midori-san **to** atta*
Mr Yamada met with Midori.

7.5.7 Experiencer

Section 7.1 stated that the particle が marks the subject. There are some cases in which が is used for the object. When the object is marked by が, the subject functions as the **experiencer**. Instead of being an agent who initiates or instigates an action, the experiencer refers to someone who experiences, or lives with, the denoted action. When Mr Yamada wants to have a lover, he experiences a feeling of desire (103). When he does not understand the Japanese language, he lives with the process of not understanding it (104). Likewise, his emotional experience is evoked when he likes, needs, or does not get along with Midori (105).

(103) 山田さんが恋人**が**ほしい。
*Yamada-san ga koibito **ga** hoshii*
Mr Yamada wants to have a lover.

(104) 山田さんが日本語**が**分からない。
*Yamada-san ga nihongo **ga** wakaranai*
Mr Yamada does not understand Japanese.

(105) 山田さんがみどりさん**が**好きだ・必要だ・苦手だ。
*Yamada-san ga Midori-san **ga** sukida / hitsuyōda / nigateda*
Mr Yamada likes/needs/does not get along with Midori.

Activity 3

Identify the particles from the newspaper report about Somalia, Africa, and explain their functions. Include topic は.

Text 7.13

無政府状態　銃が支配

1　ソマリアの首都モガディシオは、かつてインド洋に面した美しい町
だった。青い海を背に、白い石造りの政府の建物や銀行が並び、金

> 細工の店がにぎわっていた。こぢんまりした家庭的なホテルもあっ
> た。その町並みは、１０年以上続く内戦で廃墟と化していた。砲撃
> **5** で壁は崩れ落ち、白い廃墟だけが残る。人影はなく、波の音が大き
> く聞こえた。

© 2004 *Asahi Newspaper* 14 February

Translation:
Anarchy (無政府状態 *musēfu-jōtai*) prevails in Somalia. Guns rule Mogadishu. The capital city (首都 *shuto*) of Somalia was once a beautiful city facing (面した *menshita*) the Indian Ocean. Having the blue ocean as their background, government buildings made of white stones were on the streets and goldsmith's stores (金細工の店 *kinzaiku no mise*) were flourishing. There were also snug, homely hotels. This picture turned into ruins as a result of the civil war (内戦 *naisen*), which lasted for more than 10 years. Walls fell down due to bombardments (砲撃 *hōgeki*), and now only white ruins (廃墟 *haikyo*) remain. There is no soul. One could hear the sound of loud waves.

Commentary

The following table presents suggested answers to Activity 3.

Table 7.5 *Answers to Text 7.13*

Examples	Line	は	が	を	に	と	で	Functions
銃 *jū*	Head		○					Subject
モガディシオ	1	○						Topic
インド洋 *yō*	1				○			Location
海 *umi*	2			○				Object (figurative)
背 *se*	2				○			Location
銀行 *ginkō*	2		○					Subject
店 *mise*	3		○					Subject
町並み *machinami*	4	○						Topic
内戦 *naisen*	4						○	Instrument
廃墟 *haikyo*	4					○		Change
砲撃 *hōgeki*	5						○	Instrument
壁 *kabe*	5	○						Topic
廃墟だけ	5		○					Subject
人影 *hitokage*	5	○						Topic
波の音 *nami no oto*	6		○					Object

は appears four times. The first topic モガディシオ (line 1) is related to the theme of the article because the author is concerned with what happened to this city. その町並み *sono machinami* (line 4) takes は, since it refers to what is described in the previous sentence – the beautiful parts of Mogadishu. Using その 'that' strengthens the connection between two sentences.[3] 壁 *kabe* (line 5) takes は because the wall forms a part of the buildings in the city (e.g., 政府の建物 *sēfu no tatemono* 'govermental build-ings' and 銀行 *ginkō* 'bank') mentioned previously. The use of は in 人影はなく *hitokage wa naku* (line 5) is related to the previous description of the city now being in ruins.

The particle が appears five times. The first four serve as subject and the final as object. 波の音 *nami no oto* is the object that the journalist, an experiencer, can hear.

を *o* is attached to 海 *umi* (line 2). This use of を resembles (79); を refers to the ocean as a spatial domain against which the writer's image of the city of Mogadishu takes shape – similar to the way one runs or walks in a park. The difference is that を in the text frames a meta-phorical space.

に *ni* is used twice to express location; one refers to the location of Mogadishu on the Indian Ocean (line 1), and the other refers to the location of the blue ocean behind the buildings (line 2).

と *to* appears in 廃墟と化している *haikyo to kashite iru* (line 4). Here the function of と is not reciprocity; instead it expresses a change, since the verb 化す 'to turn into' takes と to express the change.

で *de* in 内戦で *naisende* (line 4) and 砲撃で *hōgekide* (lines 4–5) functions as an instrument: by means of the civil war, the city turned into ruins, and by means of the bombardments, the wall fell in.

What has not been dealt with in section 7.5 is the function of the case particle の *no*. の has two main functions: one is possession (e.g., 私の人形 'my doll') and the other is associativeness (e.g., 数学の先生 'maths teacher') (Iwasaki 2002: 175–176). In Text 7.13, の imparts various associative meanings, but none of them is assigned a genuine possessive meaning. 政府の建物 is an ambiguous case because it can be interpreted as possessive as well as associative. Table 7.6 (p. 196) suggests the functions of associative uses of の.

7.6 Basic sentence patterns and spoken language

Having examined the behaviour of particles in section 7.5, Japanese sentences can now be classified according to the way in which the verb takes different particles. The next fifteen classifications are considered 'basic' in the sense that they demonstrate the minimum requirements of the predicate necessary to form a grammatical sentence using case

Table 7.6 Functions of の

Examples	Line	Meanings
ソマリアの首都 *somaria no shuto*	1	Existential: 首都 exists in Somalia
白い石造りの政府の建物 *shiroi ishizukuri no sēfu no tatemono*	2	Material: 建物 is made of white stones
政府の建物	2	Possessive: 建物 is possessed by 政府 Attributive: 政府 specifies what kind of 建物 it is
金細工の店 *kinzaiku no mise*	3	Attributive: 金細工 specifies what kind of 店 it is
波の音 *nami no oto*	6	Juxtaposition: 波 equals 音

particles. The topic marker は is not included. These basic patterns convey the information needed to make sense of the entire meaning of a sentence. For example, 散歩する *sanpo suru* 'to take a walk' needs only a subject to form a grammatical sentence (see 1 below), but it also requires を *o* to provide locative information essential to the activity of walking, that is, the place where the walking takes place (see 3 below). Look now carefully at each pattern and move on to Activity 4, in which you will contrast these patterns with spoken Japanese, which allows the frequent occurrence of ellipsis.

1   が + Verb
    山田さん**が**散歩します。
    Yamada-san ga sanpo shimasu
    Mr Y takes a walk.
    つくえ**が**あります。
    Tsukue ga arimasu
    There is a desk.

2   が + を (thing) + Verb
    山田さん**が**焼き鳥**を**食べます。
    Yamada-san ga yakitori o tabemasu
    Mr Y eats barbecued chicken.
    山田さん**が**お茶**を**飲みます。
    Yamada-san ga ocha o nomimasu
    Mr Y drinks a cup of tea.

3   が + を (location) + Verb
    山田さん**が**公園**を**散歩します。
    Yamada-san ga kōen o sanpo shimasu
    Mr Y takes a walk in the park.

4 が + へ (direction) + Verb
山田さん**が**会社**へ**行きます。
Yamada-san ga kaisha e ikimasu
Mr Y goes to the company (= to work).

5 が + に (location) + Verb
つくえ**が**教室**に**あります。
Tsukue ga kyōshitsu ni arimasu
There is a desk in the classroom.

6 が + で (location) + Verb
山田さん**が**ディスコ**で**踊ります。
Yamada-san ga disuko de odorimasu
Mr Y dances at discos.
山田さん**が**図書館**で**勉強します。
Yamada-san ga toshokan de benkyō shimasu
Mr Y studies in a library.
山田さん**が**会社**で**働いています。
Yamada-san ga kaisha de hataraite imasu
Mr Y works for a company.

7 が + で (instrument) + を (object) + Verb
山田さん**が**フォーク**で**ステーキ**を**食べます。
Yamada-san ga fōku de sutēki o tabemasu
Mr Y eats a steak with a fork.

8 が + に (location) + Verb
山田さん**が**会社**に**就職しました。
Yamada-san ga kaisha ni shūshoku shimashita
Mr Y found employment in a company.
山田さん**が**会社**に**勤めました。
Yamada-san ga kaisha ni tsutomemashita
Mr Y worked for a company.

9 が + に (receiver) + を (transferred object) + Verb
山田さん**が**みどりさん**に**花**を**贈ります。
Yamada-san ga Midori-san ni hana o okurimasu.
Mr Y gives flowers to M.
山田さん**が**みどりさん**に**ネックレス**を**あげます。
Yamada-san ga Midori-san ni nekkuresu o agemasu
Mr Y gives a necklace to M.

10 が + に (target) + を + Verb
山田さん**が**かべ**に**油絵**を**掛けます。
Yamada-san ga kabe ni aburae o kakemasu
Mr Y hangs the oil painting on the wall.
山田さん**が**机の上**に**本**を**置きます。
Yamada-san ga tsukue no ue ni hon o okimasu
Mr Y puts a book on the desk.

197

11   が + と (reciprocal) + Verb
山田さん**が**みどりさん**と**結婚します。
*Yamada-san **ga** Midori-san **to** kekkon shimasu*
Mr Y marries M.
山田さん**が**みどりさん**と**喧嘩します。
*Yamada-san **ga** Midori-san **to** kenka shimasu*
Mr Y has a row with M.

12   が + へ・に (direction) + Verb
山田さん**が**学校**へ・に**行きます。
*Yamada-san **ga** gakkō **e/ni** ikimasu*
Mr Y goes to school.
山田さん**が**駅**へ・に**向かいます。
*Yamada-san **ga** eki **e/ni** mukaimasu*
Mr Y goes toward the station.

13   が + に (direction) + Verb
山田さん**が**みどりさん**に**会います。
*Yamada-san **ga** Midori-san **ni** aimasu*
Mr Y meets/bumps into M.
山田さん**が**電車**に**乗ります。
*Yamada-san **ga** densha **ni** norimasu*
Mr Y gets on the tram.

14   が₁ + が₂ + Verb
山田さん**が**焼き鳥**が**好きです。
*Yamada-san **ga** yakitori **ga** suki desu*
Mr Y likes barbecued chicken.
山田さん**が**日本語**が**わかります。
*Yamada-san **ga** nihongo **ga** wakarimasu*
Mr Y understands Japanese.

15   が + Adjective + です
みどりさん**が**かわいいです。
*Midori-san **ga** kawaī desu*
M is pretty.

Activity 4

This activity asks you to compare the basic sentence patterns shown in 7.6 with spoken language in a drama. Text 7.14 is a passage taken from ふぞろいの林檎たち *Fuzoroi no ringo-tachi* III 'Uneven Apples' (Yamada 1991). Try to identify the forms typical of spoken Japanese, and explain on the basis of the patterns in 7.6 why you think they are structurally different from the basic forms. The conversation is carried out between four people (陽子 *Yōko*, 健一 *Ken-ichi*, 実 *Minoru*, 良雄 *Yoshio*), who know each other well, and it takes place right outside the hospital where 陽子 works as a nurse. The three males had been visiting their female friend 晴枝 *Harue*, who is now hospitalized, and on the way back they decided without notice to see 陽子. One salient feature of spoken Japanese is the occurrence of **ellipsis** (or omission) when forms are inferable from the context (see also JLU: Chapter 3, section 3.7, for ellipsis).

Text 7.14

準夜勤を終えて、白衣の上からコートを羽織り、帽子をとりながら
駐車場の方へ行きかかる陽子。美しい。

1　陽子「（ドキリと動きを止めかけながら前を見る）」

　　健一「（離れて立っていて）しばらく」

　　陽子「フフ、なに？（動揺がある）」

　　実「しばらく（と横に並ぶ）」

5　陽子「あ」

　　良雄「しばらく（と横にならぶ）」

　　陽子「あ（咄嗟に考え）晴枝——？」

　　良雄「たいしたことないようだった」

　　陽子「そう——」

10　健一「でね、こっちへ来た」

　　実「折角、三人で逢ったから」

　　良雄「じゃあ、陽子ちゃんにも逢おうじゃないかって」

　　健一「へとへと？」

　　陽子「いいけど、そっちこそいいの？こんな時間（と車の方へ歩き

15　出す）明日、仕事あるんでしょう？」

　　良雄「あるけど——」

　　実「すっごく久し振りだしさ」

　　陽子「そうね」

　　良雄「すぐ別れるの、つまらないような気がしてね」

199

20 健一「また一年も二年も会わないことになりそうだし」

　　陽子「ほんとね」

　　良雄「顔だけ見ようって」

　　実「逢えてよかった」

　　陽子「私、そこ、車あるの（と前方を指し）車？

25 （と実にきく）」

　　実「うん、こいつのに（と健一を指す）」

　　健一「正門入ってすぐ脇に停めてあるんだ」

　　陽子「（車のところへ来て）どうする？私のに乗る？そっちへ行

　　く？」

30 良雄「どっかへ行く？」

　　陽子「だって、これで別れるんじゃ」

　　健一「疲れていない？」

　　実「どこ行くかだよな」

　　陽子「うちへ来ない？この下、白衣なの。着替えるの面倒くさくて」

35 良雄「いいの？」

　　陽子「いいわよ、久し振りじゃない」

© 1991 Yamada, Taichi / *Fuzoroi no Ringo-tachi* (pp. 14–15), Magazine House

Commentary

Six structural characteristics of spoken Japanese are found in this passage.
{ } provides an alternative that contains omitted parts.
First, the subject is unexpressed.

- でね、∅こっちへ来た　{**それ**でね、**僕たちが**こっちへ来た}
  (line 10)

Second, が *ga* (a subject marker) and に *ni* (a location marker) are often
unexpressed. Only the nouns are verbalized.

- 明日、仕事∅あるんでしょう？　{明日、仕事**が**あるんでしょ
  う？}(line 15)

- すぐ別れるの∅、つまらないような気がしてね　{すぐ別れるの**が**、つまらないような気がしてね} (line 19)
- 私、そこ∅、車∅あるの {私、そこ**に**車**が**あるの} (line 24)

Third, the object and its particle are unexpressed since they can be inferred from the conversation. The explicit verbalization of the name here would sound too private and emphatic.

- ∅逢えてよかった　{**陽子に**逢えてよかった} (line 23)

Fourth, predicates are unexpressed. Copulas (i.e., です, だ) tend to be unexpressed very often, as shown by the first three examples.

- なに∅?　{なん**です**か} (line 3)
- しばらく∅　{しばらく**です**} (line 4)
- へとへと∅?　{へとへと**です**か} (line 13)
- 顔だけ見ようって∅　{顔だけ見ようって**ことになったんだ**} (line 22)
- だって、これで別れるんじゃ∅　{だって、これで別れるんじゃ**つまらないよ**} (line 31)

Fifth, many sentences do not have a subject and predicate. Interrogatives are not marked by か; instead, the question mark is used.

- 晴枝∅——?　{晴枝**のことですか**} (line 7)
- 車∅?　{車**で来ましたか**} (line 24)

Sixth, some sentences do not contain the case particle that expresses temporal location or direction.

- こんな時間∅　{こんな時間**に**} (line 14)
- どこ∅行くかだよな　{どこ**へ**行くかだよな} (line 33)

In general, spoken language is shorter than written language because of the frequent occurrence of **ellipsis**. This happens by virtue of the nature of spoken language, which lays special emphasis on the **context** in which the conversation is carried on (see JLU: Chapter 2, section 2.3, for the concept of context). When the speaker's intention is inferable from the context, the speaker does not, or does not need to, express it explicitly. Conversations such as the above do not strictly obey the basic sentence patterns, precisely because spoken language is not concerned with 'grammatical correctness' but with 'facilitating communication' in a given speech situation.[5]

7.7 Noun modifications

Speakers or writers use various means to construct sentences to make them meaningful. By assigning a topic to a sentence or by making the predicate more complex, sentences become more explicit and meaningful. As we have seen in Activity 4 (pp. 198–201), simplifying the sentence can also enhance the degree of communication. This final section demonstrates another means of constructing a meaningful sentence. It deals with **noun modification**, in which the referent of the noun is made more explicit by being modified by the preceding element.

Nouns are modified in various ways in Japanese. Students learn adjectives at their initial stage of language learning. When saying 親切な日本人 *shinsetsu na nihonjin* 'kind Japanese', an adjective 親切な modifies the following 日本人. When saying 働き者の日本人 *hatarakimono no nihonjin* 'hard-working Japanese', the noun 働き者 functions like an adjective since it modifies the following noun. Noun modification differs from the adjectival construction in that the noun is modified by a verb or a verbal element. Consider (106) and (107), where 日本人駐在員 *nihonjin-chūzaiin* and マレーシア are modified by the verbal expression 働いている and イスラム教徒である, respectively.

(106) シンガポールで**働いている日本人駐在員**は大きな家に住んでいる。
*Singapōru de **hataraite iru nihonjin-chūzaiin** wa ōkina ie ni sunde iru*
Japanese expatriates working in Singapore are living in a big house.

(107) 国民の６０パーセント以上が**イスラム教徒であるマレーシア**は日本人にとって異質な国だろう。
*Kokumin no 60 pāsento ijō ga **isuramu-kyōto dearu marēsia** wa nihonjin ni totte ishitsu na kuni darō*
Malaysia, with a more than 60 per cent Muslim population, may be a unique country for the Japanese.

As may be seen, the semantic relation between the modifier and the noun is not always the same. In (106) the modifier 'describes' what the referent of the noun (i.e., 日本人駐在員) does in Singapore, while in (107) the modifier 'characterizes' the referent of the noun (i.e., マレーシア).

The following examples demonstrate the semantic relations between Modifier and Noun. The verbal elements are always expressed in the plain form, either in past or non-past tense. Noun modification has two major functions. The first is to represent the relations encoded in case particles, as illustrated in (108) to (113). Modifier and Noun bear a relationship represented by **case particles** (see section 7.5). For example, (110) represents an accusative relationship in that Modifier (歩いた *aruita*) and Noun (公園 *kōen*) can be combined by using an object marker を. Let us call this type of noun modification **grammatical**.

(108) お金を**盗んだ泥棒**が警察に捕まった。{泥棒がお金を盗んだ}
*Okane o **nusunda dorobō** ga keisatsu ni tsukamatta*
The thief who stole the money was caught by the police.

(109) マリ子さんが**作ったケーキ**はとてもおいしい。{ケーキ を 作った}
*Mariko-san ga **tsukutta kēki** wa totemo oishī*
The cake Mariko made is very tasty.

(110) ここは昔よく**歩いた公園**だ。{公園 を 歩いた}
*Koko wa mukashi yoku **aruita kōen** da*
Here is the park where I often took a walk.

(111) ここが国際学会が**開かれた大学**だ。{大学 で 国際学会が開かれた}
*Koko ga kokusai-gakkai ga **hirakareta daigaku** da*
Here is the university at which the international conference was held.

(112) 昔**住んでいた町**の名前を忘れた。{町 に 住んでいた}
*Mukashi **sunde ita machi** no namae o wasureta*
I forgot the name of the town in which I used to live.

(113) 私は佐藤さんが**結婚した女性**に会った。{女性 と 結婚した}
*Watashi wa Satō-san ga **kekkon shita josē** ni atta*
I met a woman whom Mr Sato married.

Not all case particles are compatible with noun modification. The relationship expressed by the case particle へ or で (i.e., direction and instrument, respectively) cannot be included in noun-modified clauses, as shown in (114) and (115).

(114) ×**行った郵便局**がしまっていた。{郵便局 へ 行った}
The post office I went to was closed.

(115) ×これは子どもたちが学校へ**通った自転車**だ。
{自転車 で 通った}
This is a bicycle children used to go to school.

The second function of noun modification is to represent **appositive** relationships between Modifier and Noun. Modifier elaborates on the content of Noun without recourse to a grammatical relationship between the two. To illustrate, the noun ニュース 'news' is elaborated on by saying what exactly the content of this news is, as in (116).

(116) 友達が**結婚したニュース**を聞いた。
*Tomodachi ga **kekkon shita nyūsu** o kīta*
I have heard the news that my friend had got married.

This elaboration is generally based on what one 'hears', 'perceives', 'observes', 'details' or 'witnesses' regarding the referent of the noun (see also Iwasaki 2002: 190). In other words, only certain groups of nouns that are eligible to express specific meanings can form this type of noun modification. The appositive use of noun modification falls under six types, as shown in Table 7.7 (adopted from Iwasaki (2002: 189) slightly modified by the author).[4]

Table 7.7 Appositive uses of noun modification

	Type of nouns	Examples
I	Communication	ことば *kotoba* 'words', うわさ *uwasa* 'rumour', ニュース *nyūsu* 'news', 命令 *meirē* 'order', 知らせ *shirase* 'news', 手紙 *tegami* 'letter', 警告 *kēkoku* 'warning'
II	Facts	こと *koto* 'fact', 事実 *jijitsu* 'fact', 事件 *jiken* 'incident', 状態 *jōtai* 'situation', 場面 *bamen* 'scene'
III	Mental action	考え *kangae* 'thought', 想像 *sōzō* 'imagination', 夢 *yume* 'dream', 疑い *utagai* 'doubt', 約束 *yakusoku* 'promise', 感じ *kanji* 'feeling', 予感 *yokan* 'premonition', 恐怖心 *kyōfushin* 'fear'
IV	Visual stimulus	顔 *kao* 'face', 写真 *shashin* 'picture', くせ *kuse* 'habit'
V	Non-visual stimulus	におい *nioi* 'smell', 音 *oto* 'sound', 声 *koe* 'voice', 感触 *kanshoku* 'sensation'
VI	Cause and result	原因 *gen-in* 'cause', 結果 *kekka* 'result', おつり *otsuri* 'change', つけ *tsuke* 'sequel'

(117) 山が**崩れる音**がした。
　　　*Yama ga **kuzureru oto** ga shita*
　　　I heard the sound as the mountain was falling.

(118) 何か**焦げるにおい**がした。
　　　*Nanika **kogeru nioi** ga shita*
　　　I smelt something being burnt.

(119) いい仕事が**見つからないかもしれない恐怖心**がある。
　　　*Ī shigoto ga **mitsukaranai kamoshirenai kyōfushin** ga aru*
　　　I am terrified by the idea that I may not find a good job.

(120) 明日の夕方友人と**会う約束**がある。
　　　*Ashita no yūgata yūjin to **au yakusoku** ga aru*
　　　I have an appointment to meet my friend tomorrow evening.

What the examples in (117) and (118) have in common is that the referent of Noun, 音 *oto* and におい *nioi*, is made explicit by specifying what the speaker hears or smells. When a mountain falls (e.g., because of heavy rain), we normally 'hear' the sound of this happening. When something burns, it 'emits a smell'. What (119) and (120) have in common is that Modifier elaborates on Noun by giving more details about the nature of the referent of Noun. Failing to find a job is what one perceives as fear. Meeting with my friend is the content of my appointment.

(121) **うそをついたつけ**が今やってきた。
　　　***Uso o tsuita tsuke** ga ima yatte kita*
　　　I now have a sequel to my lies.

Type VI is slightly different from the others, since Modifier elaborates on Noun by serving as the cause for the rise of Noun (see Masuoka 1994: 9–10). A good example is つけ 'sequel' in (121). The speaker realizes that he now has a sequel to his lies in the past.

Activity 5

Text 7.15 is taken from *Calling You*. In this passage, a narrator わたし 'I' describes what she experienced while she was on the bus. She met a woman who looks mature for her age. Using her 'brain telephone' (頭の電話 *atama no denwa*), she reports her encounter with this woman to シンヤ *Shinya*, who had gone on a journey. This passage contains instances of noun modification. Find the forms and explain their functions. The distinction between 'grammatical' and 'appositive' is a convenient tool for your explanation.

Text 7.15 Noun modification

---

1 次の日。

わたしの乗ったバスは渋滞で遅れていた。車内は空港へ向かう人で

埋まっていた。隣に、白色のコートを着た女の子が座っていた。

年齢はわたしと同じくらいだろう。しかし、化粧をして、わたしよ

5 り大人びた、きれいな人だった。彼女は大きな鞄を膝に載せて座っ

ていた。

「ここ数年で、一番の寒さだと朝のテレビで言っていたよ」

頭の電話に向かってシンヤに説明する。一時間前の彼は、今ようや

く飛行機に乗り込んだところだった。彼がシートに座って、はるか

10 下に広がる地面を眺めている場面を想像する。微笑ましい。わたし

たちの会話は実際に声を出すわけではない。だから、隣に座った女

の子は、わたしのことを、ぼんやり窓の外を眺めているだけだと思

っただろう。

暖房でほてった頭を、冷たい窓ガラスに押し付けるのが好きだった。

---

15 曇った窓の一部分を手でふき取ると、そこからわずかに見える空に

は、今にも雪の降り出しそうな低い雲が広がっていた。太陽はなく、

人通りの少ない町の中を冷たい風が通り抜けているだけだった。

一切の色を奪い去られたように、風景が灰色に見えた。

© 2003 Otsu, Ichi / *Calling You* (p. 31), Kadokawa

Commentary

Table 7.8 illustrates nine instances of noun modification.

Table 7.8　*Functions of noun modification in Text 7.15*

Line		Examples	G or A	Transforming into a basic pattern
①	2	乗ったバス	G	バスに乗った
②	2	空港へ向かう人	G	人が空港へ向かう
③	3	コートを着た女の子	G	女の子がコートを着た
④	10	下に広がる地面	G	地面が下に広がる
⑤	10	眺めている場面	A	–
⑥	11–12	隣に座った女の子	G	女の子が隣に座った
⑦	14	ほてった頭	G	頭がほてった
⑧	15	曇った窓	G	窓が曇った
⑨	15	見える空	G	空が見える

A striking feature of this passage is the frequent occurrence of grammatical noun modification. There is only one instance of the appositive use of noun modification ⑤. Here, it is not possible to transform Modifier and Noun into a basic causal pattern, since there is no grammatical relation between the two. This example contains 場面 *bamen* 'scene' as Noun, which is elaborated by Modifier. Noun modification here refers to the scene in which シンヤ *Shinya* is looking down towards the ground of the earth through the airplane window.

　　　Having examined the nature of noun modification, the question that can be raised is 'what is noun modification actually for?', in other words, 'what is the advantage of using this construction?'. Take a closer look at ⑦ほてった頭 *hotetta kao* 'overheated head' (line 14). As shown in the rightmost column of Table 7.8, Modifier + Noun can in most cases be transformed into a clause in which Noun becomes a subject. Thus, the underlying sentence of ほてった頭 can be 頭がほてった 'The head became overheated', whereby 'head' is a subject predicated by 'became overheated'. If we did not use noun modification, the single sentence (i.e., 'I like holding my overheated head against the cold window pane') on line 14 would be divided into two clauses, as demonstrated in (122). This solution may not be economical because 頭 'head' is used twice. The narrator's main intention might be to highlight the 'overheated head' – not the head that became overheated – and to contrast it directly with the 'cold' window pane. Only the complex noun phrase can do justice to the realization of the contrast between hotness and coldness. In short, noun modification 'joins' two concepts to get the writer's intentions across economically.

(122) a. 暖房で頭がほてった。
      Danbō de atama ga hotetta
      The **head** became overheated with the heating.
      b. 頭を冷たい窓ガラスに押し付けるのが好きだった。
      Atama o tsumetai madogarasu ni oshi-tsukeruno ga suki datta
      I liked to hold my head against the cold window pane.

Exercise

Try looking for any additional instances of noun modification in different genres of written texts, such as newspapers or magazines to which you have access, based on the explanations you have learned in this chapter.

Notes

1   See Hinata and Hibiya (1988: 30–34) for more examples.
2   This type of verb is called 'quasi-intransitive' in Martin (2004: 294), and the objects such verbs take are distinguished from direct objects by being called 'traversal objects'.
3   The semantic relation between the description of the scenery of Mogadishu (lines 2–4) and the expression 町並み *machinami* pertains to the hyponym and hypernym in Chapter 6, section 6.1.5.
4   Grammatical and appositive relations are also mentioned as 内の関係 *uchi no kankeē* and 外の関係 *soto no kankeē* in Japanese linguistics (Teramura 1975–1978, cited in Masuoka 1994).
5   We deal with 'naturally occurring conversation' in Chapter 5, *Japanese Language in Use*, which is distinguished from spoken conversation shown here.

References

The references listed here include works quoted in the book and consulted during the writing of it.

Alfonso, A. (1966) *Japanese Language Patterns. A Structural Approach.* With the co-operation of Y. Hirabayashi. Tokyo: Sophia University.

An Encyclopedia of Contemporary Words [Gendai Yōgo no Kiso-chishiki] (2003) Tokyo: Jiyū Kokuminsha.

Asahi Editorial Board [Asahi Shinbun Ronsetsu Iinkai] (1986) *Heaven's Voice, Men's Words with English Translation. 1985 Winter* [Tensei-jingo. Eibun Taishō 85 Fuyu]. Tokyo: Hara Shobo.

Asano, Y. (1981) *Vocabulary: Handbook of Japanese for Teachers* [Goi: Kyoshiyō Nihongo Handobukku]. Tokyo: The Japan Foundation, International Japanese Center.

Backhouse, A. E. (1993) *The Japanese Language: An Introduction.* Oxford/ Auckland/New York: Oxford University Press.

Chino, N. (1991) *All about Particles: A Handbook of Japanese Function Words.* Tokyo/New York/London: Kodansha International.

Davenport, M. and Hannahs, S. J. (2005) *Introducing Phonetics and Phonology* (2nd edn). London: Arnold.

Frawley, W. (1992) *Linguistic Semantics.* Hillsdale, New Jersey/Hove/London: Lawrence Erlbaum.

Hinata, S. and Hibiya, J. (1988) *Discourse Structure* [Danwa no Kōzō]. Tokyo: Aratake.

Hoshino, A. (1976) 'About body-parts vocabulary', in T. Suzuki (ed.), *Japanese Vocabulary and Expressions* [Nihongo no Goi to Hyōgen]. Tokyo: Taishukan, pp. 153–181.

Ikegami, Y. (1978) 'DO-language and BECOME-language', in W. U. Dressler and W. Meid (eds), *Proceedings of the Twelfth International Congress of Linguists.* Innsbruck, pp. 190–194.

Inazuka, E. and Inazuka, H. (2003) *An Introduction to Japanese Phonetics: Explanations and Exercises* [Nihongo no Onsei Nyūmon: Kaisetsu to Enshū]. Tokyo: Baberu Press.

Iwasaki, S. (2002) *Japanese.* Amsterdam/Philadelphia: John Benjamins.

Jacobson, W. M. (1992) *The Transitive Structure of Events in Japanese.* Tokyo: Kuroshio.

Japanese Pronunciation and Accent Dictionary [Nihongo Hatsuon Akusento Jiten] (1985) Tokyo: NHK.

Kageyama, T. (1990) *Comparison between Japanese and English Vocabulary* [Nihongo to Eigo no Goi no Taishō]. Tokyo: Meiji Shoin.

Kaiser, S., Ichikawa, Y., Kobayashi, N. and Yamamoto, H. (2001) *Japanese: A Comprehensive Grammar*. London/New York: Routledge.

Kamiya, T. (2001) *The Handbook of Japanese Verbs*. Tokyo/London/New York: Kodansha International.

Katamba, F. (1989) *An Introduction to Phonology*. London: Longman.

Katō, K., Ashihava, K., Yoshizawa, Y. and Yuda, M. (2003) *Living Japanese Through Comics. Life in Japan*. Tokyo: ASK.

Kess, J. and Miyamoto, T. (1999) *The Japanese Mental Lexicon*. Philadelphia/ Amsterdam: John Benjamins.

Kindaichi, H. (1998 (1982–1983)) *Japanese Language Classroom* [Nihongo Kyōshitsu]. Tokyo: Chikuma Shobo.

Kodansha's Furigana Japanese-English Dictionary [Kōdansha Furigana Wa-ei Jiten] (1995). Tokyo: Kodansha International.

Komai, A. and Rohlich, T. H. (1991) *An Introduction to Classical Japanese*. Tokyo: Bonjinsha.

Makino, S. and Tsutsui, M. (1986) *A Dictionary of Basic Japanese Grammar*. Tokyo: The Japan Times.

Makino, S. and Tsutsui, M. (1995) *A Dictionary of Intermediate Japanese Grammar*. Tokyo: The Japan Times.

Mangajin's Basic Japanese through Comics (1998 (1993)) vol. 1. New York/Tokyo: Weatherhill.

Martin, S. E. (2004) *A Reference Grammar of Japanese* (revised edn). Hawai'i: University of Hawai'i Press.

Masuoka, T. (1994) *Conjoining Patterns of Noun Modification – Focusing on Content Clauses* [Mēshi Shūshoku no Setsuzoku Kēshiki – Naiyōsetsu o Chūshin ni]. Tokyo: Kuroshio.

Matthews, P. H. (1997) *The Concise Oxford Dictionary of Linguistics*. Oxford/New York: Oxford University Press.

Maynard, K. S. (1990) *An Introduction to Japanese Grammar and Communication Strategies*. Tokyo: The Japan Times.

Maynard, K. S. (1998) *Principles of Japanese Discourse: A Handbook*. Cambridge: Cambridge University Press.

McClure, W. T. (2000) *Using Japanese. A Guide to Contemporary Usage*. Cambridge: Cambridge University Press.

Mey, J. L. (2001) *Pragmatics: An Introduction* (2nd edn). Oxford: Blackwell.

Miura, A. (2002) *Japanese Words and Their Uses* II. Rutland/Boston/Tokyo: Tuttle.

Modern Chinese-Reading Dictionary with Examples [Gendai Kango Reikai Jiten] (1992) Tokyo: Shogakukan.

Morita, Y. (1989) *A Dictionary of Basic Japanese* [Kiso Nihongo Jiten]. Tokyo: Kadokawa.

New Concise Japanese Accent Dictionary [Shin-mēkai Nihongo Akusento Jiten] (2006 (2001)), H. Kindaichi and K. Akinaga (eds). Tokyo: Sanseido.

Ō, N. (1996) 'Single sound level' [Tan-on reberu], in K. Saji and S. Sanada (eds), *Sounds, Vocabulary, Letters and Writing Systems* [Onsei, Goi, Moji to Hyōki]. Tokyo: Tokyo Hōrei, pp. 16–52.

Obana, Y. (2000) *Understanding Japanese: A Handbook for Learners and Teachers.* Tokyo: Kuroshio.

Ōno, S. (1974) *Tracing the Japanese Language* [Nihongo o Sakanoboru]. Tokyo: Iwanami.

Reading Japanese History in English [Eibun de yomu nihonshi] (1996) Tokyo: Kodansha International.

Rubin, J. (1998) *Making Sense of Japanese: What the Textbooks Don't Tell You.* Tokyo/New York/London: Kodansha International.

Saeed, J. (2003) *Semantics* (2nd edn). Oxford: Blackwell.

Sakairi, I., Sato, Y., Sakuragi, N., Nakamura, K., Nakamura, H. and Yamada, A. (1991) *100 Questions Foreigners Frequently Ask to Japanese Teachers* [Gaikoku-jin ga Nihongo-kyōshi ni Yoku Suru 100 no Shitsumon]. Tokyo: Baberu Press.

Sanada, S. (1989) *Variations in Japanese* [Nihongo no Bariēshon]. Tokyo: ALC.

Shibatani, M. (1990) *The Languages of Japan.* Cambridge: Cambridge University Press.

Tagashira, Y. and Hoff, J. (1986) *Handbook of Japanese Compound Verbs.* Tokyo: Hokuseido.

Teramura, H. (1975–1978) *Essays by Hideo Teramura: Japanese Grammar* [Teramura Hideo Ronbun-shū I: Nihongo-bunpō-hen], vol. 1. Tokyo: Kuroshio.

The New Oxford Dictionary of English (1998) Oxford: Clarendon Press.

Trask, R. L. (1996) *Historical Linguistics.* London/New York: Arnold.

Tsujimura, N. (1996) *An Introduction to Japanese Linguistics.* Cambridge, Mass./Oxford: Blackwell.

Vance, T. J. (1987) *An Introduction to Japanese Phonology.* New York: State University of New York Press.

Yamaguchi, T. (2005) *Basic Japanese Vocabulary: An Explanation of Usage.* Selangor Darul Ehsan: Pelanduk.

Yamaguchi, T. (forthcoming) *Japanese Language in Use: An Introduction.* London/New York: Continuum.

List of authentic texts

Academic texts

Ikeda, Y. (2000) *An Easy Guide to Japanese: Phonology/Phonetics* [Yasashī Nihongo Shidō: On-in/Onsei], vol. 5. Tokyo: International Japanese Education Center [Kokusai Nihongo Kenshū Kyōkai].

Nishiguchi, K. and Kono, T. (1994) *Kanji in Context. A Study System for Intermediate and Advanced Learners.* Tokyo: The Japan Times.

Children's books

Aman, K. (1977) *The Colour of the Car is the Colour of the Sky* [Kuruma no Iro wa Sora no Iro]. Tokyo: Poplar.

Kanzawa, T. (1977) *A Bear Cub Uf* [Kuma no Ko Ūfu]. Tokyo: Poplar.

Comics

Adachi, M. (1996) *Full of Sunshine* [Hiatari Ryōkō]. Tokyo: Shogakukan.
Adachi, M. (2001) *Always Misora* [Itsumo Misora]. Tokyo: Shogakukan.
Fujiko, F. F. (1995) *Doraemon*: *Kandō-hen*. Tokyo: Shogakukan.
Fujiko, F. F (2002) *Doraemon*: *Nobita-Grafity*. Tokyo: Shogakukan.
Takahashi, S. (2004) *Good-natured Man* [Ī Hito]. Tokyo: Shogakukan.

Drama

Yamada, T. (1991) *Uneven Apples* III [Fuzoroi no Ringo-tachi III]. Tokyo: Magazine House.

Internet

www.asahi.com

Newspapers

Asahi Newspaper [Asahi Shinbun]. Tokyo.
Mainichi Newspaper [Mainichi Shinbun]. Tokyo.
Yomiuri Newspaper [Yomiuri Shinbun]. Tokyo.

Novels

Yoshimoto, B. (2003) *Hagoromo*. Tokyo: Shinchosha.

Magazines

'Traveling the world by car' [Sekai no michi o kuruma de tabi-suru] (2002) *Newsweek Japan* [Nyūzu-uīku Nihon-ban] 1/8 May. Tokyo: Hankyu Communications, pp. 64–93.

Short stories

Otsu, I. (2003) 'Calling You', in I. Otsu, *Lost Story* [Ushinawareta Monogatari]. Tokyo: Kadokawa, pp. 5–47.

English index

Japanese index

219

CPSIA information can be obtained at www.ICGtesting.com
Printed in the USA
LVOW09s1619280814

401258LV00019B/82/P